Lecture Notes in Information Systems and Organisation

Volume 39

Lecture Notes in Information Systems and Organization—LNISO—is a series of scientific books that explore the current scenario of information systems, in particular IS and organization. The focus on the relationship between IT, IS and organization is the common thread of this collection, which aspires to provide scholars across the world with a point of reference and comparison in the study and research of information systems and organization. LNISO is the publication forum for the community of scholars investigating behavioral and design aspects of IS and organization. The series offers an integrated publication platform for high-quality conferences, symposia and workshops in this field. Materials are published upon a strictly controlled double blind peer review evaluation made by selected reviewers.

LNISO is abstracted/indexed in Scopus

More information about this series at http://www.springer.com/series/11237

Alena Siarheyeva · Chris Barry ·
Michael Lang · Henry Linger ·
Christoph Schneider
Editors

Advances in Information Systems Development

Information Systems Beyond 2020

Springer

Editors
Alena Siarheyeva
130 impasse Louis Bonamici
Résidence le Gouverneur B2
Toulon, France

Chris Barry🆔
Cairnes School of Business and Economics
National University of Ireland Galway
Galway, Ireland

Michael Lang🆔
Cairnes School of Business and Economics
National University of Ireland Galway
Galway, Ireland

Henry Linger🆔
Faculty of Information Technology
Monash University
Melbourne, VIC, Australia

Christoph Schneider🆔
IESE Business School
University of Navarra
Barcelona, Spain

ISSN 2195-4968   ISSN 2195-4976   (electronic)
Lecture Notes in Information Systems and Organisation
ISBN 978-3-030-49643-2   ISBN 978-3-030-49644-9   (eBook)
https://doi.org/10.1007/978-3-030-49644-9

This Springer imprint is published by the registered company Springer Nature Switzerland AG
The registered company address is: Gewerbestrasse 11, 6330 Cham, Switzerland

Preface

The **International Conference on Information Systems Development** (ISD) is an academic conference where researchers and practitioners share their knowledge and expertise in the field of information systems (IS) development. As an affiliated conference of the Association for Information Systems (AIS), the ISD conference complements the international network of general IS conferences (ICIS, ECIS, AMCIS, PACIS, HICSS). The ISD conference continues the tradition started with the first Polish-Scandinavian Seminar on Current Trends in Information Systems Development Methodologies, held in Gdansk, Poland, in 1988. This seminar has evolved into the International Conference on Information Systems Development.

Throughout its history, the conference has focused on different aspects, ranging from methodological, infrastructural, and educational challenges in the ISD field to bridging the gaps between industry, academia, and society. Advancements in information systems foster technological developments. The deployment of the resulting technologies in all areas of society, including the public and private sectors, the community, and people's homes is greatly beneficial. ISD has always promoted a close interaction between theory and practice that has set a human-centered agenda focused on advancing the methods, tools, and management of IS development.

This volume is a selection of papers from ISD2019, the 28th Information Systems Development Conference hosted by the Higher Institute for Electronics and Digital Training (ISEN Yncréa Méditerranée) and held in Toulon, France, from August 28–30, 2019. All accepted papers have been published in the AIS eLibrary, which is accessible at https://aisel.aisnet.org/isd2014/proceedings2019. This volume contains extended versions of the best papers, as selected by the ISD2019 Proceedings Editors.

The theme of the conference was *Information Systems Beyond 2020*. It focused on the latest developments in ISD and particularly on emerging concepts, novel approaches, and ideas that are likely to shape information systems research in the 2020s. The conference provided a forum for discussing research and developments in this field.

The ISD2019 conference attracted contributions in the general area of information systems development, as well as in more specialized topics including *Society, Trust, and Ethics in ISD*, *New Media in ISD*, *ISD Methodologies*, *ISD Education*, and *Managing ISD*. ISD2019 focused on these and associated topics in order to promote research into theoretical and methodological issues and ways in which these advances enable better synergies between theory and practice.

We believe that the innovative papers assembled in these lecture notes will inform the reader of important contributions in this regard.

Alena Siarheyeva
Chris Barry
Michael Lang
Henry Linger
Christoph Schneider

Conference Organization

Conference Chair

Alena Siarheyeva

International Steering Committee

Chris Barry
Michael Lang
Henry Linger
Christoph Schneider

Track Chairs

Society, Trust, and Ethics in ISD

Chris Barry
Michael Lang

Exploring New Media in ISD

Jean-Rémy Chardonnet
Ruding Lou
José Tiberio Hernández
Manolya Kavakli

Information Systems Methodologies and Education

Mikko Rajanen
Dorina Rajanen
Monica Vladoiu

Managing ISD

Miguel Mira da Silva
Emilio Insfran
Ana Cristina Ramada Paiva

Current Topics in ISD

Karlheinz Kautz
Sabine Madsen
Sharon Coyle

Reviewers

Jon Aaen
Parisa Aasi
Silvia Abrahao
Ademar Aguiar
Muhammad Ovais
  Ahmad
Jan Aidemark
Asif Akram
Rafael Almeida
Vasco Amaral
Bo Andersson
Elina Annanperä
Joao Araujo
Leena Arhippainen
Doris Aschenbrenner
Rogerio Atem De
  Carvalho
Cheuk Hang Au
Eduard Babkin
Per Backlund
João Barata
Chris Barry
Peter Bellström
Olivia Benfeldt Nielsen
Peter Bernus
Gro Bjerknes
Dominique Blouin
Keld Bødker
Veera Boonjing
Ross Brown
Jeremy Brown
Noel Carroll
Priscila Cedillo
Luca Cernuzzi
Narayan Ranjan
  Chakraborty
Jean-Rémy Chardonnet

Witold Chmielarz
Cesar Collazos
Zoran Constantinescu
Sharon Coyle
Daniela Danciulescu
Duong Dang
Duy Dang Pham
Denis Dennehy
Sean Duignan
João Faria
Marta Fernández-Diego
Jennifer Ferreira
Justin Filippou
Owen Foley
Martin Gellerstedt
Ahmad Ghazawneh
Abel Gómez
Fernando González
Daniel Peter Gozman
Carmine Gravino
Patrick Guillemin
Figen Gul
Darek Haftor
Eija Halkola
Anne Vorre Hansen
Heidi Hartikainen
Henrik Hedberg
Seamus Hill
Mairéad Hogan
Netta Iivari
Yavuz İnal
Emilio Insfran
Amin Jalali
William Jobe
Björn Johansson
Gustaf Juell-Skielse
Miranda Kajtazi

Dimitris Karagiannis
Pasi Karppinen
Karlheinz Kautz
Manolya Kavakli
Rónán Kennedy
Marianne Kinnula
Dina Koutsikouri
Erdelina Kurti
Markus Lahtinen
Arto Lanamäki
Michael Lane
Michael Lang
Birger Lantow
Jouni Lappalainen
Michael Le Duc
J Ola Lindberg
Henry Linger
Ruding Lou
Ulrika Lundh Snis
Sabine Madsen
Monika Magnusson
Tim A. Majchrzak
Jabier Martinez
Raimundas Matulevicius
Frederic Merienne
Miguel Mira Da Silva
Tonja Molin-Juustila
Phelim Murnion
Priyadharshini
  Muthukannan
Makoto Nakayama
Andrés Adolfo Navarro
  Newball
Lene Nielsen
Ovidiu Noran
Behnaz Norouzi
Lena-Maria Öberg

Mairead O'Connor
Thuy Duong Oesterreich
Raphael Pereira De
  Oliveira
Christian Ostlund
Ana Paiva
Malgorzata Pankowska
Nearchos Paspallis
Ruben Pereira
Guillaume Perocheau
John Persson
Daranee Pimchangthong
Tomas Pitner
Dijana Plantak Vukovac
Claudia Pons
Natallia Pshkevich
Iman Raeesi Vanani
Claudia Raibulet
Mikko Rajanen
Dorina Rajanen
Marios Raspopoulos
João Reis

António Rito Silva
Alberto Rodrigues Da
  Silva
Christoph Rosenkranz
Bruce Rowlands
Paulo Rupino Da Cunha
Mikko Salminen
Kurt Sandkuhl
Sanem Sariel
Wilson Javier Sarmiento
Boubker Sbihi
Helana Scheepers
Christoph Schneider
Ulf Seigerroth
Alena Siarheyeva
Ashok Sivaji
William W. Song
Michiel Spape
Zlatko Stapić
Karen Stendal
Stefan Stieglitz
Janis Stirna

Frantisek Sudzina
Ann Svensson
Torben Tambo
Barney Tan
Kimmo Tarkkanen
José Tiberio Hernández
Justas Trinkunas
Fanny Vainionpää
Juan Manuel Vara
Tero Vartiainen
Christopher Vendome
Monica Vladoiu
Liisa Von Hellens
Neven Vrcek
Ulrika H. Westergren
Anna Wingkvist
Karen Young
Bo Yu
Alfred Zimmermann
Miguel Angel Zúñiga
  Prieto

Contents

Advancing Conceptual Modeling Education Towards a Generalized Model Value Proposition

Ana-Maria Ghiran, Cristina-Claudia Osman, and Robert Andrei Buchmann[✉]

Business Informatics Research Center, Babeş-Bolyai University, Cluj-Napoca, Romania
{anamaria.ghiran,cristina.osman,robert.buchmann}@econ.ubbcluj.ro

Abstract. This paper proposes a teaching method and artifact for Conceptual Modeling education, motivated by a challenge in the authors' university of bridging the gap between bachelor-level studies and research work on topics related to Conceptual Modeling. At bachelor-level, Conceptual Modeling is subordinated to Software Engineering or Business Process Management topics, making extensive use of available standards for graphical documentation purposes. However, at doctoral level and in project-based work, modeling methods must be scientifically framed within wider-scoped paradigms – e.g. Knowledge Management, Enterprise Modeling – or tailored for domain-specific scenarios. The teaching artifact presented in this paper is an example of an "agile modeling method" that can be iteratively evolved together with students through a metamodeling approach in support of a course flow that argues for a generalized model value proposition and modeling languages acting as "schema" that can be tailored and migrated to accommodate explicit requirements from any application domain.

Keywords: Agile Modeling Method Engineering · Metamodeling · Teaching Conceptual Modeling · Resource Description Framework

1 Introduction

This paper extends a proposal on improving Conceptual Modeling education presented at ISD 2019 [1], by enriching the proposed teaching artifact with details regarding the course flow that frames it, the rationale of its design decisions and further justification on the choice of tooling and methodology.

Conceptual Modeling education can be tackled as a design problem to address common preconceptions identified in the students' understanding, and possibly in the stance of educators who strictly employ Conceptual Modeling for common use cases (e.g. database design, business process modeling). The hereby advocated teaching approach introduces Conceptual Modeling to students as a purposeful activity that has a value proposition for a diversity of domains, among which databases design or control flow modeling are only a selection of (popular) use cases. Others, such as service design [2],

---

A prior version of this paper has been published in the ISD2019 Proceedings (http://aisel.aisnet.org/isd2014/proceedings2019).

A. Siarheyeva et al. (Eds.): ISD 2019, LNISO 39, pp. 1–18, 2020.
https://doi.org/10.1007/978-3-030-49644-9_1

smart city simulations [3], value analysis [4] or even a knowledge management approach to something as trivial as cooking recipes [5] can equally benefit from this discipline, as it provides means for capturing structured conceptualizations on a mitigation layer between human-oriented knowledge representation and machine-readable knowledge representation. When we add the ingredient of *agile metamodeling*, modeling languages become schemata that enable domain-specific knowledge retrieval – something that can be convincingly presented by analogy with how a database schema enables SQL queries for data-driven system or decision.

In the authors' university, the students graduating bachelor programs in Business Information Systems or Computer Science come in contact with Conceptual Modeling topics as chapters of courses on software engineering or business process management. On the other hand, a wider and deeper understanding is required in research work – i.e., project-based industry collaborations, doctoral and postdoctoral studies, some master dissertations (especially in industry collaborations where domain-specificity tends to be a key requirement). In master or doctoral studies it is not sufficient to wear the hat of a modeling tool "user" (who takes a modeling language for granted), but it is often necessary to be capable of exercising abstraction abilities, of expanding standards, of hybridizing modeling dialects or developing model-based proof-of-concept experimentation and evaluation.

This gap in perception is comparable to the one between "database users" (who operate on data records, while taking a database design for granted) and those able to migrate or deploy their own database for evolving needs. While for database courses this gap is easily bridged (even during the same semester), it is not the same for Conceptual Modeling which is dispersed in "aspects" of other disciplines. This turns Conceptual Modeling education into a "design problem" (in the sense of Design Research) – a problem we are investigating along the full engineering cycle, from contextual requirements to proposed treatments. As a possible treatment to this problem, we hereby present a teaching artifact that aims to stimulate students' lateral thinking – the main learning objective is to show that a modeling language is a *knowledge schema* to be tailored and migrated in the same sense as a database schema, in order to ensure the semantic richness necessary for some selected purpose (which may go well beyond graphical documentation, e.g. interoperability with external systems). Software Engineering is thus repositioned as an application domain that benefits from standards, best practices and consensus; but at the same time, a more general notion of "model value" is introduced - one that transcends application domains and follows learning design recommendations from the literature [6].

The proposed teaching artifact is a "modeling method" (cf. the definition of [7]) that showcases to students, through a minimalist approach: (i) a modeling method's building blocks, prototyped in the form of a domain-specific modeling tool; and (ii) a conceptualization and implementation process based on the Agile Modeling Method Engineering framework [8] to enable the agile migration of a modeling prototype assuming evolving requirements. Therefore, the Design Research challenge for which this artifact was developed is *How can we teach Conceptual Modeling in a way that stimulates productivity and creativity of students in research work, expanding their understanding of modeling purpose and model value beyond traditional application areas and use cases?*

The short answer, for which the proposed artifact was developed, is *by revealing the "agile schema" function that a modeling language can fulfil and by demonstrating its evolvability driven by requirements.* The targeted success measure in our university's case was to enable master students to publish scientific contributions for the first time in international venues on Conceptual Modeling topics, derived from their own dissertations, thus easing their learning curve towards project-based work and potential doctoral studies.

The remainder of the paper is organized as follows: Sect. 2 clarifies the working terminology and provides justification for the choice of tools. Section 3 outlines the requirements for the proposed teaching artifact and provides an overview on the proposed solution. Section 4 presents the teaching artifact and how it fits in the overall teaching method and course flow. Section 5 discusses observed outcomes. Section 6 comments on related works. The paper ends with conclusions.

2 Working Terminology and Justification

In this work's interpretation, the term *Conceptual Modeling* refers to a "standalone discipline that uses or creates conceptualizations for any domain" [9], resulting in diagrammatic abstractions relevant to that domain and driven by some requirements. The longstanding conference series on Conceptual Modeling (ER), although often presenting Software Engineering use cases, generally recognizes this wide scope - covering from philosophical foundations [10] to expanding application areas, e.g. Enterprise Architecture Management [11]. However, in education (and educational research) this wide scope is obscured; consequently, junior researchers face a steep learning curve when they suddenly discover that modeling is not limited to ancillary techniques they routinely employ for documenting their work in other disciplines.

This paper is motivated by direct observation on the study programs where authors are involved, which is backed by a recent literature survey [12] showing that, perhaps due to how the ACM/AIS curriculum on Information Systems [13] is designed, the research literature on Conceptual Modeling education is dominated by Software Engineering scenarios – e.g. [14, 15], with a minority (quarter) of surveyed works pertaining to Business Process Management and only isolated works tackling other application areas (e.g. [16]) - although the diversity of available modeling languages is otherwise well represented outside educational contexts (from work on extending standards like Archimate [4] to domain-specific projects [17]). Some academic courses where Conceptual Modeling is positioned as a standalone discipline can also be identified [18, 19] but these are tightly coupled to Software Engineering contexts.

The engineering process for this artifact (and the associated tutorial flow) is a simplification of a metamodeling approach called Agile Modeling Method Engineering (AMME) [8], which employs notions of "model", "instance" and "metamodel" similar to the Meta-Object Facility [20] but is independent of the UML language family and aims to support a full production line of modeling tools. Its formal foundation is the FDMM formalism published in [21] aligned with the meta-metamodel of the ADOxx platform [22] that assumes a graph-like underlying structure for any diagrammatic representation. This is also the metamodeling platform employed to develop the artifact together with students, due to its (i) free availability, (ii) rapid prototyping features that help students produce something usable before (or in parallel with) acquiring theoretical foundations or programming experience, (iii) open access to a diversity of modeling tools that students can dissect and repurpose, hosted within the Open Models Laboratory ecosystem [23]. The design decisions to be presented in this paper aim for educational qualities, a minimization of prerequisite skills and of domain expertise, therefore they should be easy to translate to other preferred platforms, with only few limitations (e.g. built-in model interoperability features are quite diverse among metamodeling platforms and may require some implementation effort on the educator's part).

3   Requirements for the Teaching Artifact

Several meta-requirements have been distilled as motivation for the proposed teaching artifact. These are synthesized in Table 1 together with their rationale, paralleled by suggestions on how they are addressed *(Solution Approach)*.

Table 1. Requirements on the proposed teaching artifact and means of addressing them

Requirement	Solution approach	Rationale
A. *To position Conceptual Modeling as a Design Science approach*	The notion of "modeling method" [7] (including a modeling language) is introduced as an artifact subjected to its own engineering process driven by "modeling requirements" The engineering process produces specific deliverables guided by situational requirements and evaluation criteria (derived from generic criteria proposed in [24])	Students should gain the ability to create and customize modeling methods that are purposeful and situational, and to productively prototype them in the form of modeling tools
B. *To position Conceptual Modeling within the Knowledge Management paradigm*	Considering the existing works on revisiting Nonaka's knowledge conversion cycle [25] through the lens of Conceptual Modeling (e.g., [26]), modeling is presented as a means of Knowledge Externalization. The "knowledge representation" quality of models is stressed by showcasing the ability of applying semantic queries on models, employing the Resource Description Framework (RDF) [27] as a model storage format	Students should gain the ability of tailoring a modeling method for Knowledge Externalization purposes, to satisfy knowledge retrieval requirements (semantic queries or reasoning). A modeling language must be understood as a knowledge schema that can be migrated just like a database schema (with models taking on the role of "records")
C. *To emphasize domain-specificity as a common situational requirement*	Inspired by the existing tradition in domain-specific language development and domain engineering [17, 28], the approach highlights means of assimilating domain-specificity in modeling languages, or to apply such specificity to all building blocks of a modeling method	Students should gain the ability of extending standard modeling languages or to create new ones, for domain-specific purposes and having in mind knowledge retrieval goals (model queries and possible interoperability with model-driven systems)

(continued)

Table 1. (*continued*)

Requirement	Solution approach	Rationale
D. *To reveal the agility potential of modeling methods.*	The Agile Modeling Method Engineering [8] methodology is employed to evolve a modeling method through two iterations driven by additive requirements, with the help of fast prototyping (metamodeling) platforms	Students should gain the ability to evolve a modeling tool according to changing requirements

Traditionally, there has been a significant gap between these requirements and the dominant perception of students on diagrammatic Conceptual Modeling, as acquired during bachelor studies. Most of our master students come from Business Information Systems or Computer Science bachelor programs, with a minority (<10%) from Business Administration programs. Their experience with modeling is dominated by UML and ER diagrams (or BPMN, for a minority of Business Administration students) – employed strictly as graphical documentation for bachelor theses (typically using drawing tools with diagramming "templates").

The value of models *as purposeful knowledge representation* is thus lost or diluted by the common use case of graphical documentation. We aim to reinforce that value by repositioning a modeling language as a knowledge schema that supports easily demonstrable pragmatic goals – model queries, rule-based mechanisms or interoperability to enable model-driven engineering. The graphical representation thus becomes only a superficial layer for semantically rich knowledge structures. By raising the abstraction level, modeling goals are attached to paradigms such as Design Science or Knowledge Management, thus suggesting theoretical frames for students who want to further pursue research on these topics.

In addition to the requirements summarized in Table 1, several pragmatic goals have been distilled from feedback on earlier attempts to design our teaching artifact [5]:

- **Minimalism:** The development of the modeling method should be demonstrable in 2 meetings × 3 h each, plus an additional meeting for discussion (to map the hands-on experience on theoretical background provided by parallel lectures, also suggesting potential extensions for student homework). The modeling language should introduce in its first iteration not more than 3 concepts (and necessary relations), thus reducing the complexity to a "Hello world" kind of demonstration – however one that *touches all building blocks of a modeling method and is still aligned with the meta-requirements* in Table 1;
- **Intuitive constructivism:** Hands-on experience of students should clash against their dominant preconceptions in order to generate transformations across the educational objectives specified by Bloom's framework [29] - Knowledge, Comprehension, Application, Analysis, Synthesis, and Evaluation. Students with heterogeneous background should be able to follow and replicate the demonstration;
- **Domain-specificity (without domain expertise)** should manifest in various aspects of the modeling method, suggesting further means of expanding this specificity.

However, specificity should be minimal to avoid prerequisite domain expertise and distractions pertaining to domain understanding;

- **Generalizability** (only loose coupling to software engineering): The proposed artifact should be detached from Software Engineering standards (UML, ER). At the same time, it should be re-attachable to software engineering purposes through means that illustrate the "models are knowledge" principle (i.e., model queries instead of the tight coupling of code generation);
- **Familiarity:** Existing modeling experience should be leveraged through analogies (with e.g. activity modeling), further suggesting how students could develop their own customization of existing standards.

The teaching artifact introduced to satisfy these requirements is therefore a minimalist modeling method – sufficiently rich to showcase the core principles of Agile Modeling Method Engineering and, at the same time, open-ended for further extensions in student homework. The building blocks of this artifact are shown in Fig. 1, each mapped to their enabling technologies (free versions for educational purposes are available for all of these):

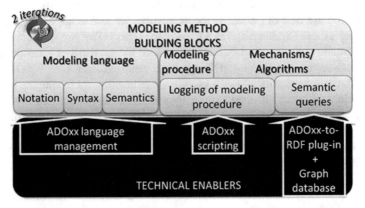

Fig. 1. Building blocks and enablers of the proposed teaching artifact

1. ADOxx [22], a metamodeling platform for rapid prototyping of modeling tools (including notation, syntactic rules, semantics or model-driven functionality);
2. ADOScript, the built-in scripting language of ADOxx for implementing model-based functionality;
3. GraphDB [30], an RDF graph database server with ontological capabilities (to store models as knowledge graphs and demonstrate model queries outside the modeling environment);
4. ADOxx-to-RDF [31], a plug-in for converting diagrammatic models to machine-readable RDF graphs, regardless of the modeling language used to create them; the graphs are stored in GraphDB to expose model content to semantic queries (SPARQL [32]) from arbitrary clients.

4 Methodology and Artifact

4.1 Application Domain for the Teaching Artifact

The research method underlying this work is subordinated to the Design Science research paradigm [33] – i.e., we designed an artifact (a "modeling method") that is needed to improve a problem context - to enable master students to think not only as users of established modeling tools (taken for granted and bound to a modeling procedure), but also as knowledge creators guided by specific requirements in a narrow application domain where a modeling layer must be employed to bridge human understanding and a technological execution environment. Thus the artifact is iteratively built to defuse the discussed fallacies and to satisfy the requirements formulated in Sect. 3, enabling new innovation competences in our Information Systems study programs, as well as an open-ended understanding of the benefits of Conceptual Modeling as a knowledge creation activity.

The application domain targeted by the teaching artifact is the Internet of Things, for which Conceptual Modeling can be used not only for traditional goals (e.g., system design), but also as a knowledge representation technique that is amenable for both analysis by humans and semantic processing by machines. The proposed modeling method is introduced in relation to Knowledge Management requirements in a maintenance company. A knowledge base must accumulate diagnosing or repair procedures mapped on maintained devices and their diagnosing sensors. A modeling tool is required to build this knowledge base in diagrammatic form.

4.2 Teaching Method and Course Flow

The teaching method is based on live tutorial demonstration of small implementation increments, mirrored by students. The progress has a "gradual revealing" nature, with metamodeling theorization provided in parallel lectures, to reflect back on the hands-on experience and by comparison with known modeling tools or languages. Each modeling method building block is showcased by a minimal example enriched across two iterations.

The tool development method employed for hands-on exercising is a simplification of the Agile Modeling Method Engineering (AMME) methodology. This is an iterative metamodeling approach where each iteration (i) starts with the definition of domain knowledge and modeling requirements (which here take the form of diagram mock-ups and the purpose of retrieving some information from models) and (ii) ends with the deployment of a usable modeling tool. More details on the AMME phases are available in [8], but for teaching purposes it is reduced here to its *Design* and *Develop* phases, quickly leading to a usable result even in the absence of introductory metamodeling theorization.

The two teaching iterations are exemplified in this paper, with the initial iteration satisfying the constraint of "not more than 3 concepts" and the second one splitting the modeling language into two types of models with machine-readable links, editable attributes and interactive notation. A third iteration may be left for students' homework, allowing them further individual exploration. The theoretical exposition that parallels the hands-on experience follows a learning flow suggested in Fig. 2, where the argumentation cascades along the following steps:

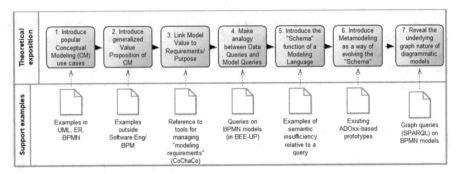

Fig. 2. Conceptual learning flow and support examples for each step

1. Introduce popular Conceptual Modeling use cases. This acts as a reminder of previous student experience from bachelor programs, where first contact with modeling involves the use of one or more of ER, UML, BPMN for the purpose of graphically documenting student projects;

2. Formulate a generalized "model value" proposition: first, by revealing (or reminding) that the models at the previous step may also have other purposes than graphical documentation - e.g. SQL code generation and BPMN process path simulation can be quickly demonstrated with open educational tools like BEE-UP [34]; next, the semantic coverage and domain-specificity of modeling languages is expanded towards other application areas and other purposes – e.g. Archimate, Value modeling, Designer components in Robotic Process Automation;

3. Link "model value" to Requirements/Purpose. This aims to make explicit the niche class of "modeling method requirements" (for which recent research proposed dedicated Requirements Engineering methods – see [35]). In the general sense, this reveals the nature of modeling languages/tools as Design Science artifacts subjected to requirements that trigger specific engineering cycles;

4. Make analogy between Data Queries and Model Queries to benefit from existing student experience with relational databases. Use the simplest examples that support the analogy – e.g. "select all tasks of a certain participant in a BPMN model". Use a tool that where model queries can be easily demonstrated directly in the modeling environment, e.g. BEE-UP [34];

5. Introduce the "schema" function of a modeling language. Reveal that model queries are enabled by a model schema ("metamodel"), similarly to how SQL queries are enabled by a database schema (and that the model schema must be sufficiently rich to satisfy the query). Provide examples of semantic insufficiency (e.g. how to retrieve ingredients and quantities from a BPMN diagram repurposed as a cooking recipe) – this will argue for the possibility of agile schema adaptation;

6. Introduce Metamodeling as a way of adapting the model schema to make it adequate for certain model queries (themselves derived from Requirements/Purpose). Show existing prototypes of open modeling tools and present Metamodeling platforms as means for editing their "model schema" and for the rapid (re)prototyping of a modeling tool according to the changed schema;

7. *Introduce the underlying graph-like nature of diagrammatic models* and the possibility of enabling model queries outside a modeling environment. A handy example can again benefit from BEE-UP, as it provides an option to export BPMN or UML models to RDF graphs, making them available to semantic processing. This will also be shown in the teaching artifact developed with students, thus establishing a bridge towards the next course module (on semantic technology).

4.3   Initial Iteration of the Teaching Artifact

The teaching artifact is demonstrating starting with introducing the scenario (Sect. 4.1) immediately followed by the initiation of AMME's Design phase by (i) sketching a mock-up of how diagrams should look in the language being developed and (ii) identifying the distinct types for each element present in the mock-up diagram. The types (node types and connector types) will form the *metamodel*, introduced here as the "language vocabulary" or "knowledge schema", thus simplifying the traditional notions of meta-modeling established in the MOF specification [20] to one easily involved in the data-models analogy.

Figure 3 shows such a mockup depicting a rudimentary process flow (simple sequence of maintenance steps), where each step can be connected either to a sensor or a device it acts upon; additionally, sensors should be attachable to devices.

The language vocabulary is introduced as the aggregate answer to four questions: (i) what types of nodes are used in the mock-up? (ii) what types of connectors are used? (iii) what types of nodes should be linked by each connector (i.e., the domain and range of each relation)? (iv) how should the types be unified in order to have a single domain and range for each relation? (i.e., a generalized RESOURCE concept is introduced, to allow a maintenance step to act on both SENSORs and DEVICEs).

Non-specialized wording is employed ("types/concepts", "connectors", "generalization", "language vocabulary") to support Business Administration students while at the same time allowing those with computer science background the mapping to a more technical dialect ("classes", "inheritance", "metamodel").

Following this design, students are guided to stepwise implement it in the language engineering component of ADOxx. Implementation phases are clearly distinguished by the building block they address: (i) abstract syntax (the definition of types and their syntactic constraints – i.e., domain, range, cardinality); (ii) notation (the custom graphic symbols attached to each concept and connector); (iii) semantics (the meaning attached to each symbol).

The importance of semantics is stressed as the core benefit of Conceptual Modeling in contrast to free sketching/drawing. Human interpretation and machine interpretation are thus distinguished – the first relying on expressive labeling and visual cues; the second requiring machine-readable (possibly domain-specific) annotation properties that will be later exposed to model queries and model-driven systems. These properties must conform a schema that can be tailored for each concept. In this case, to DEVICEs we add a TYPE property (as a way of distinguishing meaning without having to add new

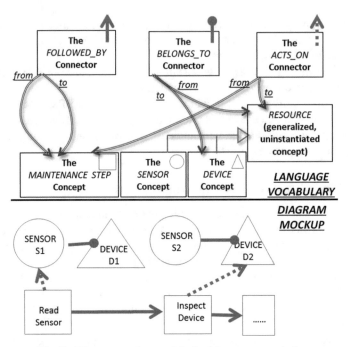

Fig. 3. Diagram mockup and derived language vocabulary

graphical symbols to the language) and a DOCUMENTATION property (a hyperlink to some device documentation available outside the modeling tool). Both labels and annotations will later become the basis of running semantic queries against the RDF graph structure that can be derived from models.

Figure 4 shows a model created with the initial modeling tool implementation. The model is still limited in its capability of expressing information, relying on the labels attached to the concepts and not so much on the graphical representation. It is also very simplistic in terms of attributes that it exposes to model queries.

After the initial language implementation, the other two building blocks of a modeling method are demonstrated: *mechanisms* and the *modeling procedure*. A minimal demonstrative mechanism is scripted with the help of ADOxx's internal scripting language. The script shown in Listing 1 captures the event of drawing a connector instance and writes in a log file information about the created connector (which objects have been connected, in what model). It showcases the machine-readable nature of models – through functions that retrieve the objects and types associated to a modeling event (here, connector creation) while at the same time accessing the external file system to produce some output based on model contents.

This is presented as a toy example of traditional model-driven approaches such as code generation. It also introduces the third component of a modeling method, the "modeling procedure" (i.e., the recommended steps for creating models). If the modeling procedure is simple enough to be formalized as a sequence of modeling actions, a "reference sequence" can be compared with logged sequences with the help of similarity

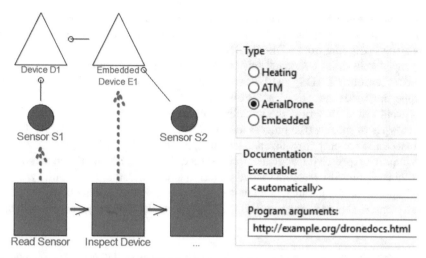

Fig. 4. Model created with the initial language iteration (left) and concept-level schema for DEVICE annotations (right)

metrics – e.g., Levenshtein distance. Recent works concerned with the effectiveness of teaching Conceptual Modeling show a growing interest in measuring modeling actions as means of assessing learning outcomes [36] (an approach that we label as "modeling procedure analysis").

```
ON_EVENT "AfterCreateModelingConnector"{
CC "Modeling" GET_ACT_MODEL
CC "Core" GET_MODEL_INFO modelid:(modelid)
CC "Core" GET_CLASS_NAME classid:(classid)
CC "Core" GET_OBJ_NAME objid:(fromobjid)
SET sourcename:(objname)
CC "Core" GET_OBJ_NAME objid:(toobjid)
SET targetname:(objname)
CC "AdoScript" FWRITE file:"C:\\log\\log.txt" text:("In model
"+modelname+" you created a connector of type "+classname+ " from
object "+sourcename+" to object "+targetname+"\n") append:yes}
```

Listing 1. ADOxx script for logging modeling actions

4.4 Advanced Iteration of the Teaching Artifact

Coming from initial modeling experiences in software engineering, students tend to perceive modeling languages as invariants. However, agility principles may also be adopted for modeling languages/methods - this is demonstrated in our teaching case by evolving the "modeling requirements", followed by a quick reprototyping of the modeling tool. Examples of requirements driving the new iteration are the following:

- The maintenance procedure should be more than a sequence of STEPs. DECISIONs may also be necessary (which leads to the necessity of writing the progress condition on arrows outgoing from a DECISION);
- To avoid "construct overload" (cf. [37]), the ACTS_ON relation must be specialized for sensors (READS_VALUE) and devices (ACTS_ON_DEVICE), consequently supporting model queries with this distinction;
- To avoid visual cluttering, the modeling language should be partitioned in two distinct types of models (the process and the resources); consequently, the ACTS_ON connector is not only specialized, but also replaced with hyperlinks between models;
- To improve expressivity, domain-specificity should also be assimilated in notation (as visual cues, plus the freedom to load preferred icons instead of the default symbols);
- To improve interoperability, domain-specificity should be assimilated in semantics as well (sensors should have a live ADDRESS property that directly gives access to their value stream).

Figure 5 shows diagrams created with the new iteration of the modeling tool and the two model types that separate the process aspect from the resource aspect.

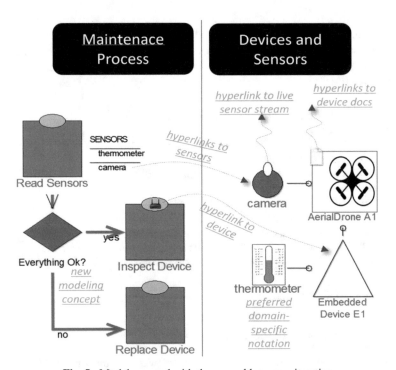

Fig. 5. Models created with the second language iteration

Modeling standards, since they establish consensus, provide a foundation for model compilers and roundtrip engineering. Since in this case we are advocating a non-standard, unpredictable customization of a modeling language, the benefits of consensus do not apply. However, software artifacts can still benefit from the knowledge captured in diagrammatic form by resorting to the Resource Description Framework.

For this purpose an ADOxx plug-in can convert any type of model (created with any language/tool implemented on ADOxx) to RDF graphs according to certain transformation patterns available in the literature [38]. The derived graphs are hosted by a graph database and some simple model query examples can be demonstrated with students, suggesting the possibility of building client applications that are "aware" of model contents and their "knowledge schema". This specific type of model-driven software engineering method has been discussed in more detail in [39].

An example of a (SPARQL) query is provided here in Listing 2. It retrieves all the devices inspected during a selected procedure and the components attached to them on any decomposition level. At this point RDF and semantic queries are not necessarily mastered by students - this is an introductory example for a subsequent Knowledge Representation module that complements the Conceptual Modeling module by delving into semantic technology and showing how their interplay establishes a bridge between human-oriented (visual) knowledge and machine-readable knowledge graphs.

```
SELECT ?device ?component
WHERE {
GRAPH :MaintenanceProcedure
{?x :ActsOnDevice ?device.?device :describedIn ?model}
GRAPH ?model
{?component :BelongsTo+ ?device}
}
```

Listing 2. SPARQL queries on model contents enabled by the second iteration

5 Outcomes

The hands-on demonstration and exercise have proven successful in defusing the fallacies detailed in Sect. 3 and in establishing a uniform baseline for students regardless of their background. Success is mainly manifested in the sense that more sophisticated model-driven thesis projects have been enabled, moving away from a "blueprint thinking" towards lateral thinking, revealing a more general value and application possibilities for Conceptual Modeling. Specifically, we can revisit the meta-requirements in Table 1 through the lens of Bloom's taxonomy of educational objectives. Confining students to the role of users (of a modeling language) locks them in limited comprehension, whereas the proposed teaching artifact opens new layers of:

- *comprehension* ("I understand the role of knowledge schema that a modeling language fulfils, regardless of the application domain") – this level satisfies meta-requirement B from Table 1;
- *analysis* ("I can distinguish the building blocks of a modeling method, I know which is affected by an agile change request") – this level satisfies meta-requirements A and D;

- *synthesis* ("I can synthesize a new method/tool based on my knowledge of those building blocks") – this level satisfies meta-requirements A and C;
- *application* ("I can implement a domain-specific modeling tool") – this level satisfies meta-requirements A and C;
- *evaluation* ("I can relate a modeling method to the requirements/purpose for which it was built") – this level satisfies meta-requirements A and D.

Regarding a quantified success of the approach, the proposal is part of a master exam that reflects a normal distribution of grading and student interest, like any other typical exam (about 25% of students propose new domains and bring novelty in their exam projects; 45% do not bother to innovate but are capable of extending the developed prototype; 30% show little interest or have difficulties passing the exam – this is however not a discrepancy from other exams).

A more relevant outcome than the grading distribution is the fact that our master students were for the first time able to publish scientific works on Conceptual Modeling topics at prestigious international conferences: ENASE 2018 [39], ICEIS 2018 [40], CAISE 2018 workshops [41], PoEM 2018 workshops [42], BIR 2019 [43]. Furthermore the learning curve for junior researchers starting project work was shortened by an estimated 2 months for those attending strictly this module or by 6 months for those following the full program, which includes additional related topics: dissecting open source implementations of known modeling languages (e.g., the BEE-UP tool supporting UML, BPMN, ER, EPC and Petri Nets [34]); further reading on the benefits of domain-specific or situational method engineering [28, 44]; exercises with graph databases and semantic technology. The estimation is based on isolated cases as the module was only recently launched and we do not have yet alumni data for a longitudinal survey – but the measurable success that was targeted by this "education design problem" is that of unprecedented scientific output on Conceptual Modeling topics from master students.

6   Related Works

Recent works show growing preoccupation with deploying teaching methodologies for Conceptual Modeling. A recent panel discussion made the following position statement referring to Conceptual Modeling education [45]: "Supportive means such as text books, case examples are hardly available. In many cases teaching may boil down to an art being passed on to students. […] (basic) courses are dominated by the coding exercise, i.e., students' efforts in mastering simulation software, or, to a lesser degree, statistics associated with model elements or outputs. Hence little time is left for Conceptual Modeling." The work at hand tries to address this discontinuity which, in the authors' experience is often met between bachelor programs and more advanced studies or research project work.

Works such as [36, 46] employ analysis of modeling action logs to assess different dimensions of learning and educational objectives when teaching software engineering-oriented Conceptual Modeling (e.g., UML). Another work that quantifies UML model creation errors by novices is [3]. In [47] authors proposed a tool for monitoring the interactions and mistakes done during using an established modeling language. In comparison, our work focuses on empowering students to take control over their modeling method and tool, while being aware of and guided by a purpose and related requirements.

This work was also inspired by previous publications detailing teaching experiences that make use of similar resources (i.e., ADOxx): the modeling tool presented in [48] is much more complex and does not target our specific learning objectives (e.g., iterative minimalism and knowledge retrieval); the case of [14] is closer in scope to our work – however it is subordinated to teaching Software Engineering (SQL generation from Entity Relationship diagrams). A long-term teaching experience report oriented towards system architect practitioners, rather than students, is presented in [15]. A generalized framework for teaching Conceptual Modeling has recently been published in [49], using a revised variant of Bloom's taxonomy as a motivational starting point. Our future work will provide further analysis of our proposed artifact through the analytical lens established by that publication.

7   Conclusions

The paper introduced a minimalist modeling method as a teaching artifact that can be created together with students, with the help of open use educational resources. Its qualities are minimalism, intuitive constructivism, open-endedness, domain-specificity, detachment from standard practices (while still showing relevance for Software Engineering). The methodological and technological enablers of the proposed artifact are the Agile Modeling Method Engineering framework, the Resource Description Framework and openly available tooling supporting these frameworks.

The framework proposed very recently by [49] will be employed in the next phase of our work to dissect the hereby proposed teaching artifact in terms of the knowledge and cognitive dimensions of the revised Bloom taxonomy. Future work will also be invested in defining variations of this artifact for other domains and timeframes. Examples of candidate domains are Service Design (for marketing experts), Narrative Structure Analysis (for communication theorists), Model-driven Robotics (for engineering schools).

We aim to further reshape this demonstration in order to fit the 2–3 h frame typically allowed in conference tutorials, as well as to fit it in the curriculum of the Next Generation Enterprise Modeling summer school series [50] and later make it available as an educational resource in the OMiLAB portal [23].

Acknowledgements. This work was supported by a mobility grant of the Romanian Ministry of Research and Innovation through UEFISCDI project number PN-III-P1-1.1-MC-2019-1953, part of the programme PNCDI III.

References

1. Ghiran, A.M., Osman, C.C., Buchmann, R.A.: A metamodeling approach to teaching conceptual modeling at large. In: Siarheyeva, A., Laville, A., Pérocheau, G., Barry, C., Lang, M., Linger, H., Schneider, C. (eds.) Information Systems Development: Information Systems Beyond 2020 (ISD2019 Proceedings). Toulon, France (2019)

2. Boucher, X., Medini, K., Fill, H.-G.: Product-service-system modeling method. In: Domain-Specific Conceptual Modeling, pp. 455–482. Springer, Cham (2016). https://doi.org/10.1007/978-3-319-39417-6_21

3. Kayama, M., Ogata, S., Masymoto, K., Hashimoto, M., Otani, M.: A practical Conceptual Modeling teaching method based on quantitative error analyses for novices learning to create error-free simple class diagrams. In: Proceedings of 3rd Advanced Applied Informatics (IIAI 2014), pp. 616-622. IEEE (2014)

4. Sales, T. P., Roelens, B., Poels, G., Guizzardi, G., Guarino, N., Mylopoulos, J.: A pat-tern language for value modeling in Archimate, In: Giorgini, P., Weber, B. (eds.) Advanced Information Systems Engineering. CAiSE 2019. vol 11483, pp. 230–245.. Springer, Cham (2019). https://doi.org/10.1007/978-3-030-21290-2_15

5. Buchmann, R.A., Ghiran, A.M.: Engineering the cooking recipe modelling method: a teaching experience report. In: CEUR-WS vol. 1999, paper 5 (2017)

6. Strecker, S., Baumol, U., Karagiannis, D., Koschmider, A., Snoeck, M., Zarnekow, R.: Five inspiring course (re-) designs. Bus. Inf. Syst. Eng. **61**(2), 241–252 (2019)

7. Karagiannis, D., Kühn, H.: Metamodelling platforms. In: Bauknecht, K., Tjoa, A.M., Quirchmayr, G. (eds.) E-Commerce and Web Technologies. EC-Web 2002. LNCS, vol. 2455, p. 182. Springer, Heidelberg (2002)

8. Karagiannis, D.: Conceptual modelling methods: the AMME agile engineering approach. In: Silaghi, G.C., Buchmann, R.A., Boja, C. (eds.) Informatics in Economy (IE 2016). Lecture Notes in Business Information Processing, vol. 273, pp. 3–19. Springer, Cham (2018)

9. Buchmann, R.A., Ghiran, A.M., Döller, V., Karagiannis, D.: Conceptual modeling education as a "design problem". Complex Syst. Inform. Model. Q. **21**, 21–33 (2019). https://doi.org/10.7250/csimq.2019-21.02

10. Embley, D.W., Liddle, S.W., Lonsdale, D.W.: Principled pragmatism: a guide to the adaptation of ideas from philosophical disciplines to conceptual modeling. In: De Troyer, O., Bauzer Medeiros, C., Billen, R., Hallot, P., Simitsis, A., Van Mingroot, H. (eds.) Advances in Conceptual Modeling. Recent Developments and New Directions (ER 2011). LNCS, vol. 6999, pp. 183–192. Springer, Heidelberg (2011)

11. Moser, C., Buchmann, R.A., Utz, W., Karagiannis, D.: CE-SIB: a modelling method plug-in for managing standards. In: Mayr, H.C., Guizzardi, G., Ma, H., Pastor, O. (eds.) Conceptual Modeling. Enterprise Architectures (ER 2017). LNCS, vol. 10650, pp. 21–35. Springer, Cham (2017)

12. Rosenthal, K., Ternes, B., Strecker, S.: Learning Conceptual Modeling: structuring overview, research themes and paths for future research. In: Proceedings of ECIS 2019, paper 137, Association for Information Systems (2019)

13. Association for Computing Machinery (2018). Curricula Recommendations. https://www.acm.org/education/curricula-recommendations/. Accessed 14 Oct 2019

14. Glässner, T.M., Heumann, F., Keßler, L., Härer, F., Steffan, A., Fill, H.G.: Experiences from the implementation of a structured-entity-relationship modeling method in a student project. In: Proceedings of the 1st International Workshop on Practicing Open Enterprise Modeling within OMiLAB (PoEM 2017), vol. 1999 (2017)

15. Muller, G.: Challenges in teaching conceptual modeling for systems architecting. In: Jeusfeld, M., Karlapalem, K. (eds.) Advances in Conceptual Modeling, ER 2015. LNCS, vol. 9382, pp. 317–326. Springer, Cham (2015)

16. Bider, I., Henkel, M., Kowalski, S., Perjons, E.: Teaching enterprise modeling based on multi-media simulation: a pragmatic approach. In: Benyoucef, M., Weiss, M., Mili., H. (eds.) Proceedings of the 6th International Conference on E-Technologies. Montréal, Canada, pp. 239–254. Springer, *Cham* (2015)

17. Karagiannis, D., Mayr, H.C., Mylopoulos, J.: Domain-specific Conceptual Modeling. Springer, Switzerland (2016)

18. Kastens, U., Büning, H.K.: Modellierung: Grundlagen und formale Methoden, Hanser (2008)
19. Seidl, M., Brandsteidl, M., Huemer, C., Kappel, G.: UML@ Classroom, Dpunkt (2012)
20. OMG: Meta-Modeling and the OMG Meta Object Facility. https://www.omg.org/ocup-2/doc uments/Meta-ModelingAndtheMOF.pdf
21. Fill, H.G., Redmond, T., Karagiannis, D.: Formalizing meta models with FDMM: the ADOxx case. In: Proceedings of ICEIS 2012. LNBIP, vol. 141, pp. 429–451. Springer, Heidelberg (2012)
22. BOC GmbH: ADOxx metamodeling platform – official website. http://www.adoxx.org/live/ home. Accessed 24 June 2019
23. OMiLAB, Modeling Method Projects. https://austria.omilab.org/psm/exploreprojects? param=explore
24. Prat, N., Comyn-Wattiau, I., Akoka, J.: Artifact evaluation in information systems design-science research-a holistic view. In: Proceedings of the 19th Pacific Asia Conference on Information Systems (PACIS 2014). AIS (2014)
25. Nonaka, I., von Krogh, G.: Perspective - tacit knowledge and knowledge conversion: controversy and advancement in organisational knowledge creation theory. Organ. Sci. **20**(3), 635–652 (2009)
26. Karagiannis, D., Buchmann, R., Walch, M.: How can diagrammatic conceptual modelling support Knowledge Management? In: Proceedings of the 25th European Conference on Information Systems (ECIS 2017), pp. 1568–1583 (2017)
27. W3C: Resource Description Framework – official website. http://www.w3.org/RDF. Accessed 24 June 2019
28. Frank, U.: Domain-specific modeling languages: requirements analysis and design guidelines. In: Reinhartz-Berger, I., Sturm, A., Clark, T., Cohen, S., Bettin, J. (eds.) Domain Engineering, pp. 133–157. Springer, Berlin, Heidelberg (2013)
29. Bloom, B.S.: Taxonomy of educational objectives: the classification of educational goals: handbook I: cognitive domain, D. McKay (1956)
30. Ontotext: GraphDB - official website. http://graphdb.ontotext.com/. Accessed 24 June 2019
31. OMILab: ADOxx-to-RDF download page. http://austria.omilab.org/psm/content/comvan tage/downloadlist?view=downloads. Accessed 24 June 2019
32. W3C: SPARQL 1.1 Query Language. http://www.w3.org/TR/2013/REC-sparql11-query-201 30321. Accessed 24 June 2019
33. Wieringa, R.J.: Design Science Methodology for Information Systems and Software Engineering. Springer, Heidelberg (2014)
34. OMiLAB: Bee-Up – official website. http://austria.omilab.org/psm/content/bee-up/info. Accessed 24 June 2019
35. Karagiannis, D., Burzynski, P., Utz, W., Buchmann, R.A.: A metamodeling approach to support the engineering of modeling method requirements. In: Proceedings of the 27th International Requirements Engineering Conference (RE 2019), Jeju Island, South Korea, pp. 199–210. IEEE CS, (2019). https://doi.org/10.1109/RE.2019.00030
36. Snoeck, M.: Conceptual modelling: how to do it right? In: Proceedings of 11th Research Challenges in Information Science (RCIS 2017). IEEE (2017)
37. Moody, D.L., Heymans, P., Matulevičius, R.: Improving the effectiveness of visual representations in requirements engineering: an evaluation of i* visual syntax. In: Proceedings of 17th Requirements Engineering Conference (RE 2009), pp. 171–180. IEEE (2009)
38. Karagiannis, D., Buchmann, R.A.: Linked open models: extending Linked Open Data with conceptual model information. Inf. Syst. **56**, 174–197 (2016)

39. Buchmann, R.A., Cinpoeru, M., Harkai, A., Karagiannis, D.: Model-aware software engineering - a knowledge-based approach to model-driven software engineering. In: Damiani, E., Spanoudakis, G., Maciaszek, L. (eds.) Proceedings of the 13th International Conference on Evaluation of Novel Approaches to Software Engineering (ENASE 2018), pp. 233–240. ScitePress (2018)

40. Harkai, A., Cinpoeru, M., Buchmann, R.A.: Repurposing zachman framework principles for "enterprise model"-driven engineering. In: Hammoudi, S., Smialek, M., Camp, O., Filipe, J. (eds.) Proceedings of the 20th International Conference on Enterprise Information Systems - Volume 2 (ICEIS 2018), pp. 682–689. ScitePress (2018)

41. Harkai, A., Cinpoeru, M., Buchmann, R.A.: The what facet of the zachman framework: a linked data-driven interpretation. In: Matulevičius, R., Dijkman, R. (eds.) Proceedings of CAISE 2018 Workshops. LNBIP, vol. 316, pp. 197–208. Springer, Cham (2018)

42. Chis-Ratiu, A., Buchmann, R.A.: Design and implementation of a diagrammatic tool for creating RDF graphs. In: CEUR-WS, vol. 2238, pp. 37–48 (2018)

43. Cinpoeru, M., Ghiran, A. M., Harkai, A., Buchmann, R. A., Karagiannis, D.: Model-driven context configuration in business process management systems: an approach based on knowledge graphs. In: Pańkowska, M., Sand-kuhl, K. (eds.) Perspectives in Business Informatics Research. BIR 2019. LNBIP, vol. 365, pp. 189–203. Springer, Cham (2019). https://doi.org/10.1007/978-3-030-31143-8_14

44. Bucher, T., Klesse, M., Kurpjuweit, S., Winter, R.: Situational method engineering. in: situational method engineering: fundamentals and experiences. In: Ralyté, J., Brinkkemper, S., Henderson-Sellers, B. (eds.) IFIP — The International Federation for Information Processing, vol. 244, pp. 33–48. Springer, Boston (2007)

45. van der Zee, D.J., Kotiadis, K., Tako, A.A., Pidd, M., Balci, O., Tolk, A., Elder, M.: Panel discussion: education on conceptual modeling for simulation – challenging the art. In: Proceedings of the 2010 Winter Simulation Conference (WSC 2010), pp. 290–304. IEEE (2010)

46. Bogdanova, D., Snoeck, M.: Domain modelling in bloom: deciphering how we teach it. In: Poels, G., Gailly, F., Serral Asensio, E., Snoeck, M. (eds.) The Practice of Enterprise Modeling (PoEM 2017). Lecture Notes in Business Information Processing, vol. 305, pp. 3–17. Springer, Cham (2017)

47. Ternes, B., Strecker, S.: A web-based modeling tool for studying the learning of conceptual modeling, Modellierung 2018, Gesellschaft für Informatik, pp. 325–328 (2018)

48. Bork, D., Buchmann, R., Hawryszkiewycz, I., Karagiannis, D., Tantouris, N., Walch, M.: Using conceptual modeling to support innovation challenges in smart cities. In: Proceedings of IEEE 14th International Conference on Smart City (SmartCity 2016), pp. 1317–1324. IEEE (2016)

49. Bork, D.: A framework for teaching conceptual modeling and metamodeling based on bloom's revised taxonomy of educational objectives. In: 52nd Annual Hawaii International Conference on System Sciences (HICSS 2019), pp. 7701–7710 (2019)

50. OMILab: NEMO Summer School Series. http://nemo.omilab.org/2018/. Accessed 24 June 2019

Beyond Reading Media and Interaction Behavior: Self-reported User Satisfaction and Cognitive Implications of Digitized Reading Patterns

Dorina Rajanen[✉]

University of Oulu, Oulu, Finland
dorina.rajanen@oulu.fi

Abstract. This paper examines the reading and navigation (browsing) behavior and the user satisfaction when interacting with a traditional and digital newspaper during an experiment. The qualitative, visual inspection of the interaction behavior allowed to identify the reading and navigation patterns specific to the reading media. The patterns were quantified as duration to assess the amount of time dedicated for reading, in contrast to navigation. The results show that, in the paper reading condition, the reading time was higher when compared to the tablet condition. In contrast, the navigation time was generally higher in the tablet than in the paper condition, with possible consequences on cognitive load. Users' satisfaction with the traditional newspaper was higher than in the case of digital reading. The findings are discussed considering the limited capacity of mediated message processing model. Implications for designing digital reading interfaces are formulated.

Keywords: Reading behavior · Newspaper reading · Digital reading · Cognitive processing · Limited capacity model of mediated message processing · User satisfaction

1 Introduction

The morning newspaper, a bundle of newsprint paper smelling of freshly printed ink, has been an integral part of the morning routine of many since 17th century, becoming an institution of its own right, with its established design, development, and content providing traditions and ways of reading. The term newspaper itself points to a collection of news that has been printed on a paper. However, the emergence of digital online newspapers on computers in 1980s and 1990s and on mobile devices in 2000s has challenged this status quo. On the other hand, the printed newspaper is not disappearing any time fast, since studies have shown that newspaper readers perceive print and digital

A prior version of this paper has been published in the ISD2019 Proceedings (http://aisel.aisnet.org/isd2014/proceedings2019).

A. Siarheyeva et al. (Eds.): ISD 2019, LNISO 39, pp. 19–36, 2020.
https://doi.org/10.1007/978-3-030-49644-9_2

newspapers as complementary to each other and are not ready to choose one over the other [1, 2]. Nevertheless, the existing newspaper design traditions of printed newspapers cannot be transferred as such into the digital newspapers read on mobile devices, which creates a challenge to designers, developers, content providers, and readers of digital newspapers.

Despite there exist numerous isolated studies comparing digital and traditional reading, most of them focus on comparing performance such as reading speed (e.g., [3]), as well as high-level information processing like recall, comprehension, and creativity (e.g., [4]). The findings are often controversial showing contradictory findings [4–6], while the topic lacks a systematic approach on causes or implications in relation to human information processing. In contrast, most of the studies are limited to identifying differences in effects rather than pointing out behavior that leads to those effects. As such, there are still gaps in the research comparing printed and digital newspapers and reading on paper and reading on a digital device in general, especially concerning the fundamental reading behaviors and patterns such as user actions, as well as identifying the implications in a systematic way.

In this paper, the differences between the two media, print paper and a tablet computer, are examined with respect to the reader's interaction behavior. Reading and navigation (browsing) patterns during newspaper reading are derived and identified. The research question guiding this study is: *What differences are there between tablet and paper media in terms of reading and navigation patterns?* An experiment for studying media experience was conducted in which the participants read the largest Finnish newspaper in two conditions: the traditional paper version and digital tablet version[1]. Each participant took part in the study individually and read/browsed the newspaper of the day for 15 min in each condition. The data analyzed in this paper consists of video-recorded user actions during the two reading sessions. Furthermore, self-reported user satisfaction in terms of quality of interaction, usability, interestingness of contents, attention, emotional responses, and overall media experience has been collected and analyzed. Based on the collected data regarding the reading and navigation behavior, two findings are observed: 1) effective reading time on tablet was lower than on paper; and 2) navigation time and navigation-tasks diversity were higher on tablet than on paper.

These findings indicate that the two media inherently may facilitate two kinds of reading behavior: traditional paper enables better sustained reading as compared to digital reading; on the other hand, digital reading requires the user to allocate more time and resources on navigation when compared to the traditional reading medium. However, these implications should be explored in further research. As a step in this direction, the paper examines the findings in light of the model of limited capacity of mediated message processing (see Lang [7]) as an approach to frame the implications of media-specific reading behaviors on the actual processing of information displayed on digital media. In turn, this fact has implications and challenges on how to design mobile reading interfaces that are optimal for the intended purpose.

---

[1] The experiment was part of a large project ("Next Media") related to the development of the Finnish media industry and media experience concepts. (see http://virtual.vtt.fi/virtual/nextme dia/573139/en/read/page.html).

The paper is structured as follows. Section 2 summarizes the existing research on comparing digital and paper reading. Section 3 briefly describes the limited capacity model of mediated message processing. Sections 4 and 5 describe the methods and the results, respectively. The last sections discuss the results and their implications to design and conclude the paper.

2   Related Work

Print paper and digital media have been empirically compared since the introduction of personal computers in work and everyday tasks, namely since 1980s. Whereas in early comparisons, the paper medium showed some sort of advantages over the screen, nowadays, with the advances in technology and computer literacy, these differences blur [3, 8–10]. However, one can still argue that each medium has its own strengths. The strengths of the print paper are natural/quick navigation, flexibility of the spatial layout (e.g., unfolding the papers), serial presentation and, not less important, the subjective preference of the readers. The benefits of digital reading include the automatic search, updating of content, hyper-linking, multimedia, accessibility, colors, and the fact that people have become more computer literate [3, 11–13]. In addition, the size and weight of computer tablets and the improvement in screen quality make reading from mobile devices increasingly acceptable, especially in conditions where a paper version is not convenient [1, 3]. In the following, two types of related work are summarized: 1) reading behaviors from various perspectives especially oculomotor activity and reading styles, and 2) cognitive processing implications of differences in reading media.

2.1   Reading Behaviors Associated with Digital and Paper Media

Liu [14] investigated the reading behavior in digital environment and examined the evolution of reading behaviors. The findings showed that electronic reading involved more browsing and scanning, keyword spotting, selective reading, and that people spent less time in concentrated reading when compared to paper reading. Moreover, reading on digital media came with a loss of reader attention. Liu pointed out that some differences in reading behavior between paper and tablet might be explained by the fact that the paper medium is associated with thorough reading (of, for example, books), while electronic reading is often "for fun" and, thus, more selective and less concentrated. Hillesund [15] examined the way in which proficient readers handle print paper and digital texts and explained the concepts of continuous and discontinuous reading, and the combination of those two. Chen et al. [16] found that navigation patterns specific in digital and paper reading do not affect reading comprehension; however, navigation style was the main factor affecting the process of reading.

In a study on news reading on a screen versus paper, Holmqvist et al. [17] employed eye-tracking and found that online news readers scanned more and read less than the traditional newspaper readers. That is, readers of online newspapers spent more fixation time on the link lists (scanning) than on the article areas (reading). On the other hand, a more recent eye-tracking study [18] found no significant differences between reading on the mobile devices and paper in terms of oculomotor behavior, though when comparing computer displays with tablets and other e-readers, the mean fixation duration was significantly longer in reading on the computer screen. Another study [19], based on data about reading patterns collected in 2013 from a readership study and automatic logs of a Swedish newspaper, found that print readers and online readers differ in the articles and pages they select for reading, but the amount of time spent on each article becomes closer in the two reading conditions.

2.2 Cognitive and Emotional Implications of Digital and Paper Reading

Reading comprehension is extensively studied in comparisons of digital and paper reading, and majority of the studies report better performance associated with paper medium than with screen (see [4, 20]). However, some studies report equal performance on reading comprehension [5, 6], which may also be due to the increasing familiarity with the digital medium (see [16]). Among the research showing superior reading comprehension when using paper compared with a computer screen, [4] also showed that levels of stress and tiredness were higher for the participants in the computer-screen condition. The authors' explanation emphasized the difference of text configuration in the two media, which makes the acquisition of information to proceed slowly in the case of the screen presentation compared with the paper. For the screen presentation, the authors argue, that more cognitive resources are invested due to the deficiency of the information presentation. In addition, in the case of reading from a screen, there is higher workload due to both reading itself and operating the computer. Chen et al. [16] compared tablet, computer, and paper reading and found that reading comprehension is also affected by the familiarity with the medium, as people with a higher level of tablet familiarity had better deep level comprehension than the ones with lower tablet familiarity.

Regarding emotions and motivation, earlier and recent studies (e.g., [11, 21]) pointed out that people prefer the print medium and feel more familiar with it. A national survey on the newspaper reading trends in Finland [1] showed that media consumers are still committed to printed newspapers and magazines and they want to read both electronic and print media, rather than choosing one of them. Flavian and Gurrea [2] have studied the motivations behind reading newspapers online vs. print and if the two media can be seen as substitute products. They showed that both formats are considered as information conduits and not as substitutive products. However, motivations that could be satisfied by both media positively affect the level of perceived substitutability between the reading media in contrast to the motivations driven by the differential attributes of each medium.

Noyes and Garland [12] pointed out that the physical nature of a computer screen also evokes additional processing during task execution compared with a paper condition, which in turn leads to greater perceived and actual workload. Moreover, the differences in the way information is retrieved on screen and paper has been found to result in differences in memory due to the nature of visual input [12]. D'Haenens and Heuvelman [22], in an experiment on how readers consume and recall news presented in online and paper versions of two Dutch newspapers, showed that the news consumption was not influenced by the news format, but rather by the news category or reader's characteristics. However, no systematic differences were found to distinguish between the readers of the print paper and digital formats. The only difference found was that the participants reading printed newspapers recalled the news better. Mangen and Kuiken [23] studied narrative engagement when reading on booklet and tablet and found that level of experience with digital reading did not affect reading engagement. Tablet reading was found generally generating lower engagement with the text and handling of the medium. On the other hand, booklet readers reported better transportation and empathy than tablet readers.

Hou et al. [24] compared recently paper and digital reading of a comic book and found that reading comprehension, fatigue, and immersion were similar in the two conditions if the digital reading was not disruptive. The methodology used in their study enabled them to conclude that the reading outcome is not influenced by the materiality of the presentation medium (e.g., screen vs. paper, or tactile dimensions of the medium), but rather by the way the text is presented and facilitates the reader to construct cognitive maps of the text structure. The cognitive map mechanism is also found useful to explain why paper books are better for readers to form a coherent cognitive map of the text than digital texts [25] which have consequences on increased reading outcomes and performance [24].

Despite the many benefits of digital reading such as providing different levels of navigation support for the manipulation of the digital text, and presenting capabilities for analytic reading (e.g., annotation, highlighting, indexing), Brown [26] acknowledges that the paper medium is more suitable for sustained reading. However, Brown also posits that the reading habits change with the development and pervasiveness of reading technology, and that reading is a multidimensional act that involves many strategies depending on the goals of reading such as pleasure and enjoyment, information and learning. Moreover, it is recognized that in paper reading, readers feel omnipotent, they dominate text, and they have a feel of orientation given the physical and tactile properties of the medium [26]. This natural navigation is not encountered when using digital reading media and the loss of context may hinder the motivation and attention. Thus, the navigation in digital reading media is essential for creating a positive reading experience and Brown points out that software development in this direction is a promising research area which has also implications in creating new habits of reading.

3 Limited Capacity Model of Processing Information

The limited capacity model of information processing developed by Lang [7] is founded on the assumption that the ability of people to process information is limited (see also [27, 28]). Accordingly, the cognitive resources (for attending the different stimuli from the environment, encoding new information into the working memory, and/or performing other cognitive processes) are limited and compete for different processing tasks [7]. The model is useful to explain and understand how mediated messages are processed and has been applied in media and communication research, for example in the context of television viewing [7] and communication (see e.g., [29]).

The model of limited capacity of information processing or limited capacity of mediated message processing (LCMMP henceforth) turns the focus from behavior to information processing (see [30]), following the paradigm shift in psychology started in the late 70's (see [31]). Accordingly, media in the term "mediated messages" is conceptualized as a complex set of stimuli characterized by multiple variables that are psychologically relevant and continuously change in time such as attention, encoding, storage, resource allocation, effort, and elaboration [31]. The LCMMP model can thus provide a sound theoretical basis to the information systems (IS) and human-computer interaction (HCI) research to explain and understand implications of digital media design for reading on both the design of better interfaces and optimal human information processing. Currently, the model is not applied as such in IS and HCI communities.

According to the LCMMP, three elements are interacting in mediated message processing: *the viewer, the medium, and the message or information* [32]. The viewer (user in computer science) is the information processor; his/her ability to process information is limited. The medium is seen as a set of structural features used to present audio or visual information. The message is characterized by different attributes such as the topic, genre, and information contained in a message. Media use (as well as computer use) can be defined as the "allocation of a limited pool of processing resources to the cognitive processes required for viewers to make sense of a message" [32]. Moreover, processing a message "includes (but is not limited to) the parallel cognitive subprocesses (or tasks) of encoding, storage, and retrieval" [32]. The subprocesses occur simultaneously while the user attends different stimuli contained in the message as well as in the medium. The user selects (on a conscious or sub-conscious basis) which information in the message to encode and store, because it is not possible to encode and store all the information. The selection is based on the amount of resources available for processing (encoding, storing, and retrieving), and these resources in turn are affected by all elements involved: the user, the message, and the medium. Thus, besides the user's interest and familiarity, and the message contents characteristics, the presentation medium itself plays a crucial role in information processing.

The LCMMP facilitates the understanding of how users of digital reading interfaces successfully attend the relevant information, encode it, store it, and comprehend it, and enables the operationalization of the challenges faced by digital readers in terms of cognitive processing. If too many resources are allocated for automatic processing and/or for controlling/operating the interface, there can be left insufficient resources for encoding, storing, and retrieving the relevant information, with negative consequences on comprehension and other higher-level cognitive tasks. In addition, controlling/operating the interface affects the perceived ease of use, tiredness, and stress experienced by readers. Therefore, this model provides a theoretical basis to IS and HCI research for the design of reading systems and interfaces that compensate the effort to manipulate the interface and bound the unnecessary orienting responses that distract readers' attention from the relevant information presented on the digital medium.

4   Methods

A laboratory experiment was conducted during February–April 2012 with participants individually reading a newspaper on a digital tablet and a traditional print paper. The participants were recruited via email by sending invitation letters to student mailing lists. The incentive to participate in the experiment was three movie tickets. The experiment was conducted by employing the ethical principles stated in the Declaration of Helsinki regarding human research subjects [33]; written consent was collected from all the participants.

4.1 Participants

All participants, but one, were students within the age range of 19–40 ($M_{age} = 24$, $SD = 4.2$). The sample size was 29, where 8 were men and 21, women. Most of the participants (96.6%) had reported no experience to little experience with a digital tablet or a similar gadget; thus, this sample represents rather novice users of a tablet computer. Fourteen participants (44.8%) were at the moment of the experiment subscribed to the newspaper. Of all selected participants, 19 (65.5%) reported themselves as regular readers.

4.2 Study Design, Materials, Task, and Data Collection

The design of the experiment was within-subjects[2]. Each participant was exposed to two conditions; reading the print version of the largest newspaper in Finland, Helsingin Sanomat, and reading the digital version of the same newspaper. An iPad 2 tablet, which supported a dedicated iPad application of the newspaper, was utilized as the digital platform. The order of the conditions was counterbalanced. Each reading session lasted 15 min. The participants were free to select for reading in each condition the news articles they wished. The contents of the articles were not controlled; instead a fresh issue of the newspaper was provided for reading in the experiment day, resulting in 23 different issues being used in the experiments (one or two experiments were carried out per day).

The arrangement was planned such that to provide a laboratory setting that resembles natural reading in an everyday situation. For this reason, also the digital reading on the tablet was set up by utilizing the online version of the newspaper, with all inherent connection and live events that may occur when using an online system. Participants were instructed to skip reading the ads and the weather. The reading behavior was video recorded; for the tablet also screen capture was recorded. During the experiment, self-reports using questionnaires were also gathered after each reading session.

4.3 Measures of User Satisfaction

In the Next Media project[3], the multidisciplinary project team developed a comprehensive model of media experience based on an extensive literature review [36]. Furthermore, the team developed a media experience scale for empirical data collection [37]. This scale was utilized in the experiment reported here to measure the media experience in its various dimensions.

For this paper, relevant variables measuring the user satisfaction were selected from the media experience scale [37]. The selection of these variables was done so that the dimensions reflect the constructs of end-user computing satisfaction [38] and media enjoyment [39]. Thus, the dimensions of user satisfaction included in this analysis

---

[2] During the experiment psychophysiological data were also recorded, and, because individual differences affect the psychophysiological values, it is recommended to use a within-subjects study design (see [34]). The collection and analysis of psychophysiological data are reported in [35].

[3] As mentioned earlier, the experiment was part of a large project ("Next Media") related to the development of the Finnish media industry and media experience concepts. (see http://virtual. vtt.fi/virtual/nextmedia/573139/en/read/page.html).

are: Interestingness, Attention, Hierarchy, Navigation, Usability, Interactivity, Emotional responses, and Overall Media Experience. Examples of items for each of the constructs are as follows. For complete description of the constructs please see [37]. Interestingness had three items including "In the newspaper were interesting things.". Attention had five items, e.g., "The reading experience was compelling". Hiererchy: "The contents of the newspaper were well structured.". Navigation: "Sometimes I had the feeling that I was lost." (Scores are reversed to be comparable). Usability: "It is easy to find in this publication what I am looking for.". Interactivity: "The publication was easy to browse.". A single-item construct Overall Media Experience was also measured, using the statement "The reading experience was overall good." These items were rated on the 5-point scale: *Fully disagree – Fully agree.* In addition, three items for measuring emotional responses using the Self-Assessment Manikin scale (SAM) were utilized. These were rated using the SAM standard 9-point pictorial scale (see [40]). Pleasantness: "As I read the news I felt pleasant."; Arousal: "As I read the news I felt aroused."; and Dominance: "As I read the news I felt in control of the situation".

For analysis, both the scores of individual items and the aggregated indices at construct level were utilized. For example, the analysis utilized aggregated indices for Interestingness, Attention, Hierarchy, Navigation, Usability, and Interactivity.

4.4   Video Data Analysis

Video Coding and Coding Schemes. Visual inspection of the interaction behavior with the two reading-media was conducted using Noldus Observer XT. Two coding schemes of events and behaviors were produced in an iterative manner, one for each reading condition. The coding schemes for the two media have also been matched so that the findings could be compared across the media. The scrolling behavior in the digital reading condition has been coded so that to distinguish between scrolling that disrupts reading and scrolling during which reading is possible. The reason was to obtain a measure of the time during which the subject actually reads the articles of the newspaper. The final coding schemes are shown in Table 1.

Three types of behaviors were identified: 1) mutually exclusive events or states (at a time, only one of them can occur); 2) mutually exclusive behavior with no match with other media (e.g., events or states specific to one media); and 3) external behavior (behavior that can occur simultaneously with mutually exclusive states or events). Concurrent behavior in Table 1 defines behavior occurring simultaneously with reading or navigation and not affecting those in a disruptive way.

Coding Accuracy, Data Cleaning and Pre-processing. The coding was conducted as accurately as possible by three research assistants in a cooperative manner, under close supervision by the author. Most of the coding relied on visual inspection in Noldus Observer XT, and whenever needed frame-by-frame inspection was employed to achieve the greatest accuracy. The timestamps in the logs were reported with millisecond accuracy. During the experiment, there have occurred a few Internet connection errors, downloading errors, and unresponsiveness of the software. For two participants, these errors caused a relatively large disruption time, and therefore data from 2 subjects were discarded. Thus, 27 participants were retained for further analysis.

Table 1. Coding schemes for paper and tablet reading

Paper reading	Type	Tablet reading	Type
Mutually exclusive behavior		*Mutually exclusive behavior*	
Open newspaper	Start event	Open newspaper	Start event
Turn page	Navigation	Transition event	Navigation
		Select event	Navigation
Front page	Reading	Front page view	Reading
Spread open	Reading	Article view	Reading
		Section view	Reading
Disruptive distraction	Disruption	Disruptive distraction	Disruption
Mutually exclusive event with no match on tablet media		*Mutually exclusive event with no match on paper media*	
Revisit spread	Reading	Menu view	Navigation
		Error	Disruption
		Advert	Disruption
		Comic view	Reading
External behavior		*External behavior*	
Non-interruptive distraction	Concurrent behavior	Non-interruptive distraction	Concurrent behavior
Hand movement	Concurrent behavior	Holding tablet in hand(s)	Concurrent behavior
Small adjustment of the paper	Concurrent behavior	Additional content view	Concurrent behavior
		Picture view	Concurrent behavior
		Slow loading	Disruption
		No content	Disruption
		Point scroll	Reading
		State scroll	Navigation

The behavioral analysis and the coding scheme were used to quantify the reading and navigation behaviors in terms of number of pages (spreads vs. views) visited, total and average duration of visits per reading session, number of navigation events (page turns vs. view and menu transitions and selections), and total and average duration of navigation events.

4.5 Statistical Data Analysis

The data collected using the questionnaire as well as the numerical data obtained from the video data analysis was explored using descriptive statistics and statistical tests. All statistical analyses were carried out in SPSS [41]. To compare the traditional and digital media in terms of reading and navigation durations and user satisfaction, the Wilcoxon signed test was used. In addition, behavioral modeling employing linear mixed models was utilized to account for the effect of session order and individual characteristics.

5 Results

5.1 Media Differences

In the tablet application of the newspaper, the articles were organized in sections named similarly as in the traditional paper. However, each section was displayed on a separate page, and the articles were displayed on the page by headlines and a short excerpt from the article. Different types of views (pages) where reading occurred have been distinguished in tablet reading such as front-page view, section views (including comics), and article views. These views accounted for the reading behavior in the tablet reading condition (see Table 1). Other views in the tablet condition included menu, adverts, as well as popups; these were not included as reading to ensure the match between the contents of the two experimental reading conditions.

The reading patterns associated with the two media appeared to display several differences. In a paper version of the newspaper, the subject had a lot of information visible at once in one spread. Reading on paper was identified when participants were viewing the front page, had a spread open, or revisited a spread (see Table 1). In contrast, in the tablet version there is only a limited amount of text visible at any given time. Thus, the digital version of the newspaper triggers several user actions for the navigation, not only between sections and articles, but also for scrolling inside articles to advance text. One clear difference between the two media was that the number and diversity of the events and behaviors in tablet reading were larger than in the paper version (see Table 1). Two types of strategies for advancing text were observed using scrolling: 1) to enable reading at the same time (coded as point scroll), 2) fast scrolling to the extent that it is not possible to read (state scroll). This kind of fast scrolling has been coded as disrupting reading and the time allocated for this action was subtracted from reading time. Other events that have been found to disrupt reading were social media popups for sharing the article, popups regarding the wireless connection, notifications of updates for the software. These events were excluded from both the reading time and the navigation time.

To quantify the navigation, for the paper session, the main events considered were the page turns, irrespective of direction or number of pages turned at once. In tablet session, the interaction behaviors coded as navigation were the following: 1) transitions between articles, between sections, and between articles and section views; 2) menu views. Thus, the events defining the navigation behavior on the tablet newspaper comprise the transition events, select events, and menu views. The reason of including menu views into navigation and not into reading was that, typically, the menu is a means of selecting the desired options or contents; thus, it is typically employed when readers wish to change the current view.

5.2 Within-Subject Reading Behavior

Overall, across the 27 participants, the time allocated for reading in the paper reading condition was higher than in the tablet reading session. When **comparing the reading times** in the two experimental conditions, overall, the time spent on reading on paper is higher than the time spent on reading on tablet ($M_{paper} = 841.6$; $M_{tablet} = 793.2$), and this difference is statistically significant according to the Wilcoxon signed rank test ($Z = -3.15$; $p = 0.02$).

In the **paper reading sessions**, overall, the time spent on reading (namely, the time spent on open spreads) was representing 93.5% of total session time and the average variation was about 40 s (4.4%). The participants spending the least amount of time having their spreads open for reading spent a fair amount of time turning pages, 196 s and 118 s, respectively, meaning that they have used about 20% and 13% of their reading time, respectively, for browsing. On an average a subject spent 78.7 s ($SD = 46.7$ s) on a spread, including the revisited spreads.

In the **tablet reading sessions**, on an average a subject read a fairly large amount of time representing about 88.1% of all reading session with a variation among participants representing 6.2% of total reading time.

To account for **both the order of session and the reading medium**, a linear mixed methods analysis was employed. The duration of reading was significantly affected by the reading medium ($t = -2.67$; $p = 0.01$; $b_{tablet} = -49.8$). Neither the order of the session nor the interaction medium x session did affect the total duration. Thus, in the paper reading session, participants generally spent a longer time on reading as compared with the tablet reading session, regardless of the order of the sessions. When evaluating the reading duration, the subject operationalized as the intercept in the regression line was not found a contributing factor and thus was not introduced as random effect.

5.3 Within-Subject Navigation Behavior

Generally, across the 27 participants, the time spent for navigation was higher in the tablet reading condition. In the **paper reading sessions**, across the sample, the average number of page turns was 14.6 per session. The average duration of all page turns was 52.8 s per session, representing 5.9% of total session time. In the **tablet reading sessions**, across the sample, the average number of navigation events was 44.0 per session. The average duration of the navigation events was 59.0 s, accounting for 6.55% of the session duration.

When **comparing the duration of navigation events between the two media**, the difference was not found statistically significant according to Wilcoxon signed rank test ($Z = -1.55$; $p = 0.12$). However, when examining the data more closely, there were found a few outliers that had extreme durations for the navigation. Removing the outlier with the highest number of page turns (i.e., 42) from the analysis provided evidence that generally the duration of navigation time was higher in the tablet condition than in paper reading condition ($Z = -1.98$; $p = 0.048$; $N = 26$).

To account for **both the order of sessions and the reading medium**, the linear mixed methods analysis showed that the duration of navigation events was not affected by the reading medium, but by the session order ($N = 27$, $F(1,25) = 4.13$; $p = 0.05$). However, the estimate of the session order effect on navigation time was not found statistically significant. When removing the two outliers with the highest duration of page turns, the results showed that both the reading medium and the session order affected significantly the navigation duration model, but only the reading medium had a significant impact on the duration (i.e., reading on tablet was associated with an increase of navigation time by 21.18 s; $t = 2.13$; $p = 0.04$; $b_{session=1} = 21.18$). The interaction effect between medium and order was not found significant either. However, in this case, there were observed individual differences between participants, and thus the subject operationalized as intercept in the regression line was introduced as random effect.

5.4 User Satisfaction

The two reading conditions were compared in terms of self-reported user satisfaction by employing the Wilcoxon signed test. Table 2 presents the statistically significant differences across the 27 study participants. Generally, the participants reported better experience with the traditional newspaper in terms of interactivity and usability. The readers were more satisfied with the print version than with the digital version in terms of *ease of reading* the news articles, *ease of handling* the newspaper, *ease of browsing* the publication, and *ease of jumping* from one page to another page. Readers also generally felt *more aroused* when reading the traditional newspaper ($M_{paper} = 5.15$) than the tablet application ($M_{tablet} = 4.63$). And they reported the *reading experience was more compelling* in the print version than in the digital version ($M_{paper} = 3.63; M_{tablet} = 3.30$). However, these differences only approached the statistical significance (arousal: $Z = -1.80, p = 0.07$; compelling reading experience: $Z = -1.67, p = 0.095$). One positive aspect of the tablet (nearly statistically significant) was that the readers found the tablet slightly better than the print when reporting of being *less disturbed by the reflections or shine* of the publication ($M_{paper} = 4.26; M_{tablet} = 4.78; Z = 1.90, p = 0.058$).

Table 2. Statistically significant differences in terms of user satisfaction, $N = 27$

Variable	M_{paper}	M_{tablet}	Wilcoxon signed test	
			Z	p
Usability				
U2:"The articles in the newspaper were easy to read."	4.26	4.11	-2.000	0.046
U3:"The newspaper was easy to handle while reading."	3.89	3.07	-2.418	0.016
Interactivity				
I1: "The publication was easy to browse."	4.00	3.30	-2.101	0.036
I4:"While I was reading Helsingin Sanomat, I could quickly jump from one page to another."	4.19	3.00	-2.565	0.010
Overall Interactivity (mean over I1-I7)	*3.86*	*3.48*	*-2.287*	*0.022*

6 Discussion

This paper compared the reading and navigation behaviors when people interact with two essentially different media: traditional paper and digital tablet. The analysis relied on qualitative coding of the interactions of users with the digital and paper media while reading a newspaper. The reading and navigation behavior were quantified in terms of total and average duration of visits/views per reading session, and total and average duration of navigation events. In addition, user satisfaction with the two media was measured in terms of Interestingness, Hierarchy, Navigation, Usability, Interactivity, Attention, Emotional responses, and Overall Media Experience.

6.1 Differences Between Reading Media

The findings showed that the two reading media are essentially different in the way people navigate and select information. There is more information accessible at once in the paper reading; the tablet computer allows only a limited amount of information to be displayed at once. Moreover, there are more user actions and navigation possibilities in the tablet reading which require more cognitive resources to be allocated in the digital reading situation for non-reading tasks compared to the traditional paper medium (see also [4, 12]). Accordingly, the results indicate that the traditional paper medium facilitates sustained reading; there is more time allocated for effective reading in paper reading compared to the tablet reading. This confirms earlier results and assumptions that paper is a more suitable medium for sustained reading [11, 17, 26].

The navigation time was also generally higher in the tablet reading condition than in the paper reading. However, this result was not as robust as in the case of reading time; both session order and some extreme user behavior affected the stability of this finding across the sample. Thus, one limitation of the present study can be regarded as being the relatively small sample size.

There have been found also differences in terms of user satisfaction. Generally, participants preferred the usability and interactivity of the traditional newspaper. Participants liked more the print newspaper than the tablet application in terms of ease of reading, ease of browsing, ease of handling the newspaper, and ease of jumping from one page to another. However, attributes such as Interestingness, Hierarchy and Navigation were not generally perceived as being better represented in one medium than in the other. Furthermore, readers found that the media experience was more compelling and that they felt more aroused when reading the print newspaper compared to the digital newspaper. On the other hand, people felt slightly more comfortable with the tablet because its reflections and shine were less disturbing than when reading the spreadsheet. This can be due to the fact that the print newspaper was in the spreadsheet format and it was more difficult for readers to avoid the reflections of the artificial light in the extremities of the paper. The tablet was smaller and easier for participants to find the reading angle to avoid reflections. Although the experiment was carried out in a laboratory where the lighting was controlled, the spreadsheet newspaper occupied a large portion on the desk where the participants sit during the experiment. When the light was shining on the distant portions of the paper, it could have hindered the reading and induced a greater disturbance as compared to the tablet whose size fit better with the participants field of vision.

6.2 Cognitive Implications

The findings related to reading behavior showed that the paper medium elicited longer time spent on effective reading as compared to the tablet medium. In light of LCMMP model [7], it means that the paper reading condition favors the allocation of cognitive resources such as attention and memory (encoding, storing, retrieval) to processing content including news messages as well as headlines, pictures, and so forth. In contrast, the digital medium triggers a relatively smaller amount of resources to be allocated for effective reading. The duration per spread visit in the paper reading is more than double of the duration per view in the digital reading, telling that the attention of the reader is allocated a lot more to non-contents information and interface design elements. Thus, an increasing amount of resources is spent on the automatic or controlled processing of the information present in the interface that may also disrupt the reading. The consequence is that of the pool of available resources more of them are allocated to non-reading tasks in the digital reading when compared to traditional reading, with possible negative implications on higher-level cognitive tasks such as making sense of the information, comprehension, and recall. Furthermore, the necessary encoding, storing, and retrieval of information relevant for controlling the interaction and navigation make the experience of digital reading potentially more tiring and stressful especially for users who are not familiar with a specific interface. This in turn may have negative consequences in the ability to process further the news messages or to reflect and act upon the information.

These consequences are in line with the findings in earlier studies analyzing reading on the two media that showed decreased comprehension and increased level of stress and tiredness when reading from computer screen [4]. Wästlund et al. [4] argued that more cognitive resources are invested during reading in screen due to a deficiency of the information presentation and also due to a higher workload of reading itself and operating the computer. The navigation behavior observed in the two conditions supports the above predictions. There were observed more navigation events in the tablet reading, which according to the LCMMP model [7] would account for additional processing resources that would negatively influence the attention to news content and their processing. Moreover, the overall time spent on navigation and user actions to access content was generally higher in the tablet reading, strengthening the prediction that relatively more resources were employed for non-reading tasks in the digital reading.

6.3 Implications to Design

The analysis of the behavioral patterns and user satisfaction data showed that the paper medium proves to still have an advantage over the digital reading because of the natural navigation and focus on effective reading. This has implications on finding better solutions for the design of digital interfaces for reading to be as natural for the reader as the paper reading. Novel digital interfaces that are based on scrolling still lag behind paper media in performance and feeling of naturalness; scrolling can become frustrating when the pages are advancing too fast and there is no feeling of control over the content being browsed (see also [26]). On the other hand, interfaces that require clicks and selections require a lot of control from the user, who then allocates a lot of attentional resources on manipulating the interface, which may have negative effects on processing the relevant information.

Analyzing the effect that the order of the sessions has on reading and navigation behavior showed that in the digital reading, when the newspaper content is not completely new, there are a lot of scanning and browsing events. This means for designers that the digital reading interface should be designed so that the content already seen is hidden from the reader so that the access to interesting and novel information is facilitated.

Our findings showed that disruptions such as slow loading, fast scrolling, pop-ups may occur in natural digital reading as opposed to traditional reading, and thus during digital reading there are challenges for designers and developers to provide disruption-free reading experiences to facilitate flow and to avoid fragmentation of reading. This is especially relevant in light of the study by Hou et al. [24] which showed that paper and digital reading are similar in terms of comprehension, fatigue, and immersion if the digital reading is not disruptive. In addition, designers should explore different solutions to make the information presentation easily accessible through different mechanisms that prove to be optimal to the intended purpose, for example to facilitate the creation of coherent cognitive maps of the text (see [25]).

The findings showed significant differences in navigation time and more diverse navigation strategies in the tablet reading, which diverge from the natural navigation encountered when interacting with the paper medium. Thus, designers should explore novel and innovative navigation paradigms for the digital reading as they are essential for creating a positive reading experience. Brown [26] pointed out that software development in this direction is a promising research area which has also implications in creating new habits of reading.

6.4 Future Work

The present study showed also that individual differences play a role when comparing navigation behavior, but not reading behavior. The effect of certain user profiles has not been studied in detail here, however, there are studies that show that familiarity with the medium [16] influences the performance of readers such as in comprehending the text and that users' characteristics are associated with different patterns of news consumption [22]. Thus, additional research should also be conducted to study the effect of individual characteristics on both reading and navigation behavior. In this study, the random effect introduced in the linear mixed model analysis was found significant in modelling the navigation time; the individual characteristics reflected by the variable subject had a significant influence on the intercept in the regression lines, indicating that an amount of variation in the navigation time was due to individual characteristics. In addition, the analysis of the reading and navigation behavior based on partial correlation, when the effect of session order was controlled for, showed patterns that may reflect different styles of reading. As shown also in previous research, individual characteristics do influence reading behavior and preferences (see e.g., [16, 21, 22]), and research is needed in this area to profile the reading styles and readers typologies. In this respect, with data from the same experiment, it has been shown that personality and approach motivation dispositions affect the physiological responses to reading on different media such as paper and tablet [35]. The present research could be extended by including in the model of reading and navigation the individual characteristics such as type of reading (systematic, focused), and preference of news categories (see [22]), as well as personality and motivational disposition (see [35]). Moreover, new studies should be conducted with different types of users with varying level of experience with a tablet computer. At the time of the experiment, the tablet computer was a relatively novel technology, the newspaper application was just launched, and the sample comprises mainly novice users of tablet. Reading and navigation behavior may be different when users are familiar with the device and/or newspaper application.

For future research, there is a need to study the way the navigation and interaction events, states, and actions affect the overall reading experience and cognitive load by utilizing the models of limited capacity of mediated message processing [7], as well as viewer engagement (see [42, 43]). These give a basis for studying further the interaction between user actions and behavior on the one hand, and cognitive and emotional processing on the other hand.

Moreover, size of the display could also be a variable to further explore. A larger display will naturally require less navigation actions, as more information can be accommodated on a page. Additionally, having more space available, there are more possibilities to enhance the information design and layout to respond more effectively to users' needs. However, when the display size is small such as on a mobile phone or tablet, the designers have fewer practical choices for presenting the information and designing the information layout and user navigation controls. In these circumstances, the creativity of the designer in conceiving effective and attractive information layouts is important. To ensure the effectiveness of the layout and navigation from the user point of view, the information and interaction design should take into account the implications of the LCMMP model. Thus, to meaningfully address the effect of display size would reduce to designing and evaluating alternative designs for small displays and comparing their effectiveness with best practice designs for larger displays.

To summarize, for future studies it is important to examine the effectiveness of innovative designs for small displays in terms of cognitive load and reading experience. These effects should be studied in a diverse and large population in order to detect any moderating effects of individual characteristics, such as gender, age, experience with digital media, experience with newspaper reading, reading style, personality and motivational disposition.

7 Conclusions

This paper shows that, compared to the digital medium, reading on paper elicits a longer time spent on effective reading tasks. Moreover, navigation tasks are more frequent and consume more time and implicitly cognitive resources in the digital reading. User satisfaction with the traditional newspaper is generally higher in terms of usability and interactivity. Ease of reading, ease of handling, ease of browsing, and ease of navigating from page to page were generally higher when interacting with the traditional newspaper compared to the digital newspaper. This paper contributes to the understanding of reading and navigation behavior. By reflecting the results in the light of the limited capacity of mediated message processing model, the paper draws attention to designers of reading interfaces to take into account not only behavior, but also the internal processing of information to ensure optimal user engagement and experience.

Acknowledgements. This study was possible with the support of numerous people to whom I am grateful. The data collection was possible thanks to working in a project led by Professor Niklas Ravaja at Aalto University (Next Media). The coding of the video data was assisted by three students as part of their project course at University of Oulu: Pertti Karhapää, Paavo Orajärvi, and Juho Tapani. I am also grateful to Dr. Mikko Salminen for earlier comments on this study and to the three aforementioned students for their comments and insights during the project course work. The writing of the article was finalized during a research grant I have received from Jenny and Antti Wihuri Foundation (Project "Climate Change in the News").

References

1. Finnish ABC: The Finnish National Readership Survey (published report) (2013). http://yle. fi/uutiset/survey_print_still_popular_among_media_consumers/6834703

2. Flavian, F., Gurrea, R.: Perceived substitutability between digital and physical channels: The case of newspapers. Online Inf. Rev. **31**(6), 793–813 (2007)
3. Siegenthaler, E., Wurtz, P., Groner, R.: Improving the usability of E-Book readers. J. Usability Stud. **6**, 25–38 (2010)
4. Wästlund, E., Reinikka, H., Norlander, T., Archer, T.: Effects of VDT and paper presentation on consumption and production of information: Psychological and physiological factors. Comput. Hum. Behav. **21**(2), 377–394 (2005)
5. Connell, C., Bayliss, L., Farmer, W.: Effects of eBook readers and tablet computers on reading comprehension. Int'l J. Instr. Media **39**(2), 131–141 (2012)
6. Dundar, H., Akcayir, M.: Tablet vs. paper: The effect on learners' reading performance. Int. Electron. J. Elementary Educ. **4**(3), 441–450 (2012)
7. Lang, A.: The limited capacity model of mediated message processing. J. Commun. **50**(1), 46–70 (2000)
8. Lam, P., Lam, S.L., Lam, J., McNaught, C.: Usability and usefulness of eBooks on PPCs: How students' opinions vary over time. Australas. Educa. Technol. **25**(1), 30–44 (2009)
9. Mayes, D.K., Sims, V.K., Koonce, J.M.: Comprehension and workload differences for VDT and paper-based reading. Int'l J. Ind. Erg. **28**, 367–378 (2001)
10. Muter, P., Maurutto, P.: Reading and skimming from computer screens and books: The paperless office revisited? Behav. Inf. Tech. **10**, 257–266 (1991)
11. Dillon, A.: Reading from paper versus screens: A critical review of the empirical literature. Ergonomics **35**(10), 1297–1326 (1992)
12. Noyes, J.M., Garland, K.J.: Computer- vs. paper-based tasks: Are they equivalent? Ergonomics **51**(9), 1352–1375 (2008)
13. O'Hara, K., Sellen, A.: A comparison of reading paper and on-line documents. In: Proceedings of the ACM SIGCHI Conference on Human Factors in Computing Systems (CHI97), pp. 335–342 (1997)
14. Liu, Z.: Reading behavior in the digital environment: Changes in reading behavior over the past ten years. J. Doc. **61**(6), 700–712 (2005)
15. Hillesund, T.: Digital reading spaces: How expert readers handle books, the web and electronic paper. First Monday **15**(4), 4–5 (2010)
16. Chen, G., Cheng, W., Chang, T.W., Zheng, X., Huang, R.: A comparison of reading comprehension across paper, computer screens, and tablets: Does tablet familiarity matter? J. Comput. Educ. **1**(2–3), 213–225 (2014)
17. Holmqvist, K., Holsanova, J., Barthelson, M., Lundqvist, D.: Reading or scanning? A study of newspaper and net paper reading. In: The Mind's Eye, pp. 657–670 (2003)
18. Zambarbieri, D., Carniglia, E.: Eye movement analysis of reading from computer displays, ereaders and printed books. Ophthalmic Physiol. Opt. **32**(5), 390–396 (2012)
19. von Krogh, T., Andersson, U.: Reading patterns in print and online newspapers: The case of the Swedish local morning paper VLT and online news site vlt. se. Digit. Journalism **4**(8), 1058–1072 (2016)
20. Mangen, A., Walgermo, B.R., Brønnick, K.: Reading linear texts on paper versus computer screen: Effects on reading comprehension. Int'l J. Educ. Res. **58**, 61–68 (2013)
21. Kretzschmar, F., Pleimling, D., Hosemann, J., Füssel, S., Bornkessel-Schlesewsky, I., Schlesewsky, M.: Subjective impressions do not mirror online reading effort: Concurrent EEG-eyetracking evidence from the reading of books and digital media. PLoS ONE **8**(2), e56178 (2013)
22. D'Haenens, L., Heuvelman, A.: News in online and print newspapers: Differences in reader consumption and recall. New Media Soc. **6**(3), 363–382 (2004)
23. Mangen, A., Kuiken, D.: Lost in an iPad: Narrative engagement on paper and tablet. Sci. Study Lit. **4**(2), 150–177 (2014)

24. Hou, J., Rashid, J., Lee, K.M.: Cognitive map or medium materiality? Reading on paper and screen. Comput. Hum. Behav. **67**, 84–94 (2017)
25. Jabr, F.: The reading brain in the digital age: The science of paper versus screens. Scientific American, 11 April (2013)
26. Brown, G.J.: Beyond print: Reading digitally. Libr. Hi Tech. **19**(4), 390–399 (2001)
27. Baddeley, A.: Working memory. Science **255**(5044), 556–559 (1992)
28. Gevins, A., Smith, M.E.: Neurophysiological measures of working memory and individual differences in cognitive ability and cognitive style. Cereb. Cortex **10**(9), 829–839 (2000)
29. Lang, A.: Using the limited capacity model of motivated mediated message processing to design effective cancer communication messages. J. Commun. **56**(s1), S57–S80 (2006)
30. Lachman, R., Lachman, J.L., Butterfield, E.C.: Cognitive Psychology and Information Processing: An Introduction. Psychology Press, East Sussex (2015)
31. Lang, A., Potter, R.F., Bolls, P.D.: Where psychophysiology meets the media: Taking the effects out of media research. In: Media Effects: Advances in Theory and Research, pp. 185–206. Routledge, New York (2009)
32. Lang, A., Borse, J., Wise, K., David, P.: Captured by the world wide web: Orienting to structural and content features of computer-presented information. Commun. Res. **29**(3), 215–245 (2002)
33. World Medical Association: World Medical Association Declaration of Helsinki. Ethical principles for medical research involving human subjects. Bulletin of the World Health Organization **79**(4), 373 (2001)
34. Ravaja, N.: Contributions of psychophysiology to media research: Review and recommendations. Media Psychol. **6**, 193–235 (2004)
35. Rajanen, D., Salminen, M., Ravaja, N.: Psychophysiological responses to digital media: Frontal EEG Alpha asymmetry during newspaper reading on a tablet versus print. In: Proceedings of the 19th International Academic Mindtrek Conference, pp. 155–162. ACM (2015)
36. Helle, M., Ravaja, N., Heikkilä, H., Kallenbach, J., Kankainen, A., Kätsyri, J., Laine, J., Marghescu, D.: A theoretical model of media experience and research methods for studying it. Project report for Next Media–a TIVIT Programme (2011). http://virtual.vtt.fi/virtual/nex tmedia/332702/en/read/page.html
37. Helle, M., Ravaja, N., Heikkilä, H., Kallenbach, J., Kätsyri, J., Laine, J., Marghescu, D., Mensonen, A., Aikala, M., Saari, T.: Media experience: Detailed plan of empirical studies. project report for next media–a TIVIT programme (2011). http://virtual.vtt.fi/virtual/nextme dia/332702/en/read/page.html
38. Doll, W.J., Torkzadeh, G.: The measurement of end-user computing satisfaction: Theoretical and methodological issues. MIS Q. **15**(1), 5–10 (1991)
39. Tamborini, R., Bowman, N.D., Eden, A., Grizzard, M., Organ, A.: Defining media enjoyment as the satisfaction of intrinsic needs. J. Commun. **60**(4), 758–777 (2010)
40. Bradley, M. M., Lang, P. J.: Measuring emotion: The self-assessment manikin and the semantic differential. J. Behav. Therapy Exp. Psychiatry **25**(1), 49–59 (1994)
41. Field, A.: Discovering Statistics Using SPSS, 3rd edn. Sage, London (2009)
42. Diao, F., Sundar, S.S.: Orienting response and memory for web advertisements: Exploring effects of pop-up window and animation. Comm. Res. **31**(5), 537–567 (2004)
43. Smith, M.E., Gevins, A.: Attention and brain activity while watching television: Components of viewer engagement. Media Psychol. **6**(3), 285–305 (2004)

Career Choice and Gendered Perceptions of IT – A Nexus Analytic Inquiry

Fanny Vainionpää[✉], Marianne Kinnula, Netta Iivari, and Tonja Molin-Juustila

University of Oulu, Oulu, Finland
{fanny.vainionpaa,marianne.kinnula,netta.iivari,
tonja.molin-juustila}@oulu.fi

Abstract. Girls' disinterest in Information Technology (IT) careers is a persisting problem. We wanted to examine girls' perceptions of the IT field as well as factors shaping their career choices, to find ways girls might see IT/Information Systems careers as more interesting. For this purpose, we interviewed Finnish senior high school students, as senior high school is the last opportunity to influence girls' career choice in higher education. In addition, we asked senior high school IT teachers about IT education and their perceptions of students' relations to IT. Using nexus analysis as a sensitizing device, we focused on various discourses circulating around, different actors and their relations, as well as experience and background related matters that affect girls' career choice. Surprisingly gendered understandings of the IT field and career choices were still prevalent among the studied young people, and this supports educational and occupational segregation.

Keywords: IS education · IT use · IT education · Gender balance · Girls in tech · Gendering · Career choice · Segregation · Nexus analysis · Historical body · Interaction order · Teachers

1 Introduction

Due to fast-paced digitalization of our society, the Information Technology (IT) industry is prospering. However, there is a desperate need of skilled workers [49]. One solution has been to invite more women into the field [2, 33]. Herein lies an enduring challenge: girls are not interested in the IT field [8, 11]. The IT field is very segregated: the number of male specialists working in the field within the European Union has increased by 51.6% between 2008 and 2018, while the number of women has increased only by 5.1% [21], and across OECD countries only 20% of new students in the IT field were women in 2015 [48]. The gender divide is detrimental to the IT industry and the whole society as it affects the quality and coverage of IT, and delimits the responsibility of shaping of our digital lives mostly to one gender [64]. Thus, the topic should be of utmost interest in the IT field, including Information Systems (IS), among other areas of expertise.

A prior version of this paper has been published in the ISD2019 Proceedings (http://aisel.aisnet.org/isd2014/proceedings2019).

A. Siarheyeva et al. (Eds.): ISD 2019, LNISO 39, pp. 37–56, 2020.
https://doi.org/10.1007/978-3-030-49644-9_3

Unfortunately, recent IS research shows that the problem persists in IS similarly to other IT fields [49] despite the relative 'softness' of IS, compared to more technical IT fields [34], and its association with business schools and business-oriented careers. A burning question is: why girls do not see IT as their career choice?

The situation is surprising, considering that we are talking about a generation that has had the internet, mobile technology, video games, and social media as an integral part of their everyday life from early childhood (e.g. [50]). Then again, young people's IT use varies: some use IT widely with increasing competency while others' use is narrower [37]. A digital divide among young people today exists, i.e. polarization between those who have the access and ability to develop their skills related to digital technology, and those who do not [47]. Research has shown that there are various kinds of exclusions in the young people's engagement with digital technology [32]. While there must be several reasons for this, we believe that education plays an important role. Based on our research, we believe that not only education nor IT use, but even more importantly other gendered phenomena explain the persistent lack of girls in IT education; cultural and historical aspects seem to be shaping girls' career choices as well. Even though gender aspects have aroused interest in IS research throughout the years [19, 34, 49, 53, 60], IS research has remained quite negligent of the young generations and their (IS) education [39]. Digital natives have been acknowledged as a generation distinctly different from the older ones [67] and calls for addressing the education of young people have recently emerged [32, 39] but IS studies examining the (IS/IT) education of youth or specifically young girls are lacking [64].

This study aims to understand girls' perceptions and understanding of the IT field as well as factors shaping them, to find ways to get more girls interested in IT/IS careers. Theoretically, we approach the topic using nexus analysis [52] that offers a lens to study complex topics in-depth and from multiple perspectives, including social, cultural, and historical aspects [31], guiding researchers to study circulating discourses as well as the backgrounds and experiences of those involved and their mutual relationships and interactions as shaping the action [45]. In nexus analysis, social action is in focus – in this study, it entails senior high school girls making sense of the IT field and their career choice. As our research question we ask, *how do senior high school girls perceive IT and the IT field, and what seems to be shaping their career choices.* We address this question in the context of senior high school in Finland through an exploratory questionnaire study with 142 senior high school students and complement that with six in-depth interviews with students and five interviews with senior high school IT teachers. We add the teachers' perspective to this study as they have been seen as very significant in shaping students' career choices [1, 5, 71, 73].

2   Related Research

Conceptual and Theoretical Background. As a theoretical lens in this study, we use 'nexus analysis' [52], specifically its three intertwined concepts: discourses in place, interaction order, and historical body [52]. Nexus analysis [52] is an ethnographically oriented research framework that draws on cultural-historical activity theory [69], theory on social interaction [24], practice theory [13], as well as the thinking of e.g. Nishida [46] and Bateson [7]. *Discourses in place* tell us how participants position the topic as well as themselves in social space [10], e.g., the girls speaking about IT field as male-dominated and boring. *Interaction order* [25] guides us to examine the social arrangements between people. In our data, for example, this shows as mothers being important role models for girls. *Historical body* refers to life experiences of social actors. The concept comes close to the concept of 'habitus' [13] but is more closely related to participants' concrete embodied actions [52]. In our data, historical body shows, e.g., different expectations for girls' and boys' upbringing. The three concepts are used for examining the social action in focus. Use of the concepts helps examine the phenomenon of lack of girls in IT/IS. The concepts focus the analysis on interactions between individuals, always tied to the socio-cultural context. In real life these concepts are always intertwined in social action, but they can be used heuristically as analytical lenses to study the social action in focus (see e.g. [45]).

Other central concepts in this study are *gendering* and *segregation* that are seen influencing girls' views of the IT field and their career choices. With segregation we mean "the tendency for men and women to work in different occupations" [9]. This segregation impairs the overall economic efficiency [43] and affects companies' competitiveness around the world [2]. With gendering, we refer to "integrating the gender perspective in the understanding and construction of persons, phenomena, reflections, things, relationships, sectors of action, societal subsystems and institutions" [63]. We see occupational segregation and segregation emerging in higher education as problematic and gendering heavily contributing to segregation and vice versa. Next, we review existing IT literature addressing the topic. Nexus analytic lens guides us to focus on literature on girls' career choice and factors shaping it: their IT knowledge, assumptions, and experience (historical body) and other people's influence (interaction order).

Students' Career Choice. Women's decision to enter IT education is influenced by exposure at home, school, work, personal interest, salaries, and male influence to explore technology [53]. Values, perceived ability, and expectancies also explain why women do not get into computing [72]. In higher education, there is a scientific-humanistic divide (in curricula), but also a care-technical divide (in career applications), which are based on stereotypes of gender differences. Culturally ubiquitous gender stereotypes provide reasoning for gender inequality in society, where women are communal, and men are agentic. Exposure to the stereotypes can lead to supporting the system and the gender relations status. [35] There are cultural influences in attitudes about women's roles as mothers and the conflicts it creates in work life, but also the gendered cultural influences e.g. about careers, opportunities, and aptitude [61]. Cultural divide is also visible in how computing subjects are masculinized because of the technical orientation, whereas medicine leads to care-oriented jobs. Not all humanistic fields are care-oriented and not all scientific fields are technical, both divides influence career choice. [6] A newer explanation for gender gaps in engineering, math, computer science, and physics is that in post-industrial nations people choose occupations that they find highly interesting and they would love to do [16], and women in these societal contexts (e.g. Finland, Germany, and Hong Kong) tend to think computing subjects are boring [30]. With IS, students do not think IT could fulfil work values such as social interaction, work-family balance, and job security, and they think it is too technical [36]. Considering the impact of economics, a more even distribution of material and social resources enables women and men to express gender specific preferences [22].

Perception of the IT Field. IT is often used interchangeably with terms such as ICT (Information and Communication Technology), IS, and CS (Computer Science), and there is confusion about IT occupations [4, 42]. Women are not often introduced to the IT field before college, and unfamiliarity may explain the disinterest in enrolling to the studies [38]. The IT field is diverse and offers various career paths but pre-college students are not seeing them if their parents are not employed by the industry [27]. Within IT, IS occupations can be seen as more feminine (more social) but the stereotypes and educational prejudices affect the IS field as well [34]. A study with secondary school students found that girls were less likely to know the difference between IT and IS and were less confident than boys in using IT [42]. Students' knowledge of IT careers is based on what they hear in school, and it is important to determine whether the representation of the industry is suitable for both sexes [58]. Students may not choose IT because of incorrect or vague perceptions of the field. Identifying and managing students' perceptions of IT careers at a young age could increase the number of women in the IT workforce. [1, 15] If we look at cultures and history of technology, men have been inventors and designers of technology, while women have been users and consumers. This divide has established a gender division in expectations, experiences and education. [14] Programming has been associated with mathematical problem solving and masculinity [12]. The bias in our society is also visible in children's toys and computer games [56]. Considering this past, girls today need to challenge stereotypes about traditional careers for women and be one of the few girls in the class if they choose IT education [54]. Girls think the field is unwelcoming to women, based on what they see on television and newspapers [11]. The IT stereotypes are that the field is male-oriented, socially isolated, related to machines, and requires natural abilities [17], resulting in girls' lack of interest in the field [26].

IT Experiences. Gender differences show in motivations for choosing an IT major. Men's primary influence is interest in games, whereas women intend to use IT in other fields. [15] Girls use computers at home less than boys do and they are not interested in programming and games. Computer use in schools is similar for both genders. While there are few gender differences in IT skills, there are differences in attitudes, interest, and self-confidence in computer use. [68] Girls tend to be more anxious for having less practice in computer related activities, and need more experiences, exposure, and practice to develop confidence and computer self-efficacy [29]. When choosing a career in IT, hands-on learning, exposure to IT, and an interest in IT careers are motivating factors in enrolling into IT education [54]. Men tend to have better self-efficacy, more passion for computing, and less positive attitudes towards women's abilities in IT. [44] Even with good access to IT, boys have reported higher self-efficacy in high level IT tasks [59]. As experience and education are essential for occupational self-efficacy in IT [44], increasing computer experiences could help women develop confidence in knowledge and use of IT [29]. However, a recent study found that girls in some countries reported significantly higher levels of IT self-efficacy and outperformed boys (e.g. Australia, Chile, Czech Republic, Korea, Russia), indicating that traditional gender perceptions are diminishing in some countries. [28]

Gender in IT Education. IT education is not a compulsory subject in most curricula, so encouraging girls to choose IT studies in high schools is important [18]. For example, in the Finnish national high school curriculum, IT is not on the list of subjects, but you can find it integrated into all other studies. There are no guidelines for teaching IT – the teachers are free to offer any kind of courses. [74] Gender differences in course taking behavior is a problem that seems to stem from women's experiences in classroom environments, stereotypical images, and individual interactions that reduce their sense of belonging [41]. Positive experiences and introduction to IT at home and in schools can influence major selections [53]. Perceptions of meaningful and creative activities can increase interest [8]. The choice to pursue a career in IT occurs before college, and encouragement and exposure are significant factors for girls [70]. Exposing girls to IT at an early age could counteract the cultural and societal influences that connect the idea of success with IT to boys and men [53]. If interventions take place early on, in middle- or high schools, they can tackle biases and inaccurate impressions before they affect major choice [3, 72].

Teachers' Influence. Career education and guidance in schools has been recognized as a foundation for lifelong career development [71], and increasing teachers' awareness about IT careers can help inform and encourage students [1]. Other ways teachers can influence students are through their teaching practices as well as the expectations they set to students. Regarding teaching practices, experiencing learning activities as creative and relevant are important for seeing value in learning IT skills. As to teachers' expectations, they can influence students' beliefs about their abilities, more so for girls. [65] The role of study counsellors and teachers can be of a conduit; they can reduce emphasis of mathematical abilities in IT careers and inform students that a background in business and social studies is also relevant in IT field [5]. Encouraging words and experience at home and at school are likely to increase girls' self-efficacy in male-dominated fields. Parents and teachers can show it is not gender or social structures, but aspiration, effort, and commitment that lead to success. [73].

Other People's Influence. Peers, particularly boys, have an impact on girls' self-concept, self-efficacy, classroom experiences, and external goal orientation, shaping gendered career choices [40]. At home, parental support is important [66]; fathers, male peers, and male siblings have a significant influence in motivating women to take part in tinkering activities [55]. In addition, role models are often mentioned as an important influence in selecting a career in a particular field [2, 20, 23].

3   Research Setting and Methodology

The study was conducted as a first step of a project aiming at increasing the interest of senior high school girls to study IT/IS. Despite women becoming more educated, occupations have remained segregated by gender in Finland. The majority of workforce in technical fields are men and the majority in social, care, and education fields are women. [57] In the project, we offer female senior-high schoolers more information and practical understanding of the IT/IS field and its work practices, hoping to raise their interest in the studies. Due to our background in IS, we naturally emphasize IS aspects in the IT field, while other partners in the project place stronger emphasis e.g. on programming. Currently, we are in the exploratory phase, trying to gain deeper understanding on the causes of segregation in the IT/IS field. The main data for this study originates from questionnaires filled in by senior high-school students (78 girls, 60 boys, 4 other/undisclosed; ages 15/10 students, 16/69, 17/45, 18/14, i.e. born between 2000 and 2003), as pairs (altogether 71 answers; 35 girl/girl pairs, 26 boy/boy, 10 mixed) in 75-minute-long 'IT info events' at two different high schools in Finland in 2018. The students could choose who they pair up with, and they were told we are interested in their views of the IT field. The events were organized by the schools' guidance counsellors; some of them were compulsory to the students. The aim was to highlight the diversity of the IT field in general and the 'soft' side in particular (i.e. the design, innovation, business, organizational, management aspects). Students were first given basic information about the current need for employees in the IT field. We then asked them to answer a set of questions as pairs to orient them for further information: What are their plans for studies after high school; How they perceive the IT field (the work, the people, the companies); How to inspire high school students to enroll into IT studies; How they perceive IT studies in higher education (why study/not study IT, what prerequisites there are). Then we informed them about the broad spectrum of IT companies (applications and devices) with local examples; career paths in IT field (IS specialist, UI designer, SW business manager, SW engineer, project manager, game developer, test engineer, etc.); salaries; and studies. Then we asked them, based on the information they had received, what topics they would be interested in IT studies or work and did the information influence their opinions about IT careers.

We complement this data with face-to-face interviews of 6 students in May 2018 (3 girls, 3 boys, 50 min on average), recruited in the IT info events. Interview topics included study plans after high school, what or who influences their career choice, parents' occupations and how they affect the career choice, IT use experiences at home and at school, and perceptions of studies and work in the IT field, and why we need more women in IT. Particularly with girls, attention was paid to how they perceive IT and what kind of experiences they have, and if they did not consider it as an option, why was that. With boys, we were interested in their views on IT, what experiences they have, and what they think are the reasons girls are not choosing IT careers.

To get complementary perspectives on the topic, we also conducted interviews with 5 high school IT teachers (ITTs). The interviewees were recruited through high school principals. 2 female and 3 male ITTs agreed to participate in ~1 h long face-to-face interviews, conducted in January and February 2018. The ITTs were asked about their knowledge and experience in IT, their teaching and ideas for development, teachers' role in influencing students' career choice, what they think students think about IT as a subject and a field, and why we should have more women in IT.

All interviews were audio recorded and transcribed. In the data analysis, the most relevant parts of the questionnaire data and the transcribed interviews were extracted into a spreadsheet. First, the data collected from students was analyzed by the first author who looked for how IT field was constituted in the interviews (discourses in place), experiences and skills of the students and how those influence their views of the field and their career choice (historical body), and, who the students think influence their views of the field and career choices, and how (interaction order), highlighting both similarities and differences in the data. Then, the data collected from ITTs was analyzed using the same approach as the student data, looking at the teachers' perspective on the nexus of practice (choosing IT in high schools). All authors discussed the findings and interpretations together.

4 Empirical Insights

Table 1 summarizes our main findings from the survey data and interviews regarding our nexus-analytic inquiry into high schoolers' perceptions of IT field, their IT use experiences and career plans as well as their insights to issues influencing their career choices.

Table 1. A summary of students' perceptions about their career choice and IT

	Discourses	Interaction order	Historical body
Students' perceptions of the IT field	Programming, male-dominated, lonely, nerdy boring, difficult, on the computer, current, teamwork, social, versatile, requires dedication	High school does not introduce students to IT field. Media presents stereotypes of IT jobs and people; genius nerds, glued to their computers, working under pressure. Girls know fewer IT people than boys, neither know of any women	Students have no idea what IT workers do. Little knowledge about IS/IT. Students surprised about how versatile IT field is
Students' IT use and experiences	Boys more interested in IT	IT use introduced through a male in the family, mothers not in IT field. Students need to find out about IT themselves. Boys talk more about playing games	Schools increasingly digitalized. Girls and boys both play games. Students want balance in IT use. IT difficult to use
What students want	Everyone should be able to choose any profession - gender should not matter. Job should be interesting	Family influences what the students want through expectations and leading by example. Schools provide information and career guidance	Girls want social, creative, humanistic, care careers. Girls not interested in IT

(*continued*)

Table 1. (*continued*)

	Discourses	Interaction order	Historical body
What students think influence their choices	Job security important. Salary should be big enough to live comfortably	Teachers' comments and families' upbringing practices seen as gendered. Media targets boys. High schools present traditional professions. Families' gendered encouragement and expectations. Friends not seen as significant influences. Girls' role models from family, artists, social media stars, boys' role models people close to them	'Old ways' – society's gendered expectations. Gender divide deep in society

Discourses Reveal Stereotypes and Lack of Knowledge About IT Work. Students in the survey described their views of the IT field as sitting on the computer all day (39 pairs/includes 47 girls), programming (17/27) male-dominated (12/21), boring (11/15), and nerdy (10/18): "*Maybe that it's quite boring… and you just work on the computer, and you're alone.*[1]," (Girl1) Some girls said that IT jobs are unfamiliar to them: "*Not really, I just have the image that they fix phones and things, and it's not really interesting.*" (Girl2) The boys' answers were slightly less negative, and some described work in IT field as contemporary, social, and versatile. Some mentioned it can be difficult or complicated, and several used the words 'nerdy' and 'engineers': "*It's a stereotypical nerd job.*" (Boy1) Most of them knew that the employment prospects are good; salary ideas varied from bad (5 pairs) to mediocre (20 pairs) and good (21 pairs); working hours were thought to be 8–16 or flexible, with possibility for remote work. In the interviews, few students knew differences between IS and IT, and if they did, the difference was not clear: "*They haven't really been clarified for us, they're talked about in the same subject area.*" (Girl1) In the surveys, many students thought they should be able to code to apply to the IT field, and that it is too late to start in high school. Some associated IT with mathematical skills and thought it is a requirement in the field: "*Even if you're good at math, the reason you don't go there is the image of IT jobs.*" (Girl1) News and media (TV shows and movies) were mentioned as sources for these images: "*I think IT has that reputation, especially from movies, that there are those super geniuses that code a lot and it's very difficult and there's a lot of pressure.*" (Girl3) The interviewees knew IT leaders of big companies. Boys knew more people; the girls were not sure if they knew anyone. None of the students could think of a woman from the IT field. On the other hand, one girl noted that she "*wouldn't necessarily even realize that someone is from the IT field.*" (Girl1)

Historical Body and Interaction Order Shaping the Image of IT Field. IT use is a part of the everyday life for high school students. Computer use at school is differentiated from social media use: "*Well, I'm very active in social media, the computer is only for schoolwork… so Word, Excel. the basic things in high school. And then… Well, I don't really use the computer at home, e.g. coding I don't understand.*" (Girl3) During free

---

[1] All quotes are from interviews.

time, social media and games are in focus. In the interviews, two girls said they play a lot, too; boys just talk about it more: *"I play quite a lot of play station games (...) Boys talk about gaming more, that they do it for many hours per day (...) but girls don't do that."* (Girl1) The high schoolers do not want to spend all day on the computer and that is one reason for not pursuing an IT career. They do not seem to realize that in large number of occupations working with computers is a requirement. The girls seemed to expect that boys or men in the family introduce them to IT, e.g. gaming: *"We have four girls in the family so there is no boy to bring the gaming into the family."* (Girl3) *"My dad plays a lot, so thanks to my dad I've become enthusiastic about gaming."* (Girl2) One girl mentioned her brother (Girl1), and one would watch her boyfriend play. The girls told that boys have more leniency in gaming and spending time on the computer, which gives them more experience: *"In my family the expectation is that we do our homework well, and they tell you to go outside if you spend more than an hour on the phone, and boys can play for hours without interference. (...) they can become interested in coding and make a career out of it."* (Girl3).

Regarding visibility of IT field during high school, the interviewees mentioned IT courses introducing the software students need for coursework and exams. Otherwise, their schedules were so full that there is no time for IT courses as there is no matriculation exam in IT: *"I could have taken the course [on IT] but considering the matriculation exams... fitting it in would be difficult."* (Girl1) The Finnish high school does not offer many opportunities to gain experiences in IT. The students said they find information about interesting fields or ask the guidance counsellors, so the interest in an IT career needs to come from the students themselves. The IT courses that some schools offer are mostly basic programming courses, some had media courses, but most had none. The questionnaires showed that some students (4 pairs) were surprised that you do not need to know programming when beginning IT studies in the university.

Interaction Order and Historical Body Shaping Career Choice. The interviewed girls mentioned family, mothers, artists, and vloggers influencing their career choice. The boys mentioned people close to them. The students did not think they have actual role models: *"I don't really [have role models], I make my own decisions. But opinions of other people and their stories of [different] fields influence my decision, of course."* (Boy3) All of the students thought that the way they are raised has an influence on their career choice; the girls mentioned their wish for parents' approval as a motivating factor: *"Parents do influence a lot, like for me the medical school, that... you want to please them."* (Girl1) The boys said that the parents mainly encourage them to do what they want to do: *"Family has an influence but not... directly. (...) They don't have any expectations, they say 'do what you want' so there's no pressure."* (Boy1) One girl said her mother is her role model: *"My mum is in the humanities, so that could be, actually the whole family is (...) so maybe that influences my choice. (...) Is it cliché to say my mom is my role model?"* (Girl3) In general, the girls felt that family has a strong influence on their choices. None of the interviewed girls' or boys' mothers were in IT field. None of the students said that friends influence their choice: *"Friends just encourage me to do what I really want to do."* (Girl1) When asked in the interviews what else affects career choice many historical body related issues were brought up, such as personal interests, values, past experiences, and employment prospects. Both girls and boys said that personal interests and values direct career choice: *"I think personal values are important in what kind of professions you are drawn to, like, if you like animals you become a veterinarian."* (Girl1) *I've always wanted a job where I can dress nicely."* (Girl2) *"Yes, values matter. I want to study physics because I want to help make cleaner energy."* (Boy1) Salary was not seen as the most important aspect, but it would be nice to have enough to enjoy life: *"You do check how much the salaries are, it's nice to have good wages, but it's not the most important criterion."* (Girl1) Employment was also seen as important: *"You need to feel confident that if I start studies on this field I will get employed later."* (Girl2)

The interviewed students felt that 'old ways' and gendered expectations in our society influence the gender imbalance in career choices. Many students brought up the male-dominance in IT field: *"I think both genders can manage in IT just as well, but it's male-dominated because of old ways."* (Girl3) When asked whether the students saw it as an obstacle for choosing a field if they were in the minority, they would at first say no but then added that it could lead to feelings of isolation: *"Male-dominated environments would be a negative aspect, because it's different to exchange thoughts with women, I don't think I would feel like I belong."* (Girl1) *"If the guys stick together and a woman had an idea, the guys could just stick with their idea."* (Girl2) When asked why the IT field is male-dominated, the students said it was because of 'old ways' and girls are just not interested. One way to change the situation would be to introduce IT to girls earlier: *"Well like, you should catch the girls ... at a younger age, similarly as boys are caught then, or, boys find the gaming world by themselves, but girls do not know how to search for it."* (Girl3) The students saw high school's role as mostly neutral in their career choice; however, in career counselling mostly traditional occupations are introduced, and the IT field is given less attention. The students said that the interest needs to come from themselves, while they can ask guidance counsellors for help and information. One student mentioned that a teacher had been a positive influence, otherwise teachers were seen as neutral: *I think that (...) all occupations are presented openly so they don't create any prejudice."* (Girl1) When asked whether their teachers have gendered assumptions, the students said, *"sometimes someone can say 'this field will probably interest boys more than girls'"* (Girl1), which the girls took to mean that it is not for them.

Teacher's Perceptions of the IT Field. The teachers were aware of the gender imbalance in IT, and all teachers thought women could provide different perspectives in developing IT. Perceptions of gender differences showed in the discourses, related to the ways of thinking and seeing the world: women were seen as better at seeing the 'big picture,' not just the technology. In addition, the teachers saw IT as gendered due to the lack of women, the women's roles in supporting tasks in the companies, and the cultural stereotypes of who IT professionals are and what they do. Generally, the teachers described IT work as diverse, with good employment prospects. They perceived IT engineering studies to be more about hardware and IS about software and how to use it.

Table 2 summarizes our main findings from the IT teacher interviews regarding teachers' perceptions of IT field, their IT experiences and their views on student's relationship to IT and the IT field.

Teachers Shaping Students' Views in Senior High Schools. All interviewees identified stereotypical roles related to IT in their schools: the IT teachers tend to be men

Table 2. A summary of IT teachers' interviews

	Discourses	Interaction order	Historical body
Teachers' perceptions of the IT field	Versatile, good employment and salary. Gendered. Women can provide different perspectives	Read news about IT field, discuss with friends employed in IT to update knowledge	Minor studies in IT, few teachers have work experience in IT field
Teachers' IT experience	Technology is a tool that enables new ways of doing things. Education is digitized, learning to use new tools takes time. Students can be resistant	IT teachers support staff and students. IT support person usually male. Students may need a lot of support	IT use expected in national curriculum
Teachers' views on students and IT	Natural sciences are popular and fill the schedules. There is no final exam in IT that benefits applying to universities, so IT is not chosen	Students see teachers take on gendered roles with IT. Teachers can influence with example and encouragement, providing information about work life in different fields and offering experiences	Students use IT for social media and entertainment. Most lack basic computer skills; few are very proficient. IT an 'extra' subject in high school, courses offered but rarely taken

whose role is to help other staff and students in technical matters in addition to teaching the courses. A woman said, *"although I am the most highly educated person in IT in this building, I don't do anything with IT."* (ITT4) A man reflected *"the gendering is clearly visible in our work community, as the teachers interested in the subject are mostly men. Now we have a few women too."* (ITT2) This teacher saw gendering in taking on certain roles *"it's not that they say, 'come help me because I'm a woman,' but the hidden message is there if they take the role that they don't need to know how to do things."* (ITT2) In addition to providing an example, the teachers thought they can influence students through encouragement and information, and that it is not too late in high school. One of the teachers saw it as her duty to tell students about work life, while the other four said they answer questions if students come to them.

The teachers said students find information about careers from teachers, guidance counsellors, events, family, friends, and websites. When it comes to talking about work life, a teacher said, *"most teachers don't have experience from different fields."* (ITT4) We also asked what kind of discussions the teachers have with students, *"if they ask about jobs, what jobs are like and what they could be, then maybe I'll answer myself. If they ask about studying, I know some things about it but will quickly refer the student to the study guidance counsellor"* (ITT3) They said they can make suggestions; *"You can suggest like 'have you thought about this?', because they have quite a narrow view of careers.*" (ITT3) The teachers saw the importance of IT skills in any profession but were skeptical whether the students see the need. The teachers all had an interest in following news about IT. All knew people working in the field, providing some insights into what the work is like currently.

Teachers' Historical Bodies Influencing in the Background. All the IT teachers we interviewed had studied math in the university, with varying amount of studies in IT; one had taken some courses, three had a minor in IS, and one had an engineering degree in IT - and later studied math to become a teacher. The teachers had teaching experience of 5/8/10/13/18 years in high schools, their courses including firstly math, physics, and chemistry – and IT when possible. In addition, they may train the other teachers.

Teachers Views on Students' Relationship to IT and the IT Field: The IT teachers thought students' IT skills vary; some may be quite proficient due to their interest, while most students' IT use is limited to mandatory schoolwork and entertainment – resulting in lacking basic skills: *"They don't know how to use computers; they just know how to snapchat."* (ITT4) The teachers in this study said most of their students are studying advanced math and natural science, in which girls do well – deducing that it is not math but technology that the girls are not into. As IT studies (e.g. programming) will be included in earlier education, the teachers anticipate that future students will be more skilled in IT. This would mean less time spent on basic computer skills, and the teachers could do more 'interesting' things during the classes. Using computers is mandated in Finnish high schools, and IT courses can be offered as free choice studies. The teachers have the freedom to choose what they teach and how they teach these courses, but they have little time to develop new methods or content. The available IT courses were currently told to include using software systems and tools (e.g. Windows and Word), but also programming and video and image editing. Few students are taking IT courses, though, as the students focus on the subjects they will take matriculation exams in (which provide entry points to university studies). The teachers felt the students' views of career options are limited and the exams limit them further.

5   Concluding Discussion

This study was motivated by the current shortage of employees in the IT field, particularly by the lack of women. Even if one may argue the problem in IS is alleviated by the field being the 'soft' side of IT, we argue the problem has not been alleviated enough. The difference between IS and IT seems to be unknown to senior high schoolers making their major and career choices – and the IS field still suffers from a lack of women [49]. Therefore, the gender aspect was brought up in this study and we asked as our research question *how do senior high school girls perceive IT and the IT field, and what seems to be shaping their career choices.* We examined these questions from the perspective of senior high school students and IT teachers. This study contributes to IS research on gender and IT by outlying novel, surprising findings involved with young people's career choices to study IT/IS. We contribute to IS education literature by identifying a number of aspects to be considered when trying to encourage girls to study IT/IS.

IT use and Experience Does Not Bring Increased Interest in IT Career for Girls.
Our findings reveal surprisingly strong gendering and segregation in the data, manifesting
in a variety of ways in high school students' historical body. We wish to point out that
girls in our study saw IT and IT use as gender neutral but the field itself as masculine
and unattractive (see [6]). Nexus analysis guided us to study the historical bodies of
high schoolers. Even if the use of IT seems to be quite similar – and extensive – for
both genders, this did not lead to both boys and girls to consider IT field or IT career
the same way. Hence, even if this generation can be considered to represent true digital
natives [67], a very traditional and gendered understanding of IT field still prevails (cf.
[63]). Unfortunately, particularly girls seem to have a negative perception of IT careers:
IT careers are not interesting (see [30]) and they cannot fulfil girls' work values (see
[36]) even though girls play video games, use social media, and IT is an everyday tool
for them. Hence, it seems that increased, if not extensive, historical body in IT use
does not lead to increased interest in IT careers. Our data also indicates that attaching
too much importance to IT use might even strengthen the negative perception of the
IT field, as girls do not want to 'spend their time on the computer'. Perhaps this focus
on IT use overemphasizes IT and computers as complex and technical tools, instead of
viewing them as multifaceted IS systems embedded in various social practices (e.g. work
and leisure) supporting diverse, sometimes even value-sensitive aims. Interestingly, 'too
much IT use' was not considered a problem in relation to doctors, lawyers, or business
professionals. Thus, perhaps this tool-orientation has eclipsed the various meanings and
purposes of IS enabled ecosystems and we should find new approaches to introduce
IT/IS field as a creative field of design and social problem-solving with the potential of
emerging new, yet meaningful social practices of everyday life. Instead of considering
IT (non)use and (in)experience as the only explanations for exclusion of girls in IT, we
should examine the role of IT in the entire educational journey from the viewpoint of
what kind of perceptions it imprints on students. Attaching too much importance to IT use
and experience will only limit the way we understand this gender-biased phenomenon
of exclusion of girls in IT.

Discourses in Place Stereotypical and Non-informative on IT Careers. In our data,
students in senior high school did not know IT professions nor were they introduced
to those well enough during their studies. They were surprised about the diversity in
the field. Perhaps this is also connected to the way IT is introduced in high schools,
at least in Finland. Use of IT is compulsory for all, making everyone relatively competent users of IT. However, everyday use of IT does not mean that the students are
tech savvy – often their IT use is limited to entertainment (social media, games) and
schoolwork (Microsoft Office). This does not seem to increase confidence in IT skills.
More advanced courses in IT are optional and those do not tend to interest girls. Girls
assume programming skills are needed before entering higher education in IT, which
deters them from enrolling. This is not surprising as, after all, inclusion of programming
in school curricula is increasingly discussed and thus programming can be overempha-
sized in relation to IT field. Again, this behavior repeats and contributes to the prevailing
stereotypes. Therefore, it is important to break these stereotypes early on. Perhaps the
'softness' of IS field needs to be reconsidered as well. Rather than taking into focus how
'soft' or 'technical' the IT/IS fields are, we should highlight the demanding, socially

challenging practice of the IT professionals when communicating and reconciling the oftentimes conflicting demands of humans in various life situations (e.g. professionals on various fields, children, or elderly).

Teachers Trying to Make a Difference. Teachers may have a minor or a major in an IT subject but are usually firstly math teachers. IT courses may be offered but they only take place if students are enrolling. The high school course topics are basic computer skills in software use, programming, image and video editing. Teachers see the stereotypes and think their students are affected by them and try to convey a more realistic view of the field. Teachers think students' skills are lacking as they use IT mainly for entertainment, and they see this as a problem and that students need to learn computing no matter what field they end up in. Interestingly, no gender was mentioned here (see [29]). In addition, the teachers thought students have plenty of information about careers, but their knowledge about actual work life is limited. The teachers see that the girls themselves choose not to take IT courses, but also recognize the cultural and societal aspects that guide that choice. Teachers saw gendering in personnel who are interested in and teaching IT. While earlier studies have suggested that we should reduce the emphasis of math when speaking of IT [5], these IT and math teachers tend to try to motivate their students by telling the students why the subject is important in any field. It seems like math is not an obstacle based on what students and teachers said, it's the image of the IT field. Teachers think they can influence students through encouragement, example, and inspiration, and that it is not too late in high school (in line with [73]), but they did not mention the expectations they themselves set to their students (see [65]).

Gendered Interaction Orders Among Different Actors Shaping Girls' Interest in IT Careers: Expectations, Norms, Upbringing. Regarding interaction order, our data shows that our society, teachers and parents among others, play a role in gendering and segregation: they seem to have and advocate surprisingly gendered discourses, expectations, norms, and upbringing practices. Even if the students explained that everyone is expected to be able to select any career and pursue their interests freely, they also expressed very traditional and gendered career choices, girls preferring social, caring, and creative aspects, boys showing interest in technology (see [6, 16, 22, 29, 30, 44]). The students revealed that different expectations are placed on boys and girls in families and teachers may in subtle ways engage in gendering practices, hinting things that are specifically of interest to boys or girls. Our findings also suggest that males seem to introduce girls to IT (see [53, 55]). In schools, males seem to take responsibility of IT. Perhaps all this reflects the decades old male-dominant culture of the IT field in general (see [12, 54]). Since the entire IT field is known to be male-dominant, girls may unconsciously feel they need males to mediate their interest and orientation into IT. The girls also felt that the general discourses, media, and game advertisements are directed towards boys, so not much has changed in over 25 years [56]. This study corroborates the findings of existing research on the influence of society, family, and teachers on young people's career choices, including IT careers. It is surprising to find these to remain true, as the world has drastically changed through digitalization.

Vicious Cycle of Gender Segregation Upholds Itself. Based on our findings, we deduce that all the life experiences in relation to IT before choosing the major seem to play a significant role in this persistent exclusion of girls. Career choices seem to reflect not only young people's perceptions of the field but, perhaps even more importantly, the perceptions of some influential others, thus repeating the same old gender-biased views over generations: stereotypes, educational prejudices, assumptions about antisocial professions, etc. Girls' unfamiliarity of the IT field and career options makes room for influential others to have their say and thus keep the 'rat race' ongoing. We are in a vicious cycle with gender segregation in IT, particularly in the post-industrial nations such as e.g. Finland [30], the context of our study, as segregation upholds itself. Girls need role models, for example their own mothers, to consider IT field as a potential career choice. However, mothers are mostly in social/care fields. Guidance counsellors and teachers in Finnish high schools are also often women, and IT support persons typically men, and it seems that this repeats the gendered culture of women working in 'soft' professions and being less competent in IT. Encouragement and exposure [70] to the field among high school girls falls short if the social environment within the school context provides no role models. Due to lack of role models, girls do not choose the IT field and thus new role models for the next generations will not appear. To break the pattern, we need to make the women already in the field more visible [54]. Luckily, two of the interviewed IT teachers in our study were women, providing some role model for their own students. One problem is that girls think that being 'the only girl' would be lonely and socially isolated [11, 17]; we also need to increase networking between women in the field.

Exclusion and Educational Inequality. Our data indicates that girls voluntarily and intentionally exclude themselves from IT field – it is their choice (see [31]). We must also acknowledge that there are significant cultural, historical and social factors in the background, leading girls to choose this way. Nexus analysis indicates that current societal discourses, interaction orders among significant others around us, and all our historical bodies are always intermingled with our choices [52]. In research on gender and IT, earlier the focus was on intentional exclusion, while more recently the focus has changed to second generation gender bias, i.e. invisible barriers for women in IT that are based on cultural beliefs and workplace structure [51]. The girls in this study were clearly aware of the contemporary (negative) ways of talking about the IT field and professionals. They recognized that they are being shaped and influenced by their parents and their teachers. They seemed less aware of their life experiences and histories shaping their choices. This should be made more visible for the girls, we think. Regarding inclusion and exclusion, we recognize that IT is not a perfect major or career choice for everyone and exclusion from this education may be intentional and desirable for some (cf. [31]). However, exclusion of girls to such a large extent in the design of our digital futures is alarming and we must act to change that.

Our Findings Offer Valuable Insights for IS Education. We need to act and combat the digital divide to achieve equality in education. Based on the study, we identify the following as critical issues: 1) We must enter the education of young generation early on – well before senior high school as many critical choices have already been made before that phase; 2) We must make the IT field and its versatility, particularly the IS field, visible for young people; 3) We must make visible how society is still gendered and segregated – making this visible may encourage young people to question and alter the traditional ways of doing and thinking; 4) We must identify positive role models for girls in IT/IS: we need to consider what we already have and what could arouse girls' interest and admiration; 5) We must connect the field better with young people's interests, values, and desires – the IT/IS field is not in conflict with those, but the young generation does not seem to see it. IS community needs to address this problem and, building on the accumulated understanding of what keeps women away from the IS/IT field, show girls the versatile career possibilities where it is possible to fulfil various kinds of dreams, desires, and values (see [36]). We also need to remember that it is not only girls who are needed in the IS/IT field and it is not only girls in the post-industrial society who want to fulfil their dreams; we also need more boys to consider IS/IT as their career choice due to the shortage of workforce in IS/IT field. High schools and universities could work together to provide relevant and meaningful activities, with information about different career paths in IT. Further considerations are needed on how IT is integrated in education or what should be included in the IT courses. The current structure at least in Finnish curriculum seems to exclude IT as an 'extra subject' that provides little in terms of meaningful experiences.

Limitations and Future Work. This exploratory study is limited by the sample size. Next, we will interview more girls to get a more thorough understanding of girls' views of the IT field and factors shaping their career choices. In addition, we plan to collect and analyze data from women who have already entered the IT field. We will offer a more nuanced picture of girls and women in relation to IT. This analysis concentrated on summarizing the views of the informants, focusing on commonalities. Through this, we managed to show the surprisingly strong gendering and segregation still ongoing in our society. Then again, we strongly believe there are individual differences [62] among girls, and that there are other dividing factors than gender. We will pay closer attention to these aspects in our future analyses. In our project, we do not assume that girls are only interested in the soft side of IT neither do we want to push girls that way; instead, we want to give a versatile picture of the IT field to all senior high school students, boys included. It is important to note that drawing conclusions to IT/IS field in general is not possible based on our study; IT field covers such a variety. We can point out that at least in Finland, senior high school students do not see any difference between IT and IS and there is obviously a lot that could be done to help them in making well informed and meaningful career choices.

To Conclude, This is Quite a Surprising and Sad Story on How Finnish Society is Still Gendered and Segregated as Regards IT as a Career. From this nexus analytic inquiry, we can see that surprisingly gendered understandings of the IT field and career choices are still prevalent among the studied young people, and this supports educational and occupational segregation. Exclusion of women from IT education, be that intentional or unintentional, conscious or unconscious, accomplished by the excluded themselves or by others [31] indicates a potential for deep digital divide [47], especially from the perspective of people's abilities to make and shape digital technology, not only to use it [31]. Our findings concern post-industrial nations where people choose occupations that they find highly interesting and they would love to do [16], and in many studies it has been found that girls see IT as boring and unfulfilling for their work values [30, 36]. On the bright side, the teachers see they can make a difference in high schools.

Acknowledgements. Data collection for this paper has been funded by European Social Fund within the LUNO project.

References

1. Adya, M., Kaiser, K.M.: Early determinants of women in the IT workforce: a model of girls' career choices. Inf. Technol. People. **18**(3), 230–259 (2005)
2. Ahuja, M.K.: Women in the information technology profession: a literature review, synthesis and research agenda. Eur. J. Inf. Syst. **11**(1), 20–34 (2002)
3. Anderson, L., Edberg, D., Reed, A., Simkin, M.G., Stiver, D.: How can universities best encourage women to major in information systems? Commun. Assoc. Inf. Syst. **41**, 734–758 (2017)
4. Avgerou, C., Siemer, J., Bjørn-Andersen, N.: The academic field of information systems in Europe. Eur. J. Inf. Syst. **8**(2), 136–153 (1999)
5. Babin, R., Grant, K.A., Sawal, L.: Identifying influencers in high school student ICT career choice. Inf. Syst. Educ. J. **8**(26), 18 (2010)
6. Barone, C.: Some things never change: gender segregation in higher education across eight nations and three decades. Sociol. Educ. **84**(2), 157–176 (2011)
7. Bateson, G.: Steps to an Ecology of Mind: Collected Essays in Anthropology, Psychiatry, Evolution, and Epistemology. University of Chicago Press, Chicago (2000)
8. Beyer, S.: Why are women underrepresented in Computer Science? Gender differences in stereotypes, self-efficacy, values, and interests and predictors of future CS course-taking and grades. Comput. Sci. Educ. **24**(2–3), 153–192 (2014)
9. Blackburn, R.M., Browne, J., Brooks, B., Jarman, J.: Explaining gender segregation. Br. J. Sociol. **53**(4), 513–536 (2002)
10. Blommaert, J., Huang, A.: Historical bodies and historical space. J. Appl. Linguist.-Lond. **6**(3), 267 (2009)
11. Blomqvist, M.: Absent women: research on gender relations in it education mediated by swedish newspapers. In: Gender Issues in Learning and Working with Information Technology: Social Constructs and Cultural Contexts, pp. 133–149. IGI Global (2010)
12. Boivie, I.: Women, men and programming: knowledge, metaphors and masculinity. In: Gender Issues in Learning and Working with Information Technology: Social Constructs and Cultural Contexts. pp. 1–24. IGI Global (2010)
13. Bourdieu, P.: The Logic of Practice. Stanford University Press, Stanford (1990)
14. Bush, C.G.: Women and the assessment of technology: to think, to be; to unthink, to free. Read. Philos. Technol. 112–126 (2009)
15. Carter, L.: Why students with an apparent aptitude for computer science don't choose to major in computer science. ACM SIGCSE Bull. **38**(1), 27–31 (2006)
16. Charles, M., Bradley, K.: Indulging our gendered selves? Sex segregation by field of study in 44 countries. Am. J. Sociol. **114**(4), 924–976 (2009)
17. Cheryan, S., Master, A., Meltzoff, A.N.: Cultural stereotypes as gatekeepers: increasing girls' interest in computer science and engineering by diversifying stereotypes. Front. Psychol. **6**, 49 (2015)

18. Craig, A., Lang, C., Giannakos, M.N., Kleiner, C., Gal-Ezer, J.: Looking outside: what can be learnt from computing education around the world? In: Proceedings of the 45th ACM Technical Symposium on Computer Science Education - SIGCSE 2014, Atlanta, Georgia, USA, pp. 371–372. ACM Press (2014)
19. Croasdell, D., McLeod, A., Simkin, M.G.: Why don't more women major in information systems? Inf. Technol. People 24(2), 158–183 (2011)
20. Dee, H.M., Boyle, R.D.: Inspiring women undergraduates. In: Proceedings of the Fifteenth Annual CONFERENCE on Innovation and technology in Computer Science Education - ITiCSE 2010, Bilkent, Ankara, Turkey, p. 43. ACM Press (2010)
21. Eurostat: Employed ICT Specialists by Employment. Eurostat, Brussels (2019)
22. Falk, A., Hermle, J.: Relationship of gender differences in preferences to economic development and gender equality. Science 362(6412), eaas9899 (2018)
23. Fisher, J., Lang, C., Craig, A., Forgasz, H.: If girls aren't interested in computers can we change their minds? In: Proceedings of the 23rd Information Systems European Conference, Münster, Germany, pp. 1–14. AIS Electronic Library (2015)
24. Goffman, E.: Forms of Talk. University of Pennsylvania Press, Philadelphia (1981)
25. Goffman, E.: The interaction order: American Sociological Association, 1982 presidential address. Am. Sociol. Rev. 48(1), 1–17 (1983)
26. Graham, S., Latulipe, C.: CS girls rock: sparking interest in computer science and debunking the stereotypes. ACM SIGCSE Bull. 35(1), 322–326 (2003)
27. Guthrie, R., Yakura, E., Soe, L.: How did mathematics and accounting get so many women majors? What can IT disciplines learn? In: Proceedings. of the 2011 Conference on Information Technology Education, pp. 15–20 (2011)
28. Hatlevik, O.E., Throndsen, I., Loi, M., Gudmundsdottir, G.B.: Students' ICT self-efficacy and computer and information literacy: determinants and relationships. Comput. Educ. 118, 107–119 (2018)
29. He, J., Freeman, L.A.: Are men more technology-oriented than women? The role of gender on the development of general computer self-efficacy of college students. J. Inf. Syst. 21(2), 203–213 (2010)
30. Hyde, J.S.: Gender similarities and differences. Annu. Rev. Psychol. 65(1), 373–398 (2014)
31. Iivari, N., Kinnula, M., Molin-Juustila, T., Kuure, L.: Exclusions in social inclusion projects: struggles in involving children in digital technology development. Inf. Syst. J. 28(6), 1020–1048 (2018)
32. Iivari, N., Molin-Juustila, T., Kinnula, M.: The future digital innovators: empowering the young generation with digital fabrication and making. In: Proceedings of International Conference on Information Systems, ICIS 2016 (2016)
33. Jepsen, T.: Women in IT: is the pipeline still shrinking? IT Prof. 3(5), 69–71 (2001)
34. Joshi, K.D., Schmidt, N.L.: Is the information systems profession gendered? Characterization of IS professionals and IS career. SIGMIS Database 37(4), 16 (2006)
35. Jost, J.T., Kay, A.C.: Exposure to benevolent sexism and complementary gender stereotypes: consequences for specific and diffuse forms of system justification. J. Pers. Soc. Psychol. 88(3), 498–509 (2005)
36. Jung, L., Clark, U.Y., Patterson, L., Pence, T.: Closing the gender gap in the technology major. Inf. Syst. Educ. J. 15(1), 26 (2017)
37. Kaarakainen, M.-T., Kivinen, O.: Teknologia tulevaisuudessa tarvittavien ICT-taitojen ja muun osaamisen edistäjänä. In: Kuuskorpi, M. (ed.) Digitaalinen oppiminen ja oppimisym-päristöt, pp. 46–64. Kaarinan kaupunki (2015)
38. Kahle, J., Schmidt, D.G.: Reasons women pursue a computer science career: perspectives of women from a midsized institution. J. Comput. Sci. Coll. 19(4), 78–89 (2004)

39. Kinnula, M., Iivari, N., Molin-Juustila, T., Keskitalo, E., Leinonen, T., Mansikkamäki, E., Käkelä, T., Similä, M.: Cooperation, combat, or competence building–what do we mean when we are 'empowering children' in and through digital technology design? Presented at the 38th International Conference on Information Systems, Seoul (2017)
40. Leslie, L.L., McClure, G.T., Oaxaca, R.L.: Women and minorities in science and engineering: a life sequence analysis. J. High. Educ. **69**(3), 239–276 (1998)
41. Main, J.B., Schimpf, C.: The underrepresentation of women in computing fields: a synthesis of literature using a life course perspective. IEEE Trans. Educ. **60**(4), 296–304 (2017)
42. McLachlan, C., Craig, A., Coldwell, J.: Student perceptions of ICT: a gendered analysis. In: Proceedings of the 12th Australasian Conference on Computing Education, pp. 127–136 (2010)
43. Melkas, H., Anker, R.: Occupational segregation by sex in Nordic countries: an empirical investigation. Int. Lab. Rev. **136**, 341 (1997)
44. Michie, S., Nelson, D.L.: Barriers women face in information technology careers: self-efficacy, passion and gender biases. Women Manag. Rev. **21**(1), 10–27 (2006)
45. Molin-Juustila, T., Kinnula, M., Iivari, N., Kuure, L., Halkola, E.: Multiple voices in ICT design with children – a nexus analytical enquiry. Behav. Inf. Technol. **34**(11), 1079–1091 (2015)
46. Nishida, K.: Intelligibility and the Philosophy of Nothingness. Ripol Klassik (Рипол Классик) (1958)
47. OECD: Connected Minds: Technology and Today's Learners. Educational Research and Innovation, OECD Publishing, Paris (2012)
48. OECD: Education Indicators in Focus (2017). http://www.oecd.org/education/skills-beyond-school/educationindicatorsinfocus.htm
49. Oehlhorn, C.: Drawing on the underrepresentation of women in IT-professions: an analysis of existing knowledge and need for research along the stages of educational systems. In: Proceedings of the ACM SIGMIS Conference on Computers and People Research - SIGMIS-CPR 2017, Bangalore, India, pp. 197–198. ACM Press (2017)
50. Prensky, M.: Digital natives, digital immigrants part 1. Horizon **9**(5), 1–6 (2001)
51. Rogers, V.L.N.: Women in IT: The endangered gender. In: Proceedings of the ACM Annual Conference on SIGUCCS 2015, St. Petersburg, Florida, USA, pp. 95–98. ACM Press (2015)
52. Scollon, R., Scollon, S.: Nexus Analysis: Discourse and the Emerging Internet. Routledge, London (2004)
53. Serapiglia, C.P., Lenox, T.L.: Factors affecting women's decisions to pursue an IS degree: a case study. Inf. Syst. Educ. J. **8**(12), n12 (2010)
54. Silverman, S., Pritchard, A.M.: High School Girls in Technology Education in Connecticut. Connecticut State Department of Education, Hartford (1993)
55. Smith, L.B.: The socialization of females with regard to a technology-related career: recommendations for change. Meridian Middle Sch. Comput. Technol. J. **3**(2) (2000)
56. Spertus, E.: Why are there so few female computer scientists? M.I.T, Artificial Intelligence Laboratory, Cambridge (1991)
57. Statistics Finland: Segregation of fields of education by gender (2018). https://www.stat.fi/tup/tasaarvo/education/index_en.html#segregation
58. Thomas, T., Allen, A.: Gender differences in students' perceptions of information technology as a career. J. Inf. Technol. Educ. Res. **5**(1), 165–178 (2006)
59. Tømte, C., Hatlevik, O.E.: Gender differences in Self-efficacy ICT related to various ICT-user profiles in Finland and Norway. How do self-efficacy, gender and ICT-user profiles relate to findings from PISA 2006. Comput. Educ. **57**(1), 1416–1424 (2011)
60. Trauth, E.M.: The role of theory in gender and information systems research. Inf. Organ. **23**(4), 277–293 (2013)

61. Trauth, E.M., Quesenberry, J.L., Huang, H.: A multicultural analysis of factors influencing career choice for women in the information technology workforce. J. Glob. Inf. Manag. **16**(4), 1–23 (2008)
62. Trauth, E.M., Quesenberry, J.L., Morgan, A.J.: Understanding the Under Representation of women in IT: toward a theory of individual differences. In: Proceedings of the SIGMIS Conference on Computer Personnel Research: Careers, Culture, and Ethics in a Networked Environment (2004)
63. Ule, M., Šribar, R., Venturini, A.: Gendering science: slovenian surveys and studies in the EU paradigms. Obs. Soc. Sci. **4** (2015)
64. Vainionpää, F., Kinnula, M., Iivari, N., Molin-Juustila, T.: Girls' choice - why won't they pick IT? In: Proceedings of the 27th European Conference on Information Systems, Stockholm, Sweden (2019)
65. Vekiri, I.: Boys' and girls' ICT beliefs: do teachers matter? Comput. Educ. **55**(1), 16–23 (2010)
66. Vekiri, I., Chronaki, A.: Gender issues in technology use: perceived social support, computer self-efficacy and value beliefs, and computer use beyond school. Comput. Educ. **51**(3), 1392–1404 (2008)
67. Vodanovich, S., Sundaram, D., Myers, M.: Research commentary—digital natives and ubiquitous information systems. Inf. Syst. Res. **21**(4), 711–723 (2010)
68. Volman, M., van Eck, E., Heemskerk, I., Kuiper, E.: New technologies, new differences. Gender and ethnic differences in pupils' use of ICT in primary and secondary education. Comput. Educ. **45**(1), 35–55 (2005)
69. Vygotsky, L.: Interaction between learning and development. Read. Dev. Child. **23**(3), 34–41 (1978)
70. Wang, J., Hong, H., Ravitz, J., Ivory, M.: Gender differences in factors influencing pursuit of computer science and related fields. In: Proceedings of the ACM Conference on Innovation and Technology in Computer Science Education - ITiCSE 2015, Vilnius, Lithuania, pp. 117–122. ACM Press (2015)
71. Watts, A.G., Sultana, R.G.: Career guidance policies in 37 countries: contrasts and common themes. Int. J. Educ. Vocat. Guid. **4**(2–3), 105–122 (2004)
72. Zarrett, N.R., Malanchuk, O.: Who's computing? Gender and race differences in young adults' decisions to pursue an information technology career. New Dir. Child Adolesc. Dev. **2005**(110), 65–84 (2005)
73. Zeldin, A.L., Pajares, F.: Against the odds: self-efficacy beliefs of women in mathematical, scientific, and technological careers. Am. Educ. Res. J. **37**(1), 215–246 (2000)
74. Lukion opetussuunnitelman perusteet 2019 (2019). https://www.oph.fi/fi/koulutus-ja-tutkin not/lukion-opetussuunnitelmien-perusteet

I Rest My Case! The Possibilities and Limitations of Blockchain-Based IP Protection

Sofia Lopes Barata[1]([✉]), Paulo Rupino Cunha[1], and Ricardo S. Vieira-Pires[2]

[1] Centre for Informatics and Systems of the University of Coimbra, Department of Informatics Engineering, University of Coimbra, Coimbra, Portugal
{sofbarata,rupino}@dei.uc.pt
[2] Center for Neuroscience and Cell Biology and Institute for Biomedical Imaging and Life Sciences (CNC.IBILI), University of Coimbra, Coimbra, Portugal
ricardo.pires@biocant.pt

Abstract. We have identified, mapped and discussed existing research on Blockchain-based solutions for intellectual property (IP) protection, an investigation that emerged from a case in antibody production for scientific and medical applications. To that end, we have performed a systematic literature review and created an instrument that classifies the contributions according to the materiality of the object they protect (from immaterial to physical), the type of protection (authorship notarization or prevention of illegal use) and the type of research (conceptual or empirical). Our results can be used to understand which avenues to pursue in the effort to create a new generation of more effective technology-assisted IP protection systems, a priority for 152 signatory countries of the patent cooperation treaty.

Keywords: Antibodies · Blockchain · Intellectual property

1 Introduction

The global market for antibodies for research was valued at USD 2.52 billion in 2016 and it is anticipated to progress at a Compound Annual Growth Rate (CAGR) of 6.1% over 2018–2025. Antibodies are high-value proteins produced in living cells and vastly used for scientific research, medical diagnostics, and advanced therapies, namely as biopharmaceutical drugs. They originate from two sources: native and in vitro. An animal, such as a rabbit, inoculated with a vaccine X will typically respond by producing Anti-X antibodies. These can either be recovered from the blood of the animal (native source, resulting in polyclonal antibodies (pAbs)) or they can be processed with advanced methodologies to collect the genetic (DNA) information that allows in vitro production

---

A prior version of this paper has been published in the ISD2019 Proceedings (http://aisel.aisnet.org/isd2014/proceedings2019).

A. Siarheyeva et al. (Eds.): ISD 2019, LNISO 39, pp. 57–73, 2020.
https://doi.org/10.1007/978-3-030-49644-9_4

(in vitro source, resulting in monoclonal antibodies (mAbs)). Biopharmaceutical and pharmaceutical companies are heavily dependent on the use of both, pAbs and mAbs for R&D on innovative treatments for cancer and other chronic diseases, which has dictated a tremendous market traction. [37]. Monoclonal antibodies (mAbs) account for the leading share in this market. The in vitro molecular processing involved in their production enables the identification of very precise and unique genetic recipes for antibodies with specific capabilities (e.g. interacting with and killing a cancer cell). These recipes are nothing more than instructions in the form of a DNA sequence (a string of letters, A, T, G and C), that can be given to specialized living cells to produce the ultimate antibody molecule of interest. Importantly, this unique mAb recipe, becomes a high-value intellectual asset that requires special protection, since it can be used for replication and commercialization at an industrial scale. Patenting is a common route [11], but it can be very complex and costly, especially considering that the requirements needed to confer the patent may differ according to the countries in which it is applicable [22]. Additionally, patent enforcement often means expensive and long legal suits.

Thus, our research question is:

RQ: Are there Blockchain-based techniques suitable for the protection of immaterial intellectual assets, such as antibody recipes?

To investigate this issue, we started with a systematic literature review (SLR), which allows identifying, evaluating, and interpreting available research relevant to a topic area or phenomenon of interest, such as the summary of evidence concerning a given technology [9]. Our key concepts are (1) intellectual property (IP) and (2) Blockchain.

Intellectual property results from the work of the mind or intellect, which may be an idea, an invention or a process [34]. Depending on the adopted form of legal protection, the conferred rights will differ. Available forms are (1) patents, (2) trademarks, (3) copyrights, and (4) trade secrets [18], briefly described below:

- The patent is an exclusive right granted to an invention (product or a process), which prevents it from being commercially made, used, distributed, imported or sold without authorization of the patent owner [35]. It has a duration of 20 years and it is territorial, i.e., the rights are only applied in the country or region where the patent was granted, in accordance with the laws of that territory [35].
- Trademarks are used to distinguish companies, products or services by means of a word or symbol [18]. Legal owners can prevent its use by others within specific commercial limits. The trademark rights are valid for 10 years but may be renewed indefinitely [40] while the trademark is properly used and enforced [18]. It can be applied at the country or region level, or at the international level, depending on the type of registration [40].
- Copyright is an exclusive right assigned to the author or creator of a e.g. literary, artistic, musical, software products [18]. For content to be copyrightable it needs to (1) be permanently registered in some medium (e.g. paper, computer), (2) be original, and (3) exhibit creativity [18]. Copyright offers financial protection, enabling authors to license the use of their work for a fee, and also moral protection of non-economic interests [32], such as attribution or reputation. It has a finite duration that depends on the laws applied in the country/region of its use [18].

- Trade secrets are, as the name implies, secrets (e.g. formulas) that afford commercial or technical advantage [18] to a business because they are not known or easily discovered by observation [39]. Content may or may not be patentable, but if it becomes public the holder may lose all competitive advantage that the trade secret provides [18]. It has no legal protection and lasts only until discovered [18].

Blockchain is a technology originally introduced in the context of Bitcoin, to avoid the double spending of digital money, but whose underlying mechanisms have proven interesting to multiple areas where trust is a key concern [38]. This stems from the fact that transactions are recorded on a distributed, immutable, tamper-proof ledger, that is inherently auditable. Additionally, Blockchains can store and enforce smart contracts – pieces of code that are executed automatically once predetermined conditions are met – further reducing uncertainty and promoting confidence among stakeholders [30]. In the scope of our research we will focus on existing uses of Blockchain for the protection of intellectual property.

The remainder of this paper is structured as follows. Next, we describe the methodology, detailing how we obtained the data, then we present its analysis. Section 4 draws on the content of the identified papers to address the benefits, challenges, and practical applications of Blockchain-based IP protection. Section 5 maps extant research using a specially devised instrument that enables the discussion. The conclusions summarize our work and point out limitations.

2 Methodology

Our systematic literature review follows the structure defined by Webster and Watson [26]. Our goal is to identify and map relevant research about the use of Blockchain-based IP Protection. We selected the databases Science Direct (SD) and EBSCO, due to their wide coverage, complemented by AISEL for a focus on the Senior Scholars' Basket of Journals [36]. The paper search was made on the first and second weeks of November 2018. Originally, we chose the keywords "Blockchain" or "distributed ledger technology" (DLT) combined with "intellectual property" which are directly derived from the scope of our research. However, preliminary test searches in Google Scholar suggested the additional inclusion of "copyright" and "digital rights management" for the relevant hits they surfaced. The inclusion criteria were conference and journal papers, in English, published since 2008, given the fact that this was the year of publication of Nakamoto's article on Bitcoin, considered the first successful implementation of Blockchain technology [20]. Figure 1 illustrates the search process.

A full text search returned a total of 1518 hits (270 duplicates) on the selected set of databases. To narrow down the results, a second round was conducted using the same keyword combination, but constrained to title, keywords, and abstract. A total of 83 results were obtained at this stage. After eliminating six duplicates, our set was reduced to 77 articles. The date range for this subset is from 2013 to 2018. To increase validity and decrease biases, we used researcher triangulation [3, 7], in which two authors separately analysed the abstract of the papers and classified their relevance as (Yes/No/Maybe). We made final decisions on the "Maybes" in a discussion. As a result, 57 non-relevant

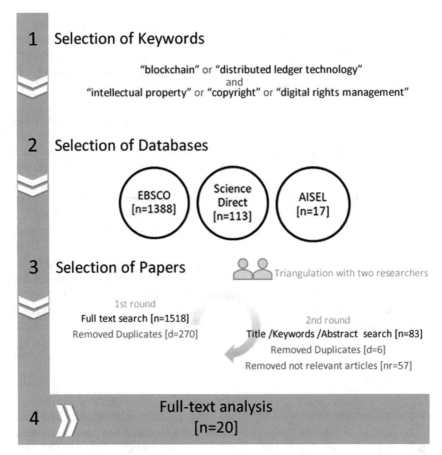

Fig. 1. Systematic literature review approach

articles were discarded and 20 remained to be analysed in-depth, by reading the full text, with the aim of extracting information about the use of Blockchain for intellectual property protection.

3 Data Analysis

The papers selected for in-depth analysis have been classified in terms of year of publication, type of research (conceptual - C, empirical - E), object of protection (e.g. music, images, software), and type of protection discussed (Authorship Notarization - AN, Use Authorization - UA). Articles that evidence the use of Blockchain for the sole purpose of authorship attribution are marked AN. If the level of protection effectively prevents illegal use or dissemination of the object, then the articles are marked UA. For every article, a brief description of the role of Blockchain was included. Table 1 presents the classification of the 20 articles analysed in-depth.

Table 1. Classification of the reviewed papers

ID	Ref	Blockchain use	Type of object	Type of protection	Year	Type of research
1	[19]	Registration of creative work, namely orphan work. With storage, dissemination, and transfer of information about copyright objects and their right holders	Creative work	AN	2017	C
2	[1]	Conception of a new ecosystem where it is possible to identify the authors, track protected content (stream), and assign a fair remuneration to the artists. The authors suggest that smart contracts could allow music royalties to be administered transparently and almost instantaneously	Music	UA + AN	2018	C
3	[2]	Normative analysis of key Blockchain technology concepts from the perspective of copyright law. Analyzes in detail the legal issues related to smart contracts and private ordering, copyright registrations, the legal regime of DRM, and fair remuneration	Digital	AN	2018	C
4	[4]	Establish ownership of the copyright, but it also helps to enforce rights (e.g. artificial intelligence could track unauthorized use on the internet, this information would be passed on to creators who could thus contact the infringer directly)	Digital	AN	2018	C
5	[5]	Analysis of the impact of blockchain on intellectual property law, namely in the registration, management and enforcement of IP rights. The authors state that Blockchain will be able to help to overcome the IP register in different legislations and dealing with different procedures	Generic	AN	2018	C
6	[6]	Analysis the possibilities of Blockchain to serve as an institution of property, and how Blockchain applications may or may not replace some aspects of legal norms and property rights	Digital	AN	2017	C

(continued)

Table 1. (*continued*)

ID	Ref	Blockchain use	Type of object	Type of protection	Year	Type of research
7	[8]	Analysis of impact in the music industry, such as, benefits, automating payments of royalties (combining streams with smart contracts), transparency and data protection and the existing, and compliance with legislation	Music	UA + AN	2017	C
8	[10]	Conception of a decentralized peer-to-peer software license validation system using cryptocurrency Blockchain technology. Licenses are validated with a unique license key that cannot be copied, reused, or regenerated. This key links the user and the device to the license	Software	UA	2018	E
9	[12]	Description of a Blockchain as a service (BaaS) architecture for DRM business models. Content is encrypted and stored in a centralized database. The rights confirmation and DRM assets consumption are made with Blockchain. Access to the data with tamper-resistant copyrights protection, digital currency for content consumption payment	Digital	UA + AN	2018	E
10	[27]	Description of a Blockchain-based scheme for digital rights management, with two isolated Blockchain application interfaces, to store plain and cipher summary information of original and DRM-protected digital content	Digital	UA + AN	2018	E
11	[15]	Analysis the main transformations and challenges that the record industry can face with Blockchain technology. Improve transparency, availability of copyright data and facilitate the near-instant micropayments for royalties	Music	UA + AN	2018	C
12	[16]	Conception of a smart contract for MANAGING digital reuse rights of research data, recording the information of the author and the conditions established for the reuse of the work	Research data	AN	2018	E

(*continued*)

Table 1. (*continued*)

ID	Ref	Blockchain use	Type of object	Type of protection	Year	Type of research
13	[17]	Analysis the impact of Blockchain on innovation in Scotland's digital design industries. Blockchain can support creative endeavour by enabling more autonomous and flexible IP management systems	Digital	AN	2017	C
14	[21]	Focus on legal aspects related to Blockchain under the copyright sphere. The role of the Blockchain in the distribution of copyrighted works in the digital realm	Generic	AN	2018	C
15	[23]	Analysis the possibilities of use and the importance of Blockchain and smart contract for attorneys	Generic	AN	2018	C
16	[24]	Adequacy of traditional ideas about property law in the context of digital assets, namely the cryptocurrency Bitcoin	Bitcoin	AN	2017	C
17	[25]	Possible use cases of IP management of Blockchain technology. Blockchain can create an immutable record of authenticity, which may include ownership, evidence, publication, and first and genuine use	Generic	AN	2018	C
18	[28]	Examination of Blockchain technologies in the "creation of proprietary digital art markets in which uncommodifiable digital artworks are financialized as artificially scarce commodities"	Digital art	AN	2018	C
19	[29]	Outset of a Blockchain-based solution for digital image rights management scheme. With Internet misuse detection based on watermark	Digital	AN	2018	E
20	[31]	Conception of a Blockchain-based scheme for an image copyright registry. A robust image feature vector is used to identify duplicate image registrations on the network where it is being used	Images	AN	2018	E

As shown in Fig. 2, the majority of papers (75%) were published in 2018 and the remainder (25%) in 2017, thus reflecting that the interest in the use of Blockchain technology for IP protection is recent and rising. Further, as seen in Fig. 3, 70% of the articles were of conceptual nature and 30% of them empirical. Considering the type of protection (Fig. 4), almost all papers addressed Authorship Notarization, in contrast to 30% of papers that indicated Use Authorization mechanisms. The analysis by type of object, more specifically the representation in a materiality continuum, will be analyzed in detail in the discussion.

Fig. 2. Spread of papers selected by year

Fig. 3. Spread of papers selected by type of analysis

Fig. 4. Spread of papers selected by type of protection

Based on the content of the papers, in the next section we will outline the key benefits and challenges of Blockchain-based in IP protection. We will also present the use cases and examples found in the literature.

4   What the Literature Says

4.1   Blockchain for IP Protection

Several authors have verified the feasibility of using Blockchain for the registration of intellectual property. The technology supports the technical, safety, and decentralization requirements for registering copyrights [19]. It can help provide tamper-proof evidence of ownership [19]. It also brings transparency and traceability over subsequent changes, increasing the visibility and availability of that information as a "Trusted Timestamping" [21], so the products are capable of "telling their own story", since their origin to commercialization [25].

Blockchain is evolving fast, but there are major challenges to address. For example, the complexity of the technology and its promise of disruptive changes raises suspicions and concerns [4]. Negative publicity associated with some use cases, like cryptocurrencies, also affects the rate of adoption of this technology [4]. The immutable nature of the Blockchain is one of its strengths, but also raises questions, such as responsibility if wrong data is registered [23].

Blockchain-based IP registers can replace existing IP databases [6, 19]. However, it is necessary to establish criteria, perform technical tests, and keep the interests of authors and users balanced [19]. The authors go further and claim that Blockchain may be considered an institution of property, such as a legal institution, but it is too early to predict whether it will replace legal norms and property rights [6]. The work of [4] also identifies the advantages of using a Blockchain-based IP system, such as simplifying the registration process, reducing associated fees, dispensing the need to register in different jurisdictions, and self-managing of IP rights by the author, without the involvement of third parties. In summary, the literature acknowledges advantages of Blockchain for IP registration, but cautions that it is not yet proven that it will be sufficient for the effective protection against illegal use of the object.

Regarding the use of Blockchain in the context of IP protection, the literature identifies some concerns, such as, where the content will be stored: in the Blockchain proper or "off-chain" [21]. In the latter case, some argue that using the Blockchain as a mere time-stamping service for "off-chain" content cannot guarantee reliability [21]. It is suggested that the use of Blockchain may disrupt the existing creative distribution networks, with [17] questioning how market will react to increased copyright control. In a nutshell, literature points to some challenges inherent to the Blockchain technology, but also raises important issues related to implementation and market acceptance.

4.2 Smart Contracts Role for IP Protection

More recently, smart contracts became a central feature of Blockchain technology [5]. These software-based contracts enforced by the Blockchain can include specific conditions for sale or licensing [2, 4]. Moreover, they enable property rights to be verified automatically [19]. Their main advantages are the possibility of control over the distribution [21], exploration of copyright-protected content [2], rewarding of the authors [1, 2, 8, 21], and enabling of near-instant micropayments [15]. Smart contracts may also allow substantially lower transaction fees [2, 15] for both, rights-owners and users [21], without the need for intermediaries [1, 8, 15]. Nevertheless, complete disintermediation is seen by some authors as somewhat challenging [15], not desirable, or even impossible to occur in some fields [2]. It is argued that, in some cases, the intermediates may continue to be necessary [1], for example, to provide seed capital and help in negotiations. Some suggest that their roles may change [15]. Generally, the authors of the analysed papers highlight the advantages of using smart contracts, namely in the protection and exploitation of copyright-protected content, however, there is no consensus of the role to be played by intermediaries in the future, if any.

4.3   Legal Support for Blockchain-Based IP Protection

Intellectual property law has emerged as a way to prevent unauthorized distribution of creative expressions due to easy mechanical, technological, and digital reproduction [28]. Some papers have researched the articulation of Blockchain with traditional copyright law [19]. In Bodó and Quintais we can find a legal analysis of the assurances granted to technological protection measures (TPM), rights Management Information (RMI), and digital rights management (DRM) according to the international copyright law, and, in certain aspects, according with the civil law tradition of authors rights (European Union) and common law copyright (United States). It also identifies the copyright domains in which the implementation of the Blockchain can be promising and challenging: smart contracts and private ordering, copyright registries, the legal regime of DRM and fair renumeration. Blockchain-based IP protection lacks legal support and some work needs to be done in order to facilitate "user's trust in Blockchain records and their good faith usage of copyrighted works based on them need to be introduced (…) as well as the status of Smart contracts and their legal consequences" [21]. It is necessary to clarify, in legal terms, the roles of online intermediaries, and define the jurisdiction and the choice of law that will involve the Blockchain since there is no centralized management and it can be distributed across the world [23]. It is evident in some of the papers that we analysed the concern with the impact that Blockchain will have on the current law and with its ability to meet the necessary legal requirements.

4.4   Blockchain-Based Solutions for IP Protection

Most papers in our literature review briefly mention examples of Blockchain-based systems or algorithms; however, only six provide an in-depth description of empirical solutions. The full list of examples, mentioned in the 20 papers we analysed, is presented in Table 2.

Half of the platforms in Table 2 are focused on the music industry. They enable registration of authorship and the fair remuneration for the use of the content. Of all the examples, only Ascribe is no longer available, and Blockai was rebranded as Binded. Next, we present the only six Blockchain-based systems that are discussed in-depth in the literature.

To prevent software piracy and preserve the rights of software vendors, Litchfield and Herbert have developed a Blockchain application, called ReSOLV [10]. It is a peer-to-peer software license validation (SLV) system that enables "software developers to protect copyrighted works" and prevents software interception and intrusion by malware. The operation is transparent to the user, with the license information being read from the Blockchain when the software is run.

In [12, 13], and [29] we can find the description of the design and implementation of a "Blockchain as infrastructure service for DRM business model", called DRMChain. This system stores the copyright information and enables the remuneration of authors in digital currency. Users can access digital content (e.g. videos, images), and if they do not have a license, they are redirected an acquisition and payment page. The latter is made directly to the author [12]. The protected content is encrypted [13] and uses a watermark mechanism for image data to avoid illegal use inside the blockchain [29].

Table 2. Examples of Blockchain-based IP Protection platforms mentioned in the papers

Platform	Ref.	Blockchain use	Object	URL
Ascribe	[17, 19]	Ascribe is no longer available. CoalaIp (protocol for intellectual property licensing) and BigChainDb (Blockchain database) resulted from the experience with this platform	Digital art	https://www.ascribe.io
Open music initiative	[1]	Open-source protocol for the uniform identification of music right-holders and creators	Music	http://open-music.org
Choon	[5]	Music streaming service and digital payments ecosystem	Music	https://choon.co
Blockai (rebranded as Binded)	[4, 19]	Blockchain solution for copyright registration and monitoring of images on several sources	Images	https://binded.com
Ujo	[5, 8, 15]	Open platform built on Blockchain technology, connecting music artists and fans. Uses smart contracts for agreements and payments	Music	https://www.ujomusic.com
Mycelia	[8, 17]	Blockchain music platform that aims to facilitate payments, collaborations, and partnerships. Ecosystem of music creators and any collaborators, publishers and distributors that might be entitled to a share of the value. It uses a creative passport that stores profile information, works, business partners, and payment mechanisms	Music	http://myceliaformusic.org
Muse	[8]	Blockchain music platform with payment management, such as royalties, music sales, merchandise and concert ticket sales. Registers copyright information and licensing conditions with smart contracts (configuration of different fees for using a song)	Music	http://www.muse.mu/
SoundChain	[8]	A Blockchain Music Ecosystem with streaming and automatic royalty payment. Users can share a link for a tune and receive a share of the royalty payment if another user listens to it	Music	https://soundchains.net

(continued)

Table 2. (*continued*)

Platform	Ref.	Blockchain use	Object	URL
Bittunes	[8]	A Blockchain Music Ecosystem based on music streaming with automatic royalty payment	Music	http://www.bittunes.com
Kodak one	[17]	Blockchain-based image rights management platform with royalty payments. The license is documented in a smart contract with copyright terms and conditions associated with each image	Images	https://kodakone.com
Screener copy	[17]	Blockchain-based forensic watermarking platform. Hosting, uploading and secure distribution of videos, with tracking of copies	Videos	https://www.screenercopy.com
Aventus	[17]	Blockchain-based event ticketing protocol where creators can track distribution and sales. Supports event organizers and inventory holders. Can track tickets as they travel through the supply-chain	Tickets	https://aventus.io
Monegraph	[28]	Blockchain platform to register, trade, sell and buy creative work	Digital art	https://monegraph.com
Publica	[17]	Blockchain end-to-end ecosystem for publishing that allows the author to obtain funds for the project and to distribute eBooks to Publica e-reader wallets. Automation of payments between authors and supporters	Books	https://publica.com
Synereo	[17]	Blockchain-enabled solution for content publishing and distribution, where the creator is paid whenever his/her work receives a "like" or "share"	Social media	https://www.synereo.com

Whenever new content is uploaded, it is checked whether it is a copy of existing work. This paper fails to identify limitations and states that the system is "reliable, secure, efficient and tamper-resistance digital content service and DRM practice".

In [31], a Blockchain-based scheme for copyright management is described. A robust image feature is used to prevent duplicate in the blockchain. However, there are no mentions to mechanisms for remuneration based on usage.

Finally, Pănescu and Manta used smart contracts to define the terms of reusing research data. The main goal is to ensure that authors control their research data, who accesses it (e.g. public or private) and under which terms. The end user of the research data benefits from a proof of compliance to the original work, opening an opportunity to integrate the proposal with existing blockchain platforms. However, this blockchain-based protection and tracing of research data also requires the participation of publishers and data repositories. The latter need to allow smart contract execution and the publishers need to confirm that the terms have been met before publication [16].

5   Discussion and Outlook

On the one hand, a vast majority of studies conclude that the use of Blockchain to register IP rights has clear advantages and can replace existing IP databases [6, 19]. On the other hand, "registering" is only part of the equation, and there are still crucial questions that remain unanswered, namely: (1) if Blockchain is enough to ensure intellectual property protection of digital objects, and (2) what could be the role of the Blockchain for different forms of IP.

Considering the main forms of intellectual property protection that we discussed: (1) patents, (2) trademarks, (3) copyrights, and (4) trade secrets [16], some research gaps have been identified. Only four of the reviewed papers mention the application of Blockchain to patents and trademarks. Furthermore, Ruzakova and Grin argue that patent and trademark registration systems do not require the use of Blockchain, because they are already managed at a governmental executive level [19]. Trade secrets are not addressed in any of the papers. Thus, these areas of IP protection should be included in future research agendas.

Most articles mention some application of Blockchain for registration and protection of copyrights. Copyright has also attracted the interest of the European Parliament, where a reform was approved in March 2019. After intense debate, the modernization of the rules in current legislation must now be transposed to the internal codes of all EU members within the next two years [33]. This is the moment to address the role of emergent technologies in supporting the IP protection.

To make sense of the very different approaches to Blockchain-based IP protection identified in the literature, we have created the instrument presented in Fig. 5. It maps existing solutions and proposals according to three dimensions:

- The materiality of the object they protect, from purely immaterial (e.g. an antibody recipe), to digital goods (e.g. music or software), to physical products;
- The type of protection they afford (e.g. if the Blockchain mechanisms are used to "merely" prove authorship, or if they effectively prevent illegal use or dissemination of the protected object);
- The type of research (e.g. conceptual, discussing possibilities, or empirical, discussing implemented systems or prototypes).

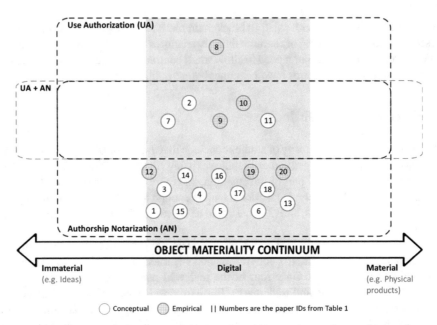

Fig. 5. Papers classified by type of object, type of protection, and type of research

The first evident observation from the use of our instrument, in Fig. 5, is that all the identified literature focusses on the digital realm. No papers discuss the Blockchain-based protection of completely immaterial forms of IP. Likewise, no papers discuss the protection of IP embedded in physical products, at the other end of the continuum. Uncovering the reasons for this bias would be a relevant topic of research. Also, specific materialities may require or enable different mechanisms for protection.

A second observation is that the majority of papers focus on some form of authorship notarization and not on mechanisms to effectively prevent illegal use or dissemination of the protected object. Important as the former is, it suffers from many of the same disadvantages of traditional forms of protection, such as patents, namely the need to resort to justice to enforce the acquired rights – an inefficient, expensive, and time-consuming endeavour, often not feasible for small and medium enterprises (SMEs).

A third observation is that the vast majority of papers are conceptual, with few discussing actual implementations. This may be due to fact that we are still at the infancy of Blockchain [14], but it also suggests that future research should strive to experiment with the technology in real cases, using pilots and proofs-of-concept.

Finally, we will discuss the reviewed literature, mapped in Fig. 5, from the perspective of our research question. Apparently, no Blockchain-based solutions exist for the effective protection of immaterial intellectual assets, of which antibody recipes (instructions, in the form of DNA sequences) are an example. Once known, these recipes can be used by unauthorized parties to manufacture and sell those particular antibodies at scale. Some proposed solutions can be adapted to provide "proof" of authorship of the recipe, but (a) enforcement would still require resorting to courts, (b) the legal value of such Blockchain-based registrations of authorship is still being debated, and (c) such an approach does not effectively impede offenders from illegally producing and selling the antibody, as it is amply demonstrated by counterfeiters. Creating effective means for Blockchain-based protection of immaterial objects is, thus, a promising line of research.

6 Conclusion

Departing from a need to protect intellectual property related to the production of antibodies for research, medical diagnostics, and advanced therapies, we carried out a systematic literature review on Blockchain-based IP protection. We identified and mapped a set of 20 relevant articles out of an initial 1518 hits that included duplicates and off-topic instances. Selected papers were read in full and their contributions categorized using a specially developed instrument. Several promising research avenues were proposed. The analysis of specific mechanisms that could prevent the spread and illegal use of the immaterial product complemented with Blockchain technology. And the identification of the benefits/disadvantages of using Blockchain-based systems for each of the types of IP protection identified, such as patents, trademarks, copyrights and trade secrets. Essentially, we did not find in the extant literature a good answer to our research question, namely, Blockchain-based techniques that are suitable for the protection of immaterial intellectual assets, such as antibody recipes. This is particularly true if we aim at mechanisms that prevent unauthorized use. This opens several research possibilities to solve the problem posed by our case company and many others with similar concerns. No solution was identified that enabled the effective protection of an immaterial assets such as an antibody production recipe, thus validating our main line of work.

As limitations of this research we can point out the relatively limited number of databases that we searched for eligible studies, even if two of them, Science Direct and EBSCO, are major aggregators. Further, in a dynamic area like Blockchain, grey literature and market initiatives often contain recent advances not yet discussed in the academic literature.

Acknowledgements. This work is partially financed by national funds through the FCT - Foundation for Science and Technology, I.P., within the scope of the project CISUC - UID/CEC/00326/2019 and by the European Regional Development Fund (ERDF), through the COMPETE 2020 - Operational Programme for Competitiveness and Internationalization and Portuguese national funds via FCT – Fundação para a Ciência e a Tecnologia, under projects projects POCI-01-0145-FEDER-030550 (BYDRUG) and POCI-01-0145-FEDER-007440l UID/NEU/04539/2019 (CNC.IBILI).

References

1. Arcos, L.C.: The blockchain technology on the music industry. Braz. J. Oper. Prod. Manage. **15**(3), 439–443 (2018). https://doi.org/10.14488/BJOPM.2018.v15.n3.a11. Stephan, C. (eds.)
2. Bodó, B., Gervais, D., Quintais, J.P.: Blockchain and smart contracts: the missing link in copyright licensing? Int. J. Law Inf. Technol. **26**(4), 311–336 (2018). https://doi.org/10.1093/ijlit/eay014
3. Denzin, N.K.: The Research Act in Sociology. Aldine, Chicago (1970)

4. Ensign, D.: Copyright Corner CLSR: Blockchain and Copyright. Kentucky Lib. **82**(3), 4–5 (2018)
5. Gürkaynak, G., Yılmaz, İ., Yeşilaltay, B., Bengi, B.: Intellectual property law and practice in the blockchain realm. Comput. Law Secur. Rev. **34**(4), 847–862 (2018). https://doi.org/10.1016/j.clsr.2018.05.027
6. Ishmaev, G.: Blockchain technology as an institution of property. Metaphilosophy. **48**(5), 666–686 (2017). https://doi.org/10.1111/meta.12277
7. Jick, T.D.: Mixing qualitative and quantitative methods: triangulation in action. Adm. Sci. Q. **24**(4), 602 (1979)
8. Khouri, G.: Music licensing. Licens. J. **37**(7), 25–27 (2017)
9. Kitchenham, B., Charters, S.: Procedures for Performing Systematic Literature Reviews in Software Engineering. Keele University & Durham University, UK (2004)
10. Litchfield, A., Herbert, J.: ReSOLV: applying cryptocurrency blockchain methods to enable global cross-platform software license validation. Cryptography **2**(2), 10 (2018)
11. De Luca, C., Trifonova, A.: Patent disclosure requirements for therapeutic antibody patents. Exp. Opin. Ther. Patents (2017). https://doi.org/10.1080/13543776.2017.1296950
12. Ma, Z., Huang, W., Gao, H.: Secure DRM scheme based on blockchain with high credibility. Chin. J. Electron. **27**(5), 1025–1036 (2018). https://doi.org/10.1049/cje.2018.07.003
13. Ma, Z., Jiang, M., Gao, H., Wang, Z.: Blockchain for digital rights management. Future Gener. Comput. Syst. **89**, 746–764 (2018). https://doi.org/10.1016/j.future.2018.07.029
14. Mougayar, W.: The Business Blockchain: Promise, Practice, and Application of the Next Internet Technology. Wiley, Hoboken (2016)
15. O'Dair, M., Beaven, Z.: The networked record industry: how blockchain technology could transform the record industry. Strateg. Change **26**(5), 471–480 (2017)
16. Pănescu, A.T., Manta, V.: Smart contracts for research data rights management over the ethereum blockchain network. Sci. Technol. Lib. **37**(3), 235–245 (2018). https://doi.org/10.1080/0194262X.2018.1474838
17. Patrickson, B.: What do blockchain technologies imply for Scotland's digital design industry? In: ISPIM Innovation Conference – Innovation, The Name of The Game, Stockholm, Sweden (2018)
18. Poticha, D., Duncan, M.W.: Intellectual property-The Foundation of Innovation: a scientist's guide to intellectual property. J. Mass Spectrom. **54**(3), 288–300 (2019). https://doi.org/10.1002/jms.4331
19. Ruzakova, O.A., Grin, E.S.: Application of blockchain technologies in systematizing the results of intellectual activity. Вестник Пермского Университета. Юридические Науки **38**(38), 508–520 (2017). https://doi.org/10.17072/1995-4190-2017-38-508-520
20. Nakamoto, S.: Bitcoin: A Peer-to-Peer Electronic Cash System (2008)
21. Savelyev, A.: Copyright in the blockchain era: promises and challenges. Comput. Law Secur. Rev. **34**(3), 550–561 (2018). https://doi.org/10.1016/j.clsr.2017.11.008
22. Storz, U.: International intellectual property strategies for therapeutic antibodies. MAbs **3**(6), 596–606 (2011). https://doi.org/10.4161/mabs.3.6.17788
23. Suzuki, B., Taylor, T., Marchant, G.: Blockchain: how it will change your legal practice. Comput. Internet Lawyer **35**(7), 5–9 (2018)
24. Szilagyi, K.: A bundle of blockchains? Digitally disrupting property law. Cumberland Law Rev. **48**(1), 9–34 (2017)
25. Vella, D., Falzon, M., Cassar, T., Valenzia, A.: Blockchain's applicability to intellectual property management. Licens. J. **38**, 10–13 (2018)
26. Webster, J., Watson, R.T.: Analyzing the past to prepare for the future: writing a review. MIS Quartely **26**(2), 12 (2002)
27. Yang, D., Li, M.: Evolutionary approaches and the construction of technology-driven regulations. Emerg. Markets Financ. Trade **54**(14), 3256–3271 (2018)

28. Zeilinger, M.: Digital art as 'monetised graphics': enforcing intellectual property on the blockchain. Philos. Technol. **31**(1), 15–41 (2018). https://doi.org/10.1007/s13347-016-0243-1

29. Zhaofeng, M., Weihua, H., Hongmin, G.: A new blockchain-based trusted DRM scheme for built-in content protection. EURASIP J. Image Video Process. **2018**(1), 1 (2018). https://doi.org/10.1186/s13640-018-0327-1

30. Zheng, Z., Xie, S., Dai, H., Chen, X., Wang, H.: An overview of blockchain technology: architecture, consensus, and future trends. In: 2017 IEEE International Congress on Big Data (BigData Congress), pp. 557–564. IEEE (2017). https://doi.org/10.1109/bigdatacongress.2017.85

31. Zhuvikin, A.: A blockchain of image copyrights using robust image. Int. J. Comput. Sci. Appl. **15**(1), 33–44 (2018)

32. Copyright. https://www.wipo.int/copyright/en/. Accessed 11 Apr 2019

33. European Commission - PRESS RELEASES - Press release - Copyright reform: the Commission welcomes European Parliament's vote in favour of modernised rules fit for digital age. http://europa.eu/rapid/press-release_STATEMENT-19-1839_en.htm. Accessed 31 Mar 2019

34. Intellectual Property | Definition of Intellectual Property by Merriam-Webster, https://www.merriam-webster.com/dictionary/intellectualproperty. Accessed 10 Apr 2019

35. Patents. https://www.wipo.int/patents/en/. Accessed 10 Apr 2019

36. Research - Association for Information Systems (AIS). https://aisnet.org/page/SeniorScholarBasket. Accessed 13 Apr 2019

37. Research Antibodies Market Size & Share | Industry Report, 2018-2025. https://www.grandviewresearch.com/industry-analysis/research-antibodies-market. Accessed 11 Apr 2019

38. The trust machine - The promise of the blockchain. https://www.economist.com/leaders/2015/10/31/the-trust-machine. Accessed 12 Apr 2019

39. Trade Secrets | Definition of Trade Secrets by Merriam-Webster. https://www.merriam-webster.com/dictionary/tradesecrets. Accessed 11 Apr 2019

40. Trademarks. https://www.wipo.int/trademarks/en/. Accessed 11 Apr 2019

Omnichannel Value Chain: Mapping Digital Technologies for Channel Integration Activities

Rehan Iftikhar[✉], Zohreh Pourzolfaghar, and Markus Helfert

Maynooth University, Maynooth, Ireland
{rehan.iftikhar,zohreh.pourzolfaghar,markus.helfert}@mu.ie

Abstract. To provide a seamless customer experience across different channels, researchers and practitioners have proposed the creation of an omnichannel retailing environment by integrating online and offline retail channels. However, retailers are struggling with the selection and implementation of suitable technologies to add value through channel integration. Despite the strong practical need, this issue has not been effectively addressed in the academic literature. This paper introduces an omnichannel value chain model underpinned by Porter's value chain and presents ten channel integration activities for value creation by carrying out a comprehensive synthesis of current research on omnichannel retailing. We also identify the technology related challenges faced by retailers in the execution of these channel integrating activities drawing upon a case study with an Irish retailer. Enabling digital technologies are then mapped to these activities that provide a guideline for retailers to select appropriate technologies for the value creation activities.

Keywords: Channel integration · Omnichannel retail · Digital technologies · Value chain · Technology mapping

1 Introduction

The retail sector is experiencing an influx of innovative methods and technologies to enhance and reform the customer experience [58]. Along with this influx, there has been a huge change in information technology (IT) provision, technology cost, and access to technology. These changes are affecting the way value creation activities are performed and the nature of the linkages among them. It is pushing the retail sector toward a new digital path i.e. omnichannel retailing [51]. Omnichannel retailing is the synergic offering of all available channels and customer touchpoints to optimize customer experience and performance across channels [51].

The most significant characteristic of omnichannel retailing is channel integration [36]. Channel integration has been shown to have a positive effect on customer experience and acts as a competitive advantage for retailers [23] which leads to stronger sales

A prior version of this paper has been published in the ISD2019 Proceedings (http://aisel.aisnet.org/isd2014/proceedings2019).

growth [14], an increase in the "perceived quality of the channels" [35] and the reduction of service inconsistencies [67]. Additionally, channel integration can achieve synergies such as "improved customer trust, improved customer awareness, consumer risk reduction, and coverage of diverse shopping preferences" [24]. Furthermore, it allows retailers to actively maintain customer contact and develop a proactive customer experience management strategy through increased customer insights [67]. Finally, the interconnection of channels makes it harder for competitors to imitate the company. It could increase the customer's value proposition and thus reduces the competitive pressure [24]. Despite all the above mentioned benefits of channel integration, retailers are still not developed enough in terms of application and implementation of technology to achieve completely integrated channels and create desired value [19, 45, 54].

Technology implementation for channel integration is a major undertaking because of constantly evolving capabilities to drive the integration [67]. Retailers trying to adopt these technologies for channel integration can easily get lost by the variety of technologies to choose from [65]. Consequently, they often select technologies without examining the potential contributions to their strategies [31]. Extant literature on channel integration addressing the issues of technology implementation or technology capabilities in retail has mainly focused on the use of some specific technologies such as RFID [2, 3], augmented reality [25], beacons [50], mobile technologies [43, 62] etc. The literature which studies multiple technologies has either focused on physical stores or online shops. For example, [44] studies the intention of customers in using the fitting room and in-store technologies in an omnichannel physical store. Similarly, [5] and [10] investigated the use of in-store digital technologies, in order to enhance the customer experience in retail stores. [43] identifies aspects of omnichannel retailing which mobile technologies can affect while [3] and [2] studied the use of RFID as an enabler for channel integration. But a clear and comprehensive picture of the digital technologies that may be adopted to create value through different aspects of channel integration and their respective roles has yet to be revealed [54]. In this paper, we will try to address this research gap by first providing a framework of value creation activities in omnichannel and then mapping the enabling digital technologies to these activities.

For omnichannel retailing to be effective and efficient, multiple channel integration activities play a pivotal role [15]. Several technologies can enable the value creation through these activities but the implementation of any technology must be guided by business value creation [15]. We, therefore, identify activities in channel integration that are necessary for value creation in omnichannel retailing underpinned by Porter's value chain model [52] and then map to these activities the digital technologies which facilitate value creation by an extensive review of the literature and real world implementation examples. Hence, this paper adds to the literature by presenting an omnichannel value chain model and mapping of the enabling technologies to the identified value creation activities.

The remainder of this paper is structured as follows. First, in section two, we introduce the research methodology followed in the presented research. Afterward, in section three, we present channel integration activities that create value for omnichannel retailers and discuss the challenges in the execution of these activities. In section four, we describe enabling technologies for channel integration and real world examples of services using these technologies. In section five, we discuss the contribution and managerial implications of this study. Finally, we conclude the paper by summarizing our study and establishing scope for further research.

2 Research Methodology

For the mapping of digital technologies to value creation activities of channel integration, we followed a multi-phase research process. First, we conducted a literature review to identify channel integration activities in omnichannel retailing. We followed the approach for the literature review proposed by [64] and [13]. We defined the scope and goal of the review in identifying the value adding activities for an integrated retail system. We applied the search using keywords channel integration, omnichannel, technology and retail in three different databases for maximum coverage of omnichannel retailing literature i.e. Scopus, Science Direct and Web of Science. We used different combinations from the keywords to better understand the occurrence of the results such as ("omnichannel" OR "omni-channel") AND ("management" or "technology"), ("channel integration" OR "integrated channels") AND ("management" OR "technology") AND "retail". This search resulted in total of 635 articles. Afterward, we excluded duplicates, articles not published in English and published before 2012. We only considered literature after 2012 as the term 'omnichannel' was coined in literature in 2011 by [53] and most of the research related to channel integration for omnichannel retailing has been published after that.

Subsequently, we examined the sum of identified articles to evaluate whether the articles could contribute to this paper and excluded articles not topic-related, for example, articles regarding foreign market channel integration. We also excluded articles from unrelated disciplines to this research such as refrigeration science and technology, chemistry, applied mechanics, etc. After screening the remaining articles for the contribution to the study, 29 articles were selected, which were then used for defining the channel integration activities for value creation.

In the second phase, we conducted a case study to identify the challenges faced by retailers who are transitioning from multichannel to omnichannel retail. In line with the recommendations from Yin [68] for choosing the case according to pre-defined sample criteria. The retailer was selected which met the criteria of currently transitioning from multichannel to omnichannel. The case retailer (called 'CR' thereafter) is an Irish company with brick and mortars as their starting point around 50 years ago. They launched their online channel in 2010. Physical stores are currently managed independently from the webshop but the company is currently looking to integrate its channels in order "to create a seamless customer experience". We followed a multi-method data gathering strategy for the case study combining interviews, observation and secondary sources [68]. We conducted semi-structured and unstructured interviews with the Strategy Director, E-Commerce Director, Marketing Manager, the Web Store Manager, the Logistics Head, Head of Store Operations and the Store Manager. In total, 8 interviews were carried out with all the CR employees. The topics addressed concerned the challenges in the implementation of the omnichannel strategy, from the point of view of each interviewee's position. All interviews lasted between 60 to 150 min. We transcribed the semi-structured interviews while the non-structured interviews were summarized. For triangulation, we used secondary sources including financial reports, website and social media pages of the retailer. In this data collection process, we followed the principles suggested by [68] to guarantee the reliability and validity of the research. A thematic analysis was conducted manually to map the challenges faced by CR for the value creation activities identified in the first phase.

In the third phase, we identified the technologies which support the channel integration activities using literature and real world usage examples to explain their implementation. For the initial selection of enabling technologies for channel integration, a literature review was conducted. The results of the search phrase ('retail' and 'technology') were analyzed to find retail technologies for channel integration activities. The search resulted in 2280 articles. We performed text analysis on these articles using NVivo to uncover potential enabling technologies for channel integration. Only those technologies were selected which were mentioned at least five times in the identified articles to support one or more channel integration activities. To improve the reliability of our analysis, we also asked retail technology experts, who are currently working in the implementation of different technology solutions in retail, to come up with a final list of technologies to be analyzed. To complement our analyses, we also used examples of the actual implementation of these technologies to better comprehend the roles of the identified technologies [4]. We mapped the technologies to relevant channel integration activities. The technology mapping has been based on [22]. We recognized the major characteristics of the particular technologies and then identified characteristics enabling the value creation activities identified in the first phase for channel integration.

3 Value Creation Through Channel Integration

Channel integration is the extent to which channels share common organizational activities as defined in Porter's value chain [52], including marketing, sales, operations, services, and logistics [69]. This leads to channel synergy, which necessitates the use of channels in such a way that the effectiveness of each separate channel increases in providing a seamless shopping experience for the customer. Channel synergy requires organizations to communicate and leverage the brand consistently across all channels [36]. Retailers have to facilitate a system where customers should be able to perceive the company as one entity and be offered various channel options that are seamlessly linked [51]. Based on the literature review, channel integration activities required for transformation to fully integrated omnichannel retail are introduced in the following sub-sections. These activities are presented in the omnichannel value chain model shown in Fig. 1. Challenges faced by the retailer in the case study for exaction of the identified activities are also described.

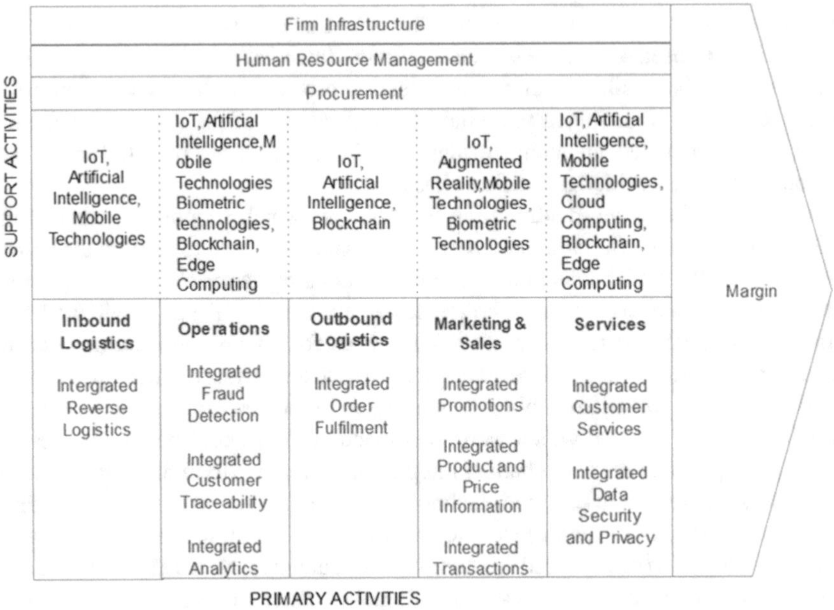
Firm Infrastructure
Human Resource Management
Procurement
SUPPORT ACTIVITIES
IoT, Artificial Intelligence, Mobile Technologies
IoT, Artificial Intelligence, Mobile Technologies Biometric technologies, Blockchain, Edge Computing
IoT, Artificial Intelligence, Blockchain
IoT, Augmented Reality, Mobile Technologies, Biometric Technologies
IoT, Artificial Intelligence, Mobile Technologies, Cloud Computing, Blockchain, Edge Computing
Inbound Logistics
Intergrated Reverse Logistics
Operations
Integrated Fraud Detection
Integrated Customer Traceability
Integrated Analytics
Outbound Logistics
Integrated Order Fulfilment
Marketing & Sales
Integrated Promotions
Integrated Product and Price Information
Integrated Transactions
Services
Integrated Customer Services
Integrated Data Security and Privacy
Margin
PRIMARY ACTIVITIES

Fig. 1. Omnichannel value chain model

3.1 Integrated Customer Service

Customer service integration refers to improving and enriching an interaction with a customer by blending the interaction simultaneously with other channels [11, 28]. Around 85% of customers who are not able to accomplish what they need in one channel such as a website will switch to other channels such as phone, mobile app, web chat, social media or email [28]. In-store customer service associates can use devices such as tablets and smartphones to provide enhanced customer service, for example by looking up information through the system to assist the consumer, thus reinforcing brand values and delivering a good shopping experience [11]. To provide in-store experience online, retailers can offer services such as virtual fitting room based on virtual reality. Fits.me is a virtual reality application used by several fashion brands (such as Hugo Boss, Twin-Set and Thomas Pink) to provide online shoppers with service which is traditionally only available in stores [41]. It offers a virtual fitting room for online shopping and suggests the garment size that is the closest match to the shopper's measurements, and enables the user to 'try on' several sizes to identify the preferred size and fit [41]. Similarly, to provide a digital experience in the physical store, services such as "on-screen customization" can be used. For instance, digitally enhanced stores such as Nike Town provide screens to customize one's shoes [11]. Similarly, customer service can be improved in social media channels by utilizing services associated to retailers' website using applications such as eBay ShopBot, which deals with consumer search enquiries on Facebook messenger and a variation of the application is now available on the Google Home device.

CR is a customer-centric company. According to their Strategy Director, "Customers are at the heart of what [CR] does. So the main thing and every decision we make is based off whether it's going to add to customer experience and if the customer is going to come back to us so growing our customer base and appreciating that and having an experiential customer experience that they want to come back to is probably number one at the top of things that we do." Being successful with this approach in their physical stores, now CR is finding it hard to exhibit similar levels of customer service in their online channels. The company recognizes this as a big challenge and their Strategy Director noted "Our customer-centricity doesn't come across in our online sites. You will not get that whole customer feel or that feel that the person is as invested in the customer as you will get if you spoke to a customer in the store. It's very different and hard to capture online."

3.2 Integrated Customer Traceability

When moving from one channel to the other, integrated customer traceability gives retailers the ability to maintain context and data continuity as the customer is moving from one channel to another channel [9, 34]. Retailers can trace the customer journey started online and finished with an offline sale [9] using mobile technologies with services such as Google's offline sales conversion tool. Retailers can track the customer who explores a product offline and then buys online [9] using Google URL Builder. Using mobile ID tracking, retailers can use the consumers' smartphone's Wi-Fi to track their journey in the store and can know the repeat visitor and analyze the departments and parts of the store visited. Mobile Decision Support System can be used to check and compare reviews posted by consumers themselves and to extract reputations of a product from weblogs [21]. While retailers track customers across channels, they collect, store, analyze and transfer a lot of personal data from customers. In doing so, they face the challenge of protecting this data from breaches [46].

CR has started to put more emphasis on connecting the customer across different channels but is struggling with technology implementation. The marketing manager noted, "We are trying to do that [add shopping links to Instagram] but we're hitting a lot of hurdles." Similarly connecting the physical store customer to online channel has been a challenge especially with the implementation of GDPR. Web-store Manager explains this issue saying "We have thousands of tourist [customers] in our different stores. So we want to try and capture their information as best we can. With GDPR obviously, we lost a big bit from our database."

3.3 Integrated Order Fulfilment

Traceability and changeability of inventory, orders and delivery points during all stages of order fulfillment across all channels is required for a fully integrated omnichannel system [29, 55]. In an integrated environment, a retailer needs to be able to see inventory across channels, that it knows where products are available and how fast it can get them to customers. With integrated order fulfillment, customers should be able to reserve products in the store using a mobile phone, web or social media (Reserve and Collect) [29] and collect products bought using mobile phone, web or social media in the physical store (Click and Collect) [39]. Customer can use their devices to reorder a product like Amazon Dash Button [29] and orders can be delivered to their place of choice in real-time like a car trunk using services such as Amazon Key delivery. Similarly, customers' needs can be predicted to have most of their regular buy in the store ready to be ordered online [59].

CR has invested in acquiring inventory systems to integrate their inventory across all channels. Logistic managers noted that the inventory system is updated very quickly across channels and said "…when it's all working fine within 30 s to a minute your [inventory system] should be updated. So, it is pretty much in real-time." But they are looking to improve further in this regard. Head of Store Operations addressing a good practice she experienced at another store said, "I was in a store recently where I was looking for an item and she [sales assistant] said, what are you looking for? And I said, Oh, do you have that in whatever size and she said not in the store but before I knew it, 10 s later, my card was in the back of an IPad, it was delivered to my house the following morning. That's what I want."

3.4 Integrated Transactions

Providing secure access to complete the transaction via all available channels constitutes integrated transactions. Regardless of how, where and within which channel the transaction is made, the relevant data should be securely retrievable by other parties in the integrated transaction system [55]. With integrated transactions, customers should be able to purchase products directly from all available channels e.g. social media outlets of the retailer and to purchase products directly from an advertisement on any channel e.g. TV or news advertisement, digital signage, catalog. Customers should be able to check out without going through a physical check out desk using other channels for payment in store e.g. Amazon Go, Mobile and Tablet check out [29], thus adding value to marketing activities of the retailer.

CR management has recognized that integrated transactions are an important part of the transition to omnichannel retail. Head of Store Operations with regards to opportunities for integrated transactions noted "I want to have iPads that I can flip over and people can pay. I want to be in a position where we don't have to bring a customer to a till all the time as well, as its too formal…I want to have something that I can use on the shop floor that they can just put their card into and just get that sale." Strategy Director mentioned on the similar lines saying "we are looking at Amazon pay actually. So they just come into Ireland recently, they want to pilot with us. So they would be someone we'd be looking at because again, they have a lot to offer, I think in terms of the checkout and how to improve us in that whole space. So I think that's an opportunity."

3.5 Integrated Product and Price Information

Integrated pricing and product information implies synchronization of the products' description, stock status, prices, and makes changes in them (e.g. discounts, availability) visible for consumers and other members of the omnichannel system instantly [55, 63]. This integration should also pick up on any mistake, mismatch, or absence of product data anywhere in the omnichannel system, and initiate the necessary corrective actions [55]. Shopify and Google's direct integration makes it easy for shoppers to discover products available in-store with Google Smart Shopping campaigns. Another example of an online-to-offline relationship is Sephora mobile application [48]. Digitally enhanced stores such as Nike Town are providing i-Kiosks to look up information digitally [11]. Retailers should also provide information based on customer social networks via different digital channels [29].

CR has adopted generally an integrated pricing strategy for its online and offline channels. As customers are now able to access online information easily when they are in physical stores, the pricing and product information needs to be consistent. But CR is struggling with providing additional information in stores such as videos which they are providing to online customers. The words of Head of Store Operations in describing this scenario were "so much technology goes into websites and what we do online and all that I think we don't have enough technology in the store to provide details around products to our customers." But on the other side, information about products is lacking on the website as well. CR is now pushing towards more information and imagery on their website. Strategy Director explained saying, "I'll be pushing the buyers now to adapt a lot more and since then, you need to come back from suppliers with content. You need to come back with imagery and you need to come back with their story because if you don't come back with that, how can you sell that product online?"

3.6 Integrated Promotions

Promotion data must be shared and available across all channels and the product's/brand's name and logo should be consistent across all channels, and the promotions should use different channels at the same time [65]. During the pre-purchase stage, retailers can use services such as digital signage showing videos, real-time pricing and product information that can be integrated with social media feeds that display consumers' reviews next to the merchandise to build the trust. Retailers can also use connected home appliances to sense customer needs and send personalized need-based offers through the mobile channel [29]. During the purchase stage of the consumer buying process, retailers can use consumer-facing in-store technology to inspire and engage with the consumer using different channels and offering personalized offers and promotions [35]. Burberry, M&S, Nike and Macy's, for instance, have adopted interactive screens (e.g. iPads, i-Kiosks, tablet computers) through which consumers get promotions during the purchase stage. Besides, adaptive digital touchpoints enable new forms of promotions. For example, by introducing firm-initiated mobile touchpoints, retailers can "provide tailored, time-sensitive, and location-sensitive advertising and promotions in store" [21].

CR is working on integrating its promotion activities across different channels. They are actively targeting the integration of their social media channels with their website. Marketing Manager commenting on their priorities said "… and just integrating better with our social media campaigns. I think there is a big disconnect there."

3.7 Integrated Reverse Logistics

Integrated reverse logistics entails providing all channels for returns to customers and return visibility in all channels as well [55]. Integrated reverse logistics links among different stages of reverse logistics and different channels involved in it. So, information around the return point(s), stock keeping point(s), and product(s) reverse flow should be retrievable, traceable, and changeable using RFID like M&S [3]. Retailers can easily provide services such as Buy online return in Store using RFID tagged products [69]. Retailers can, therefore, offer customers the ability to buy in-store and return via other channels such as using the website and get the return collected from their homes.

CR is providing the customers with the return to the store facility for products bought online but customers cannot return online (via post) the products bought in stores. Website Manager of CR said, "They [customers] can go into any of our stores and returns an online order if they have the receipt."

3.8 Integrated Analytics

Predicting customer needs and taking actions based on data available from all available channels is integrated analytics [29]. With different types of data available from various channels such as interaction data (POS, e-commerce), enterprise data (CRM and ERP) and unstructured data (social media data) which can be fused on one platform to predict customer intent and take informed actions [30]. At the same time, the route of each customer and the time they spend in different channels deciding what to purchase can be analyzed, similarly to the way it is analyzed by checking out the clicks on an e-shop browser. If combined with data, extracted by the e-shop web analytics application will allow the company to provide better and more accurate services and make product proposals, which can lead to a more gratifying interaction and raise sales [12]. Swatch and American Apparel have implemented successfully mobile tracking in their stores to track and analyze customer journeys in the store [11].

Strategy Director at CR put special emphasis on integrated analytics and capturing customer data in physical stores stating "capturing customer data [physical store customer] is a big one. And segmenting is going to make us so that we understand whether they're going to go online or whether they have the appetite to do so."

3.9 Integrated Data Security and Privacy

Omnichannel retailers should ensure that the privacy conditions are adhered to when data is integrated from different channels. Consumers are concerned about how retailers can track their location and collect data about them, and how it affects their privacy. Retailers must be aware of privacy issues, seek to comply with the law first of all but also ethically use tracking and inform consumers about the type of information collected and its purpose. Appliances and sensors that upload a large quantity of personal data to centralized databases controlled by smart device manufacturers or retailers may be exposed to serious privacy problems [16]. Customers are becoming ever more concerned about their data privacy and retailer ensuring data privacy adds to the customers' perceived value and creating trustful customer relationships [29]. Integrated data security implies keeping customers' data secure when moved from one channel to another. With the implementation of digital devices to achieve integrated channel retailers are also facing the issue of data security. Overall, this information/knowledge flow should be protected by cybersecurity solutions to limit data theft and data misuse.

CR considers capturing the customer data as a vital step in the implementation of omnichannel strategy but privacy and security concerns are not well addressed. For example, talking about the implementation of a loyalty program, Strategy Director said

"... and then absolutely the loyalty program again, I'll mention that I think we need to have a better connection to our customers physically like in terms of capturing their data and targeting them better."

3.10 Integrated Fraud Detection

Omnichannel retailing is more susceptible to frauds and needs an integrated fraud detection solution to address this new dynamic. Detecting fraud when a transaction involves more than one channel is integrated fraud detection. With digital and interconnected devices for channel integration, cyber-attacks become likely as the mobile and internet of things (IoT) devices have limited computing power to detect such attacks [66].

CR is not considering an increased risk of fraud associated with omnichannel at the time of the case study.

4 Enabling Technologies for Channel Integration in Retail

Multiple digital technologies are required to achieve total channel integration in retail [47]. According to the value chain model by Porter [52], technology development is one of the supporting activities for any organization. Also, staying current with technological advances, and maintaining technical excellence are sources of value creation. Thus, it is necessary to clearly identify the most relevant technologies and solutions to support the retailers in the transition towards the total channel integration to become omnichannel [4]. The role of digital technologies to facilitate channel integration activities identified in Sect. 3 are explained in this section. In Table 1, these relevant technologies are described. In Table 2, real-world implementation examples are presented.

Augmented Reality applications narrow the gap between online and offline shopping. They provide a sense of embodiment that results from natural interactivity and simulation of physical control over virtual offerings and sometimes exceeds what is possible in physical environments [25]. It is being used by firms like IKEA [32] to provide better product information (integrated product and price information). Mister Spex, is providing by using an AR virtual mirror an experience where customers can virtually try on different glasses from their online assortment. Walgreens offers its customers "Aisle411" application to receive digital way-finding support that helps them locate products in the supermarket aisle (integrated customer service) [25].

Blockchain offers attractive security features for distributed data processing and storage, especially when used with edge computing (Data Security and Data Privacy). Such systems are being implemented and developed in other industries such as health services. For example, using hierarchical identity-based cryptography for the handshake scheme. This scheme named as a cross-domain handshake (CDHS) scheme can be used to increase data security within integrated channels (integrated data security and privacy). Blockchain features can also be used for ensuring safe delivery to customers (integrated order fulfillment).

AI tools like machine learning extract the knowledge that is actually important in an omnichannel network. It helps the retailer to make sense of data by the transformation of

Table 1. Description of enabling technologies for channel integration in retail

Enabling technologies	Description
Augmented reality	Augmented reality integrates computer-generated objects with the real environment and allows real-time interactions [32]
Blockchain	Blockchain technology consists of blocks that are linked through cryptography [1]
Artificial Intelligence (AI)	AI augments human intelligence and for the context of this study, AI refers to machine learning, natural language processing, drones and other AI based systems [20]
Cloud computing	Cloud computing allows sharing of IT software and hardware resources over the internet, so that information can be easily stored and accessed remotely by diverse actors [4]
Internet of Things (IoT)	IoT is a sophisticated network of objects and things connected to the internet. The concept of IoT in retail consists of Radio Frequency Identification (RFID), beacons, camera networks, and other wireless sensor networks [6]
Mobile technologies	Mobile technologies refer to a set of technologies related to smartphones including mobile apps, scan and go, QR codes, location-based apps, etc. [20]
Biometric technologies	Biometric technologies are automated methods of verifying or recognizing the identity of a person based on their physiological or behavioral characters [61]
Edge computing	Edge computing refers to the enabling technologies allowing computation to be performed at the edge of the network, on downstream data and upstream data [56]

raw data into information and then information to knowledge (integrated analytics) [4, 30]. AI-based fraud detection solutions like the ones proposed by [26] can be used for detecting point of sales (POS) fraud when the system is integrated with other channels. Delivery technology based on AI such as drones facilitates the fulfillment process (integrated fulfillment). Facial recognition systems based on biometric technology are being used for identity verification e.g. Alibaba "pay with a selfie" (integrated transactions) [57]. However, the use of biometric technologies in retail is significantly affected by regulations such as GDPR in EU [46]. Methods of using biometric technologies must evolve for compliance to GDPR and sophisticated AI systems which can ensure the anonymity of the personal data processed can be a possible solution.

Cloud computing is devoted to storing raw data in structured information. Such information can be accessed by and exchanged between different channels, which may, in turn, use the structured information as the input for data analytics (integrated analytics) and customer assistant (integrated customer service) [4]. Cloud services also manage all types of raw data, but with the aim of storing structured information that may be helpful for logistics (integrated order fulfillment). Cloud computing based services can manage a multidirectional flow of information that can be used to support multiple activities like integrated product and price information, integrated promotions. Edge computing for IoT with blockchain can provide a transparent and secure alternative framework for private data management in the digitally enabled physical stores (integrated data security and privacy) [66].

IoTs play a vital role in multiple channel integration activities [15]. IoT solutions can be employed by retailers to acquire several types of data (e.g. the location of a component/product, customer data). Thereby, the data flow underlying IoTs combined with machine learning (AI) becomes a powerful resource for retailers to use for customer profiling (Integrated Analytics) and providing real-time recommendations (integrated customer service) [6]. Business to Thing Management based on IoTs can facilitate direct interactions with smart things and thus need-based promotions to the customer (integrated promotions). Edge computing is a viable way to take advantage of the explosion of the Internet of Things (IoT) which has dramatically increased the data load on networks. Integration of complex sensors, with the implementation of an efficient data fusion strategy can be used for integrated analytics and integrated customer traceability [37].

Beacon is an IoT based technology that allows retailers to send messages or notifications to consumers in the beacon's zone to promote specific products (integrated promotions) or give recommendations (integrated customer service) [18, 35]. It is used by retailers such as Macy's, Zara and H&M for communications purposes with consumers [18]. Google announced the Physical Web initiative utilizing Bluetooth beacons as an IoT gateway and proximity-based service without the need for mobile apps. Beacon gateway can be used for analyzing data from customer movements in-store (integrated analytics). Data for tracing customers can be collected using software sensors (IoT) and smartphones (Integrated Customer Traceability). RFID is being used to track products in a store and during the delivery (integrated order fulfillment) as well from a distance by using tiny microchips hooked up to miniature antennas (integrated reverse logistics) [27]. Retailers can use RFID to locate store inventory, keep track of inventory and products on the delivery route [11]. By using RFID retailers can provide customized marketing programmes (Integrated promotions) for the customers at an individual level and hence increases product and brand awareness (integrated product and price information) [40].

Mobile technology is one of the main enablers of omnichannel realization [7]. To provide services such as zero check out vision systems can be combined with other technologies and provide integrated customer service. The touchscreen functionality of mobile devices can also be exploited for reducing the physical-digital divide between the in-store and online fashion shopping experience. The QR code, a two-dimensional matrix barcode, is a technology that is changing marketing in this decade. QR code can be used to provide integrated promotions and integrated products and price information. Using mobile ID tracking, retailers can use the consumers' smartphone's Wi-Fi to track their journey in the store and can know the repeat visitor and analyze the departments and parts of the store visited. Mobile Decision Support System can be used to check and compare reviews posted by consumers themselves and to extract reputations of a product from weblogs [21]. They might either retrieve data by scanning product barcodes or QR-codes with the mobile phone camera by using special m-shopping applications [21]. H&M's have introduced a scan function in the mobile app that consumers can use in-store to scan the barcode of products and check their availability in other sizes and colors, as well as online promotions, personalized offers, and matching products.

Table 2. Overview of technologies and services for channel integration activities

Channel integration activity	Enabling technology	Examples of implementation
Integrated customer service	Cloud computing, augmented reality, mobile technology, AI	Clarke's iPad feet measurement [65], Digitally Enhanced customer Assistant, Mobile Shopping Assistant, Walmart Product Finder, eBay Shopbot
Integrated customer traceability	Mobile technologies	Tesco's Virtual coupons [8], Google Offline Attribution
Integrated order fulfilment	IoT (RFID), AI	Reserve and Pay [29], Click and Collect [9, 39], Amazon Dash Button [29], Amazon Key Delivery, Amazon Anticipatory Shipping
Integrated promotion	Mobile technologies, augmented reality, IoT (Beacon)	Taggle, Viviono social communication [25], Mobile Mirror [65], Location based recommendations
Integrated transactions	Mobile technologies, biometric technologies	Instagram Shopping [17], Amazon Go [42], Uniqul Payment, Alibaba 'Pay with Selfie'
Integrated product and price information	Mobile technologies, augmented reality	H&M Scan and Buy, Bauble Bar Interactive Display, Loreal Makeup Genius [49], Nike's product customization [25]
Integrated reverse logistics	IoT (RFID)	Buy Online Return in Store, Return Collection from Home [15]
Integrated analytics	AI, IoT	Video based emotion Analytics [60]
Integrated data privacy and security	Blockchain, edge computing	Automated access control manager [70]
Integrated fraud detection	AI, biometric technologies	POS Fraud Detection [26]

5   Research and Managerial Implications

The findings from this research offer several insights for value creation through channel integration using digital technologies and add to information systems literature on IT-enabled value creation [33]. The study investigates the extensive role of digital technologies in enabling value creation through channel integration in omnichannel retail [47]. A firm's value chain represents the linked activities that a firm executes to achieve effectiveness and efficiency. Performing value chain activities in ways that would give a firm the capability to outmatch rivals is a potential source of competitive advantage [52]. The value chain concept advocates that achieving competitive advantage begins with an effort to develop deeper organizational expertise in performing certain competitively critical value chain activities, deliberately attempting to harness those capabilities that strengthen the firm's strategy and competitiveness. This research tailors the value chain model [52] for omnichannel retailing and demonstrates how retailers can add value by utilizing appropriate technologies. Another important contribution of this study is the comprehensive analysis of the challenges faced by a retailer in execution of these activities.

Several interesting practical findings have also emerged from this study. First, IoTs, mobile technologies and AI are required for most channel integration activities as shown in Table 2 but other technologies such as blockchain and edge computing can play a substantial role in creating value through channel integration. These are not required for numerous activities like the former but are very critical for the particular activities which they support. Edge computing is a viable way to take advantage of the explosion of IoTs which has dramatically increased the data load on networks. The integration of complex sensors, with the implementation of an efficient data fusion strategy, can be used for several services which leads to better service, more sales, and lower costs [35]. For example, [12] proposed an integrated analyzer for real time analytics for the physical store and online store using mobile technologies, communication techniques which are commonly used in e-commerce applications, thus supporting hybrid systems. This method offers much better service to customers of traditional brick and mortar shops. Another important finding from our study was that some services are being employed in other domains using the identified technologies which can be easily replicated in the retail sector but are not being implemented at the moment. For example, cross-domain handshake scheme being used in the healthcare sector can be used for data security during moving data from one channel to another. Similarly sophisticated machine learning is being used in financial services for fraud detection which can be easily adopted in retail. An ideal position for a retailer would be complete customer data integration (CDI) and a single view of the customer across channels. In the context of omnichannel retailers, facial recognition or other biometric technologies can be used as a unique identifier to identify customers across different channels but there are regulatory and cultural ramifications of using these technologies which must be taken into account. For example, biometric data can only be processed in EU if consent is given explicitly.

From a managerial perspective, our mapping framework can be used as a guideline to focus on technologies identified for certain aspects of channel integration to take advantage of the complementary role of all the channels. The retailers can identify the most important value chain activity for their strategy and start with technology selection and implementation for that particular activity. For example, if CR wants to start with integrated customer service, so by using our mapping guidelines they can zoom into mobile technologies, augmented reality, AI and cloud computing and the already successful implementation of these technologies by other retailers. Secondly, retailers need to build the internal capacity and capabilities to exploit the full potential of the aforementioned technologies to fully utilize the benefits of integrated channels [29, 38]. Retailers will only be able to implement most of the technologies (e.g. IoT, AI) if they have built the required capabilities to utilize these technologies. Retail managers must develop a systemic view of the use of digital technologies in order to better seize the current and future opportunities offered by channel integration. Some retailers (e.g. Amazon, Macy, H&M, Zara) are using identified technologies to support some of the identified channel integration activities. Still, retailers are not taking full advantage of the benefits offered by these technologies for channel integration. For example, beacons have been mainly considered for fulfilling location-based customer experience and promotions but with beacon gateway, there is an aspect of using beacon technology for integrated analytics. Similarly, mobile technology is one of the main enablers of omnichannel realization [7] and its different features such as the touchscreen functionality of mobile devices can be exploited in various forms as means of reducing the physical-digital divide between the in-store and online shopping experience [41].

6 Conclusion

This paper provides a comprehensive overview of the channel integration activities for an effective and efficient omnichannel value chain and the mapping of digital technologies to these activities. This study extends our knowledge on the omnichannel value chain and the use of digital technologies in retail. Underpinned by Porter's value chain model [52], we presented twofold guidelines for transformation of the retailers from multichannel to omnichannel. First, we identified the activities required for effective channel integration and the challenges faced in the execution of these activities. Secondly, we recognized the technologies and digital solutions that act as enablers for value creation. We also underlined examples of retail companies that have already attempted to integrate the channels using the identified technologies. In particular, the proposed examples reveal the important and complementary role those technologies play for channel integration.

Most of our attention has been devoted to the selection of technologies with the perspective of the current level of technologies. Future research could be done to analyze developing trends of the enabling technologies using techniques such as patent analysis. Relatedly, an assessment of the impact that the implementation of those technologies may have had on firm financial and operational performance should be further examined. There is also a need to test in detail specific solutions to further identify why companies are struggling with the implantation of the technology based solution for channel integration. In the presented omnichannel value chain model, we describe only the role of technologies as a support activity. Future research can elaborate on how firm structure, human resource management and procurement can support primary activities in the omnichannel value chain.

Acknowledgements. This research received funding from the European Union's Horizon 2020 research and innovation programme under the Marie Skłodowska- Curie grant agreement No. 765395 and supported in part by Science Foundation Ireland grant 13/RC/2094.

References

1. Aitzhan, N.Z., Svetinovic, D.: Security and privacy in decentralized energy trading through multi-signatures, blockchain and anonymous messaging streams. IEEE Trans. Dependable Secur. Comput. **15**(5), 840–852 (2018)

2. Angeles, R.: American apparel's journey towards accurate inventory management: prelude to omnichannel retailing. In: Proceedings of the 11th IADIS International Conference Information Systems 2018, IS 2018 (2018)

3. Angeles, R.: Marks & Spencer's RFID initiative: laying the foundation for omnichannel retailing. In: Caporarello, L., Cesaroni, F., Giesecke, R., Missikoff, M. (eds.) Digitally Supported Innovation. Lecture Notes in Information Systems and Organisation, vol. 18, pp. 193–206. Springer, Cham (2016)

4. Ardito, L., Petruzzelli, A.M., Panniello, U., Garavelli, A.C.: Towards Industry 4.0: mapping digital technologies for supply chain management-marketing integration. Bus. Process Manag. J. **25**(2), 323–346 (2019)

5. El Azhari, J., Bennett, D.: Omni-channel customer experience: an investigation into the use of digital technology in physical stores and its impact on the consumer's decision-making process. In: XXIV AEDEM International Conference, London, UK (2015)

6. Balaji, M.S., Roy, S.K.: Value co-creation with Internet of Things technology in the retail industry. J. Mark. Manag. **33**(1–2), 7–31 (2017)

7. Bank, J.: Integrating online and offline worlds through mobile technology in physical stores: a quantitative study investigating the impact of technology readiness on the technology acceptance model for mobile technologies in physical retail (2018)

8. Barnes, J.D., Distler, P.H.: Providing and tracking virtual coupons. Google Patents. US 9,299,087 (2016)

9. Bell, D.R., Gallino, S., Moreno, A.: How to win in an omnichannel world. MIT Sloan Manag. Rev. **56**(1), 45 (2014)

10. Blázquez, M.: Fashion shopping in multichannel retail: the role of technology in enhancing the customer experience. Int. J. Electron. Commer. **18**(4), 97–116 (2014)

11. Bonetti, F., Perry, P.: A review of consumer-facing digital technologies across different types of fashion store formats. In: Vecchi, A. (ed.) Advanced Fashion Technology and Operations Management, pp. 137–163. IGI Global, Hershey (2017)

12. Boucouvalas, A.C., Aivalis, C.J., Gatziolis, K.: Integrating retail and e-commerce using web analytics and intelligent sensors. In: Communications in Computer and Information Science (2016)

13. Vom Brocke, J., Simons, A., Niehaves, B., Riemer, K., Plattfaut, R., Cleven, A., et al.: Reconstructing the giant: on the importance of rigour in documenting the literature search process. In: ECIS, pp. 2206–2217 (2009)

14. Cao, L., Li, L.: The impact of cross-channel integration on retailers' sales growth. J. Retail. **91**(2), 198–216 (2015)

15. Caro, F., Sadr, R.: The Internet of Things (IoT) in retail: bridging supply and demand. Bus. Horiz. **62**(1), 47–54 (2019)

16. Christidis, K., Devetsikiotis, M.: Blockchains and Smart Contracts for the Internet of Things. IEEE Access **4**, 2292–2303 (2016)

17. Dariswan, P.P., Indriani, M.T.D.: Consumers' attitude toward shopping through instagram social media. In: Proceedings of 7th Asia-Pacific Business Research Conference, pp. 25–26 (2014)
18. Fernie, J., Grant, D.B.: Fashion Logistics: Insights into the Fashion Retail Supply Chain. Kogan Page Publishers, London (2015)
19. Franco, P.P.: Digital retail and how customer-centric technology is reshaping the industry: IT-enabled digital disruption. In: Digital Multimedia: Concepts, Methodologies, Tools, and Applications, pp. 1560–1580. IGI Global (2018)
20. Grewal, D., Roggeveen, A.L., Nordfält, J.: The future of retailing. J. Retail. **93**(1), 1–6 (2017)
21. Groß, M.: Mobile shopping: a classification framework and literature review. Int. J. Retail Distrib. Manag. **43**(3), 221–241 (2015)
22. Gudanowska, A.E.: Technology mapping–proposal of a method of technology analysis in foresight studies. Bus. Theory Pract. **17**, 243 (2016)
23. Herhausen, D., Binder, J., Schoegel, M., Herrmann, A.: Integrating bricks with clicks: retailer-level and channel-level outcomes of online-offline channel integration. J. Retail. **91**(2, SI), 309–325 (2015)
24. Heuchert, M., Barann, B., Cordes, A.-K., Becker, J.: An IS Perspective on Omni-Channel Management along the Customer Journey: Development of an Entity-Relationship-Model and a Linkage Concept. Multikonferenz Wirtschaftsinformatik, pp. 435–446 (2018)
25. Hilken, T., Heller, J., Chylinski, M., Keeling, D.I., Mahr, D., de Ruyter, K.: Making omnichannel an augmented reality: the current and future state of the art. J. Res. Interact. Mark. **12**(4, SI), 509–523 (2018)
26. Hines, C., Youssef, A.: Machine learning applied to point-of-sale fraud detection. In: International Conference on Machine Learning and Data Mining in Pattern Recognition, pp. 283–295 (2018)
27. Hinkka, V., Häkkinen, M., Främling, K.: Typology of configurable RFID tracking in fashion logistics. Int. J. RF Technol. Res. Appl. **6**(2–3), 77–97 (2015)
28. Hong, D.: The omnichannel dilemma: everyone wants it but where and how do you start - Linkedin (2018). https://www.linkedin.com/pulse/omnichannel-dilemma-everyone-wants-where-how-do-you-start-daniel-hong/. Accessed 26 Mar 2019
29. Hosseini, S., Röglinger, M., Schmied, F.: Omni-channel retail capabilities: an information systems perspective. In: 38th International Conference on Information Systems, no. 4801, pp. 1–19 (2017)
30. Iftikhar, R., Khan, M.S.: Social media big data analytics for demand forecasting: development and case implementation of an innovative framework. J. Glob. Inf. Manag. (JGIM) **28**(1), 103–120 (2020)
31. Inman, J.J., Nikolova, H.: Shopper-facing retail technology: a retailer adoption decision framework incorporating shopper attitudes and privacy concerns. J. Retail. **93**(1, SI), 7–28 (2017)
32. Jung, T., tom Dieck, M.C.: Augmented Reality and Virtual Reality, Empowering Human, Place and Business. Springer, Cham (2018)
33. Kohli, R., Grover, V.: Business value of IT: an essay on expanding research directions to keep up with the times. J. Assoc. Inf. Syst. **9**(1), 1 (2008)
34. Larsen, N.M., Sigurdsson, V., Breivik, J.: The use of observational technology to study in-store behavior: consumer choice, video surveillance, and retail analytics. Behav. Anal. **40**(2), 343–371 (2017)
35. Lemon, K.N., Verhoef, P.C.: Understanding customer experience throughout the customer journey. J. Mark. **80**(6), 69–96 (2016)
36. Lewis, J., Whysall, P., Foster, C.: Drivers and technology-related obstacles in moving to multichannel retailing. Int. J. Electron. Commer. **18**(4), 43–67 (2014)

37. Li, H., Shou, G., Hu, Y., Guo, Z.: Mobile edge computing: progress and challenges. In: 2016 4th IEEE International Conference on Mobile Cloud Computing, Services, and Engineering (MobileCloud), pp. 83–84 (2016)
38. Luo, J., Fan, M., Zhang, H.: Information technology, cross-channel capabilities, and managerial actions: evidence from the apparel industry. J. Assoc. Inf. Syst. **17**(5), 308–327 (2016)
39. Ma, H., Su, Y., Oh, L.-B.: Assessing multi-channel consumers' convenience expectations of online order/in-store pickup service. Int. J. Netw. Virtual Organ. **12**. **14**(1–2), 146–159 (2014)
40. Madhani, P.M.: Business value added through RFID deployment in retail: a synthesis, conceptual framework and research propositions. Int. J. Electron. Cust. Relatsh. Manag. **5**(3–4), 305–322 (2011)
41. McCormick, H., Cartwright, J., Perry, P., Barnes, L., Lynch, S., Ball, G.: Fashion retailing - past, present and future. Text. Prog. **46**(3), 227–321 (2014)
42. McFarland, M.: Amazon Go: no cashiers, hundreds of cameras, and lots of data – CNN (2018). https://edition.cnn.com/2018/10/03/tech/amazon-go/index.html. Accessed 26 Mar 2019
43. Mladenow, A., Mollova, A., Strauss, C.: Mobile technology contributing to omni-channel retail. In: ACM International Conference Proceeding Series, pp. 92–101 (2018)
44. Mosquera, A., Olarte-Pascual, C., Juaneda Ayensa, E., Sierra Murillo, Y.: The role of technology in an omnichannel physical store. Spanish J. Mark. ESIC **22**(1), 63–82 (2018)
45. Mou, S., Robb, D.J., DeHoratius, N.: Retail store operations: literature review and research directions. Eur. J. Oper. Res. **265**(2), 399–422 (2018)
46. Nabbosa, V., Iftikhar, R.: Digital retail challenges within the EU: fulfillment of holistic customer journey post GDPR. In: 3rd International Conference on E-Education, E-Business and E-Technology, Madrid. ACM (2020)
47. Oh, L.-B., Teo, H.-H., Sambamurthy, V.: The effects of retail channel integration through the use of information technologies on firm performance. J. Oper. Manag. **30**(5), 368–381 (2012)
48. Orendorff, A.: Omni-Channel Retail Strategy: What, Why, and How (2018). https://www.shopify.com/enterprise/omni-channel-retail-strategy. Accessed 06 Nov 2018
49. Parise, S., Guinan, P.J., Kafka, R., College, B., Hall, B., Park, B., Systems, C., Francisco, S., Area, B.: Solving the crisis of immediacy: how digital technology can transform the customer experience. Bus. Horiz. **59**(4), 411–420 (2016)
50. Pierdicca, R., Liciotti, D., Contigiani, M., Frontoni, E., Mancini, A., Zingaretti, P.: Low cost embedded system for increasing retail environment intelligence. In: 2015 IEEE International Conference on Multimedia and Expo Workshops, ICMEW 2015 (2015)
51. Piotrowicz, W., Cuthbertson, R.: Introduction to the special issue information technology in retail: toward omnichannel retailing. Int. J. Electron. Commer. **18**(4), 5–16 (2014)
52. Porter, M.E.: Competitive Advantage: Creating and Sustaining Superior Performance. Simon and Schuster, New York (2008)
53. Rigby, D.: The future of shopping. Harv. Bus. Rev. **89**(12), 65–76 (2011)
54. Baskerville, R., et al.: Digital Technology and Organizational Change. In: Za, S., Rosignoli, C., Virili, F. (eds.) Reshaping Technology, People and Organizations Towards a Global Society. Lecture Notes in Information Systems and Organization, vol. 23. Springer, Cham (2017)
55. Saghiri, S., Wilding, R., Mena, C., Bourlakis, M.: Toward a three-dimensional framework for omni-channel. J. Bus. Res. **77**, 53–67 (2017)
56. Shi, W., Cao, J., Zhang, Q., Li, Y., Xu, L.: Edge computing: vision and challenges. IEEE Internet Things J. **3**(5), 637–646 (2016)
57. Smith, G.: Alibaba's Jack Ma shows off new 'pay with a selfie' technology - Fortune (2015). https://fortune.com/2015/03/17/alibabas-jack-ma-shows-off-new-a-selfie-technology. Accessed 26 Mar 2019
58. Souiden, N., Ladhari, R., Chiadmi, N.E.: New trends in retailing and services. J. Retail. Consum. Serv. **50**, 286–288 (2018)

59. Spiegel, J.R., McKenna, M.T., Lakshman, G.S., Nordstrom, P.G.: Method and system for anticipatory package shipping. Google Patents. US 8,615,473 (2013)
60. Tian, C., Zhang, R., Zhang, C., Zhao, X.: Intelligent consumer flow and experience analysis system based on cognitive intelligence: smart eye system. In: Tseng, J., Kotenko, I. (eds.) 3rd Annual International Conference on Information System and Artificial Intelligence (ISAI 2018) (2018)
61. Tripathi, K.P.: A comparative study of biometric technologies with reference to human interface. Int. J. Comput. Appl. **14**(5), 10–15 (2011)
62. Vazquez, D., Dennis, C., Zhang, Y.: Understanding the effect of smart retail brand - consumer communications via mobile instant messaging (MIM) - an empirical study in the Chinese context. Comput. Human Behav. **77**, 425–436 (2017)
63. Wang, R.J.H., Malthouse, E.C., Krishnamurthi, L.: On the go: how mobile shopping affects customer purchase behavior. J. Retail. **91**(2), 217–234 (2015)
64. Webster, J., Watson, R.T.: Analyzing the past to prepare for the future: writing a literature review. MIS Q. **26**(2), xiii–xxiii (2002)
65. Willems, K., Smolders, A., Brengman, M., Luyten, K., Schöning, J.: The path-to-purchase is paved with digital opportunities: an inventory of shopper-oriented retail technologies. Technol. Forecast. Soc. Change. **124**, 228–242 (2017)
66. Xiong, Z., Zhang, Y., Niyato, D., Wang, P., Han, Z.: When mobile blockchain meets edge computing. IEEE Commun. Mag. **56**(8), 33–39 (2018)
67. Yan, R., Wang, J., Zhou, B.: Channel integration and profit sharing in the dynamics of multi-channel firms. J. Retail. Consum. Serv. **17**(5), 430–440 (2010)
68. Yin, R.K.: Case Study Research and Applications: Design and Methods. Sage Publications, Thousand Oaks (2017)
69. Zhang, M., Ren, C., Wang, G.A., He, Z.: The impact of channel integration on consumer responses in omni-channel retailing: the mediating effect of consumer empowerment. Electron. Commer. Res. Appl. **28**, 181–193 (2018)
70. Zyskind, G., Nathan, O., et al.: Decentralizing privacy: using blockchain to protect personal data. In: 2015 IEEE Security and Privacy Workshops, pp. 180–184 (2015)

Requirements for Relief Distribution Decision-Making in Humanitarian Logistics

Mohammad Tafiqur Rahman$^{(\boxtimes)}$ and Tim A. Majchrzak

University of Agder, Kristiansand, Norway
{tafiqur.rahman,timam}@uia.no

Abstract. Making efficient and effective decisions in the chaotic environment of humanitarian relief distribution (HRD) is challenging. Decision-makers need to concentrate on numerous decision factors categorized into decision objectives, variables, and constraints. Recent HRD literature focuses on optimizing procedures while neglecting the quantification of essential requirements (decision factors) for information systems to provide decision-making support. In this article, we address this gap by accumulating affecting decision factors from both literature and practice. We investigated the practical implications of these factors in HRD decision-making by measuring the preferences of a Delphi panel consisting of 23 humanitarian experts. The results from our study emphasize the importance of the decision factors in the proposed process model for HRD in a large-scale sudden onset. Our work provides researchers not only with a comprehensive set of practically feasible decision factors in HRD but also with an understanding of their influences and correlations.

Keywords: Natural disasters · Decision support system · Decision factors · Relief distribution · Humanitarian logistics · Delphi technique · Expert preferences

1 Introduction

Although saving lives is the main aim of humanitarian relief operations, it is important to concentrate on minimizing social tension, which increases due to imbalance (inefficiency) in relief distribution (RD). For example, if two distribution centers distribute different relief items, it may fuel tension among recipients depending on which center serves them. Hence, responders need to prepare to standardize relief packages by coordinating with other responding groups and communicate with the recipients to disseminate an RD plan and during the duration of response operations. However, to meet beneficiaries' necessities, responders must know *what* the demanded items are, and *where* and *when* they are needed. For rapid, effective, and efficient response, they also require knowing the accessibility (to transport relief items), warehousing (to store

---

A prior version of this paper has been published in the ISD2019 Proceedings (http://aisel.aisnet.org/isd2014/proceedings2019).

A. Siarheyeva et al. (Eds.): ISD 2019, LNISO 39, pp. 93–112, 2020.
https://doi.org/10.1007/978-3-030-49644-9_6

them), and distributing arrangements (to reduce social tension) [1]. Moreover, for successful relief operations, understanding and assessing the overall disaster situation (e.g., environment, vulnerabilities, coping mechanisms) is necessary. Thus, responders must acquire geographical, topographical, and demographical knowledge before scheduling RD operations [7].

Identifying such influential decision factors in emergency management – especially in RD – is a complex task [47]. The humanitarian logistics (HumLog) literature proposes plenty of mathematical models and objective functions development by focusing on specific disasters as cases. Researchers utilized diverse variables and constraints in their models and functions for achieving targeted objectives. These factors need to be properly managed and utilized for rapid and effective decision making as they influence the success of the operation [46]. Failure to understand their importance for the information system will make the decision-making process more complex and time-consuming, causing delayed and inadequate responses – or potentially an overall unsuccessful relief operation [29].

By following the work of MacCarthy and Atthirawong [15], Okoli and Pawlowski [26], and Richardson, de Leeuw and Dullaert [34], we rigorously and systematically reviewed and analyzed humanitarian literature to develop a summarized list of decision factors for relief distribution. While sharing some common decision factors (objectives, variables, constraints), the review denoted that five other problem areas (DPA) influence RD decision making: facility location (FL), inventory management (IM), relief supply chain (RSC), transportation (Transp), and scheduling (Sched). For achieving better performance in the complex decision-making operation, decision-makers (DM) in RD need to concentrate on *shared* decision factors as well and assist DMs in other DPAs to achieve their objectives.

However, there has been no structured attempt in RD to identify comprehensive factors and their correlations systematically as well as to prioritize them. This study addresses this gap by empirically testing decision support requirements with the help of the Delphi technique. A worldwide Delphi panel was formed with experts from academia, governments, and national and international NGOs. Their evaluations facilitated consensus and prioritization for each factor and assisted us in answering the following research question: *What decision factors do experts prefer for effective humanitarian relief distribution decision-making?*

To answer this research question, we need to identify experts' preferences in the literature- and field-based decision factors. This investigation will assist us in finding the essential decision factors and understanding their correlations while decision-making for relief distribution. The remainder of this article is organized as follows. We provide the research background in Sect. 2. Section 3 describes our research design. Section 4 presents the results from the Delphi study, and Sect. 5 synthesizes and discusses the findings. We subsequently notify the limitations to this research and suggest implications for future research. Section 6 concludes the article.

2 Research Background

To respond to disasters in a chaotic environment, practitioners conduct complex and challenging tasks. While making decisions on RD, they face uncertainty when identifying appropriate decision factors. Not much research concentrates on recognizing factors that influence decision making in relief distribution. Peres et al. [27] classify operational research (e.g., RD) in HumLog into three DPAs (FL, IM, and network flow and Sched) without presenting influential decision factors. Gralla et al. [12] and Gutjahr and Nolz [14] respectively categorized and refined humanitarian aid operations into *efficiency* (refined into *cost efficiency*), *effectiveness* (refined into *response time, travel distance, coverage, reliability*, and *security*), and *equity* criteria. This classification, categorization, and refinement led towards identifying affecting decision factors and developing a comprehensive set of them. Although Roy et al. [37] listed some factors by dividing the RD process into four sub-processes (FL, IM, Transp, and RD decision), it was not investigated in detail to guide researchers on selecting decision variables and constraints for achieving targeted decision objectives. Safeer et al. [38] and Özdamar and Ertem [47] mapped constraints for specific objectives mainly for transportation and relief distribution but lacked a comprehensive set of decision factors, their priorities, and correlations. We know no research investigating the influences of other DPAs on the decision factors of RD.

However, to improve the disaster management process, adequate decision-making is the key, where prioritized and correlated decision factors play vital roles [4, 22, 43]. According to Li et al. [22], influential factors and their relationships need to be accumulated through proper investigation and experts' judgment. Instead of studying the entire system, current research mostly concentrates on optimizing certain procedures that are extensively case-specific and are rarely used (or unusable) in other cases. To get a holistic image, we accumulated the existing decision support models for humanitarian operations that were implemented in practice in the contexts of sudden natural disasters, thereby collecting practical decision factors. The decision factors accumulated from academic literature are evaluated and utilized in this article to develop a practice-oriented RD process model (Table 1).

3 Research Methodology

3.1 Method Selection

Several techniques were advocated in the humanitarian literature for decision making in different problem areas. We used the Delphi technique to evaluate these factors and to identify new ones. It is suitable for this kind of exploratory research where researchers need to communicate with distantly located practitioners and field experts for dealing with complex and indispensable issues [24, 34]. Although the Delphi technique was successfully utilized by MacCarthy and Atthirawong [15] for investigating and understanding decision factors, it was not widely exploited in humanitarian research. Cottam et al. [8] used the Delphi technique to assess the potential benefit of outsourcing the trucking activities for relief distribution in developing countries. Richardson et al. [34] investigated affecting factors for global inventory prepositioning locations.

Table 1. Literature-based decision factors for relief distribution decision-making

Categories	Decision factors	Literature
10 decision objectives	maximize coverage (cov), maximize transport quantity (tq), minimize travel time (tt), minimize distribution time (dt), minimize travel distance (td), minimize total cost (tc), minimize resource cost (rc), minimize penalty cost (pc), minimize number of distribution centers (ndc), minimize practical length of emergency route (pler)	[5, 6, 12, 23, 32, 33, 35, 42]
13 decision variables	travel distance (td), inventory flow and capacity (ifc), penalty cost (pc), transport cost (trc), operational cost (oc), set-up cost (stc), supply unit (su), beneficiaries access cost (bac), transport quantity (tq), demand time (det), travel time (tt), distribution time (dt), resource need (rn)	
12 decision constraints	storehouse capacity (shc), road capacity (roc), inventory holding cost (ihc), number of storehouses (nsh), budget availability (ba), demand satisfaction (ds), replenishment cost (repc), load flow (lf), transport cost (trc), travel distance (td), operational cost (oc), resource availability (ra)	

The Delphi technique provides an unbiased rating of the decision factors, which further go through ranking and consensus phases for identifying the importance and acceptance of each factor for effective decision-making in disaster-like uncertain situations [17]. Figure 1 illustrates the procedure for our Delphi study, including panel formation and research design.

We invited 76 out of 96 identified experts to participate in the survey. The questionnaire for the first Delphi round was sent to them to confirm their participation. 38 experts replied positively, and 23 finally participated in the survey (i.e., formed the Delphi panel). 17 of the 23 participants completed and returned the questionnaire, the others preferring audio-recorded interviews. We sent the questionnaire for the second round to the 17 who answered the questionnaire experts, of whom 13 responded. The panelists were anonymized according to the guidance of the Norwegian Center for Research Data (www.nsd.no) and the participants themselves. Hence, while conceptualizing panelists' thoughts in Sect. 5, we refer to them with their assigned participant identification numbers (PID in the form of P#).

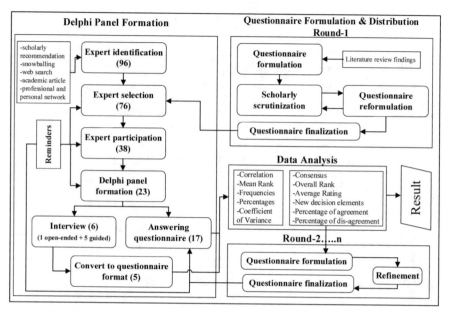

Fig. 1. The process model utilized in this Delphi Study (inspired by [21, 25])

3.2 Delphi Panel Formation

Due to their recency and severity, we targeted the Indonesia earthquakes of 2018 and the Nepal earthquake of 2015. While searching for involved experts having knowledge and interest in RD processes, we established contact with active practitioners and with their networks to gain updated knowledge on their usage of information systems (IS) for relief distribution. Besides, we utilized our contacts and the snowballing technique to bring more experts on-board. As a tentative list of potential participants was ready, we sent a study plan including information on the aim of the Delphi and its rounds, the extent and timing of the expected involvement, expected outcomes, and the potential social benefit to the ones who replied affirmatively. Finally, 23 experts from around the world participated in this Delphi study. The participating experts are listed in Table 2, along with their PID, medium of participation, affiliated organizations, countries, and contributed disasters. With an adequate panel size, according to Grim and Wright [13] and Okoli and Pawlowski [26], we proceeded to the next step. The first-round survey questionnaire was electronically distributed, along with a consent form and a non-disclosure agreement.

3.3 Research Design

Data Collection Method. Instead of starting the process with an open-ended question-naire or brainstorming sessions, as in traditional Delphi, to identify decision factors in RD [34], we approached participants with existing academic knowledge on such factors. These factors were accumulated, summarized, and clustered into three categories (decision objective, variable, and constraints). We then added them to the questionnaire for experts' evaluation. The factors were explained in the questionnaire that facilitated

Table 2. The Delphi panel

SL	PID	MPI	Affiliated Organization(s) and Country	Summary of contributed disasters
			Acronyms: PID-anonymized participant ID, **MPI**-medium of provided informantion, **Q**-questionnaire, **I'**-guided interview, **I''**-open-ended interview	
1	P2	Q	World Food Program, Nepal	Earthquake in Eastern Nepal 1988, Haiti 2010, Gorkha 2015 and several other disasters
2	P3	Q	Nepali Army Crisis Management Centre	Earthquake in Gorkha 2015 and several other disasters
3	P6	Q	Papua University, Indonesia	Disaster Risk Reduction in West Papua and several other disasters
4	P8	Q	Universitas Pembangunan Nasional Veteran Yogyakarta, Indonesia.	Merapi and Kelud volcanic disasters
5	P12	Q	Yayasan Dompet Dhuafa Republika, Indonesia	Earthquake in Lombok 2018, Central Sulawesi 2018 and several other disasters
6	P19	Q	World Food Program, Thailand	Earthquake in Haiti 2010, Indonesia 2018 and several other disasters
7	P20	Q	AHA Centre, Indonesia	Earthquake and Tsunami in Central Sulawesi 2018
8	P22	Q	AHA Centre, Indonesia	Indian Ocean Tsunami (2005 – 2008), Earthquake in Padang 2009, Central Sulawesi 2018
9	P24	I'	Kathmando Living Labs, Nepal	Earthquake in Gorkha 2015
10	P25	Q	NetHope & ICE-SA, Iceland	Earthquake in South Iceland earthquakes 2000 & 2008, Sulawesi 2018 and several other disasters
11	P26	Q	Small Wars Journal	Earthquake in Northridge 1992 and several other disasters
12	P39	Q	NetHope, Havard Humanitarian Initiative Center for Humanitarian Data, Northwestern University, USA	Earthquake in Haiti and Nepal and several other disasters
13	P40	I'	WeRobotics, Switzerland	Nearly every major humanitarian emergency for the past 15 years
14	P41	Q	Standby Task Force, USA	Earthquake in Nepal and several other disasters
15	P42	I'	TU Delft, Tilburg University, and consultant for some NGOs and Civil Protection organizations, The Netherlands	Earthquake in Haiti 2010, Philippines 2013, Nepal 2015, Indonesia 2018 and several other disasters
16	P44	Q	UNOCHA, UN Human Rights, UNDAC	Sudan 2004, Niger 2005, Lebanon 2006, Typhoon Haiyan 2013
17	P52	Q	Perkumpulan Lingkar, Indonesia	Earthquake in Jogja 2006
18	P57	I'	National disaster mitigation agency (BNPB) & Mohammodia disaster management, Indonesia	Earthquake in Jogja 2006, Selat Sunda, Sulawesi and Lombok 2018
19	P58	Q	World Food Program, Nepal	August 2017 Floods
20	P63	I''	Federal University of Rio de Janeiro, Brazil	Several humanitarian field works
21	P68	Q	Caritas Germany, Indonesia	Earthquake, Tsunami and Flash Flood
22	P69	Q	WALHI Yogyakarta, National WALHI, Sulteng Bergerak, Selat Sunda Bergerak, SHEEP Indonesia	Earthquake in Yogyakarta 2006, Selat Sunda, Sulawesi and Lombok 2018 and several other disasters
23	P71	I'	World Food Program, Indonesia	Earthquake in Selat Sunda, Sulawesi and Lombok earthquake 2018 and several other disasters

respondents to rate each decision factor on a six-point Likert Scale (inspired by [40]). Respondents were also given space to express their understanding of each of the factors and propose new factors from the practical field. However, if a participant found it complicated to answer the questionnaire, they had the opportunity to express their opinion through interview sessions (physical or online). As a result, we gained qualitative insights for the entire RD process (inspired by [44]). Additionally, to understand the depth of influences, participants were requested to mark the relationship of each decision factor of RD to the other five problem areas (FL, IM, RSC, Transp, and Sched). Thus, we incorporated relevant and in-depth information for the research quest (inspired by [18]).

Consensus and Stability. To decide on achieving consensus, we adopted the *Average Point of Majority Opinions* (APMO) technique by Kapoor [20]. A decision factor would be considered as achieving consensus if its agreement or disagreement is above the cut-off rate of APMO. Instead of considering consensus achievement as a tool to decide on further Delphi rounds, we verified how a certain percentage of votes fall within a prescribed range, i.e., how the experts react to different decision factors. We identified no clear instruction on deciding on the number of Delphi rounds for studies. Hence, by following Dajani and Sincoff [9] and Strasser [41], we calculated the *coefficient of variance* (CV) to decide Delphi rounds and check their consistencies. Finally, we utilize SPSS software to calculated *Kendall's concordance coefficient* (W) to measure the degree of agreement among panel members ($W = 0$ means perfect disagreement and $W = 1$ means perfect agreement). $W = 0.7$ is considered as an indication to achieve a higher level of general agreement in Delphi studies [39]. We demonstrate consensus and stability in Sect. 4 and discuss them in Sect. 5.

Delphi Rounds. After finalizing the list of experts, we started *round-1* by commencing the Delphi process by sending the questionnaire to each panel member in December 2018. Although an online survey is a typical mode for the Delphi technique [34, 40], emailing the questionnaire – e-Delphi – is also practical [2, 3, 25]. In addition to survey questions, the questionnaire captured the professional background for each respondent. We collected responses until February 2019. Data accumulated from the first round of the Delphi survey were extracted for descriptive analysis for finding frequencies and percentages. We utilized MS Excel and IBM SPSS to find correlations among factors and different statistics, such as the mean rank and Kendall's W. Furthermore, we utilized APMO to determine whether each factor achieved consensus. In *round-2*, the result generated from the collective feedback in the first Delphi round was shared with all the panel members in March 2019. We redesigned the questionnaire to inform about the average rating, percentage of agreement and disagreement, overall ranking, and achieving consensus for each decision factor. The respondents were provided with their previous rating for each of the decision factors and allowed to update it (inspired by [36]). The newly identified practical decision factors from round-1 were added to the questionnaire to be evaluated.

4   Results

4.1   Descriptive Information on the Participants

Most panel members have extensive working experience, some of whom worked for more than 25 years in this sector. They participated or are participating in the response operations for large-scale natural and human-made disasters worldwide, for example, the South Iceland earthquakes 2000 and 2008, the Haiti earthquake 2010, the Gorkha (Nepal) earthquake 2015, the Indonesia earthquake 2018, different devastating hurricanes and floods, the 2014–2016 Ebola outbreak in West Africa, and the Syria crisis. Their heterogeneous experiences on responding to various crises and disasters assist us in evaluating the influential decision factors.

4.2   Measurement of Stability and Stopping Criterion

To achieve stability and to stop further rounding, English and Kernan [11] quantified $0 < CV \leq 0.5$. In the first Delphi round, we had four factors in three decision-making categories (one in decision objectives and constraints, and two in decision variables) that were in the border or out of the suggested range of achieving general agreement ($CV \geq 0.5$). Besides, Kendall's W value for each category was very low (for objectives $W = 0.181$, for variables $W = 0.133$, and for constraints $W = 0.26$). Therefore, we conducted the second round, where the four decision factors achieved a good degree of consensus with $CV \leq 0.39$. Then, we measured the CV difference and defined the stopping rule as a CV difference of ≤ 0.3 (inspired by [41]). However, there were significant improvements (although still not high) in the degree of agreement in all categories in the second Delphi round (for objectives $W = 0.194$, for variables $W = 0.213$, and for constraints $W = 0.470$). Finally, receiving an absolute CV difference of ≤ 0.26 for each factor in every decision-making category and improved value for Kendall's W constituted stability, we decided to terminate conducting any additional Delphi round (inspired by [9, 10]).

4.3   Results of the Delphi Rounds

Literature-Based Decision Factors. Table 3 demonstrates the combined statistical results for two Delphi rounds. It illustrates the consensus and ranking for each deci-sion factor incorporated into three categories for relief distribution (decision objectives, variables, and constraints). We easily compare the responses in both rounds and visualize the changes made by the respondents in the second round. For convincingly presenting the result, we clustered decision factors up to the third level of importance: achieving an average rating (AR) of ≥ 5.00 was considered as *highly important* decision-making factor and placed in cluster-1, whereas factors satisfying $5.00 > AR \geq 4.00$ were con-sidered in cluster-2 as *mediocre* and the rest with $AR < 4.00$ were in cluster-3 as *least affecting* factors.

Decision Objective. In Delphi round-1, 76.8% of the experts rated all listed decision objectives as important topics in the relief distribution decision-making, whereas 19.6% found them unimportant, and 3.6% abstained from commenting. Among those decision objectives, *travel time minimization* and *coverage maximization* were placed in cluster-1 as the most important objectives that responders try to achieve without considering *minimizing* different *costs* (*total, resource, penalty*) and the *number of distribution cen-ters*, hence placed in cluster-3. The mediocre category (cluster-2) encompassed factors that were mostly related to transportation and distribution. The result suggested *trans-porting a maximum quantity* of relief items by choosing a *practically short emergency route* that would *minimize travel distance* and *distribution time*. In Delphi round-2, 78.5% of experts voted as important properties of decision making, and 21.5% voted not to consider. However, a significant change was observed in this round, where cover-age maximization was downgraded, and all the topics from cluster-3 were upgraded to cluster-2. The only topic remained in cluster-3 was resource cost minimization.

Inspecting the consensus, we can identify that transport quantity from cluster-2 and all the topics in cluster-3 did not receive general agreement from the participants in the first Delphi round. However, they continued not to receive consensus in the second Delphi round as well, but for the topic of transport quantity. Its AR was upgraded to 4.8 and secured its consensus with 92.3% vote in round-2. Except for the down-graded topic of travel distance, all topics in cluster-1 and -2 gained their votes to be importantly

Table 3. Combined statistical results for Delphi rounds 1 and 2 (inspired by [8, 41])

Acronyms: UAC: Unable to Comment; TO: Total Opinion; TP: Total Point; MP: Mean Point; SD: Standard Deviation; MR: Mean Rank; FR: Final Rank; CV: Coefficient of Variance; A.Total: Answering Total; C.Total: Consensus Total; **Please consult Table 1 for acronyms

SL	Attr**	R1 UAC #	%	Dis(1-3) #	%	Agr(4-6) #	%	TO1	Cons1	TP1	MP1	SD1	MR1	FR1	CV1	R2 Dis(1-3) #	%	Agr(4-6) #	%	TO2	Cons2	TP2	MP2	SD2	MR2	FR2	CV2	Stability (CV1-CV2)
Decision Objectives																												
1	cov	0	0	3	13.6	19	86.4	22	Y	111	5.05	1.1	6.7	3	0.22	2	15.4	11	84.6	13	Y	62	4.8	1.1	5.73	5	0.23	-0.01
2	tq	1	5	4	18.2	17	77.3	21	N	92	4.18	1.6	5.36	5	0.39	1	7.69	12	92.3	13	Y	62	4.8	1	5.96	4	0.21	0.176
3	tt	0	0	1	4.55	21	95.5	22	Y	112	5.09	0.9	6.89	1	0.18	1	7.69	12	92.3	13	Y	66	5.1	1	6.88	2	0.19	-0.01
4	dt	1	5	3	13.6	18	81.8	21	Y	109	4.95	1.6	6.89	2	0.31	2	15.4	11	84.6	13	Y	66	5.1	1.2	7.12	1	0.23	0.08
5	td	0	0	6	27.3	16	72.7	22	N	90	4.09	1.3	4.68	7	0.31	5	38.5	8	61.5	13	N	52	4	1.5	4.19	9	0.37	-0.06
6	tc	1	5	8	36.4	13	59.1	21	N	83	3.77	2	4.86	6	0.54	5	38.5	8	61.5	13	N	53	4.1	1.6	4.85	7	0.39	0.142
7	rc	0	0	8	36.4	14	63.6	22	N	85	3.86	1.4	4.52	8	0.36	4	30.8	9	69.2	13	N	51	3.9	0.8	3.88	#	0.19	0.166
8	pc	2	9	4	18.2	16	72.7	20	N	83	3.77	1.6	4.18	10	0.42	3	23.1	10	76.9	13	N	58	4.5	1.1	5.15	6	0.24	0.189
9	ndc	2	9	5	22.7	15	68.2	20	N	83	3.77	1.7	4.34	9	0.44	3	23.1	10	76.9	13	N	56	4.3	1	4.73	8	0.24	0.201
10	pler	1	5	1	4.55	20	90.9	21	Y	105	4.77	1.4	6.57	4	0.29	2	15.4	11	84.6	13	Y	62	4.8	1.2	6.5	3	0.24	0.044
A.Total		8	4	43	19.6	169	76.8									28	21.5	102	78.5									
C.Total			0			169		212	80								0		102		130	78.5						
Decision Variables																												
1	td	0	0	7	31.8	15	68.2	22	N	93	4.23	1.4	6.59	10	0.33	3	23.1	10	76.9	13	N	59	4.5	1.3	7.12	7	0.29	0.033
2	ifc	0	0	4	18.2	18	81.8	22	Y	98	4.45	1.1	6.86	7	0.24	2	15.4	11	84.6	13	Y	62	4.8	0.9	6.96	8	0.19	0.043
3	pc	2	9	7	31.8	13	59.1	20	N	78	3.55	1.8	5.09	13	0.51	5	38.5	8	61.5	13	N	50	3.8	1.2	4.38	#	0.32	0.19
4	trc	1	5	10	45.5	11	50	21	N	77	3.5	1.9	5.32	12	0.54	7	53.8	6	46.2	13	N	50	3.8	1.6	4.73	#	0.41	0.133
5	oc	0	0	8	36.4	14	63.6	22	N	86	3.91	1.5	5.68	9	0.38	4	30.8	9	69.2	13	N	53	4.1	1.2	4.96	#	0.29	0.087
6	stc	1	5	5	22.7	16	72.7	21	N	86	3.91	1.7	5.93	11	0.43	3	23.1	10	76.9	13	N	55	4.2	1	5.58	#	0.24	0.192
7	su	1	5	4	18.2	17	77.3	21	Y	94	4.27	1.4	6.75	8	0.32	0	0	13	100	13	Y	63	4.8	0.7	7.92	5	0.14	0.174
8	bac	1	5	5	22.7	16	72.7	21	Y	94	4.27	1.6	6.91	6	0.38	2	15.4	11	84.6	13	Y	60	4.6	1.1	6.96	9	0.24	0.141
9	tq	0	0	2	9.09	20	90.9	22	Y	104	4.73	0.9	7.86	5	0.19	0	0	13	100	13	Y	66	5.1	0.6	8.69	2	0.13	0.061
10	det	1	5	4	18.2	17	77.3	21	Y	103	4.68	1.6	8.43	3	0.35	2	15.4	11	84.6	13	Y	64	4.9	1.3	8.58	3	0.27	0.083
11	tt	1	5	2	9.09	19	86.4	21	Y	106	4.82	1.4	8.43	2	0.29	2	15.4	11	84.6	13	Y	64	4.9	1	8.31	4	0.21	0.08
12	dt	2	9	1	4.55	19	86.4	20	Y	104	4.73	1.8	8.27	4	0.37	1	7.69	12	92.3	13	Y	63	4.8	0.9	7.81	6	0.19	0.185
13	rn	1	5	2	9.09	19	86.4	21	Y	111	5.05	1.5	8.86	1	0.3	1	7.69	12	92.3	13	Y	67	5.2	1	9	1	0.19	0.111
A.Total		11	4	61	21.3	214	74.8									32	18.9	137	81.1									
C.Total			10			203		275	77								7		131		169	81.7						
Decision Constraints																												
1	shc	1	5	4	18.2	17	77.3	21	Y	102	4.64	1.8	7.91	2	0.39	1	7.69	12	92.3	13	Y	66	5.1	1	8.12	5	0.19	0.198
2	roc	0	0	4	18.2	18	81.8	22	Y	103	4.68	1.2	7.7	4	0.25	3	23.1	10	76.9	13	N	62	4.8	1.2	7.23	7	0.24	0.006
3	ihc	1	5	10	45.5	11	50	21	N	78	3.55	1.5	4.43	11	0.42	6	46.2	7	53.8	13	N	49	3.8	1.1	3.81	#	0.29	0.134
4	nsh	1	5	6	27.3	15	68.2	21	N	86	3.91	1.7	5.41	10	0.43	2	15.4	11	84.6	13	Y	55	4.2	0.9	5.04	#	0.22	0.213
5	ba	2	9	1	4.55	19	86.4	20	Y	99	4.5	1.9	7.52	6	0.42	0	0	13	100	13	Y	67	5.2	0.8	8.62	1	0.16	0.26
6	ds	2	9	1	4.55	19	86.4	20	Y	105	4.77	1.8	7.86	3	0.38	0	0	13	100	13	Y	65	5	0.9	8.19	4	0.18	0.194
7	repc	1	5	12	54.5	9	40.9	21	N	68	3.09	1.4	3.18	12	0.47	8	61.5	5	38.5	13	N	42	3.2	0.9	1.96	#	0.29	0.18
8	lf	1	5	3	13.6	18	81.8	21	Y	102	4.64	1.6	7.16	7	0.36	2	15.4	11	84.6	13	Y	64	4.9	1.3	7.54	6	0.26	0.101
9	trc	0	0	7	31.8	15	68.2	22	N	87	3.95	1.6	5.55	8	0.42	3	23.1	10	76.9	13	N	56	4.3	1.3	5.58	8	0.29	0.126
10	td	1	5	2	9.09	19	86.4	21	Y	102	4.64	1.4	7.59	5	0.29	1	7.69	12	92.3	13	Y	66	5.1	0.9	8.38	3	0.17	0.124
11	oc	1	5	8	36.4	13	59.1	20	N	84	3.82	1.7	5.41	9	0.44	5	38.5	8	61.5	13	N	54	4.2	1.1	5.08	9	0.28	0.165
12	ra	1	5	3	13.6	18	81.8	21	Y	106	4.82	1.6	8.27	1	0.33	2	15.4	11	84.6	13	Y	67	5.2	1.1	8.46	2	0.21	0.123
A.Total		12	5	61	23.1	191	72.3									33	21.2	123	78.8									
C.Total			12			171		252	73								8		118		156	80.8						

Test Statistics — Decision Objectives: Round 1: Kendall's W 0.181; Round 2: Kendall's W 0.194. Decision Variables: Round 1: Kendall's W 0.133; Round 2: Kendall's W 0.213. Decision Constraints: Round 1: Kendall's W 0.260; Round 2: Kendall's W 0.470.

considered in the relief distribution decision-making process. Finally, the voting for total cost was unstable (as $CV > 0.5$) in round-1 and achieved its stability in round-2.

Decision Variables. To find important decision-making variables in round-1, 74.8% of panel members positively rated the factors in this category, whereas 21.3% finds them unimportant, and 3.9% did not vote. In round-2, 81.1% voted to list them as important decision factors. However, by analyzing the voting result, we identified that resource need was placed in cluster-1 in both rounds, whereas the transporting quantity of relief items accompanied it in round-2. All costing-related topics (penalty, transportation, operational, and set-up) secured their places in cluster-3 in round-1, except beneficiaries' access cost. It was listed in cluster-2 along with travel distance, inventory flow and capacity, supply unit, transportation quantity, and demand, travel, and distribution time. There was no such significant change in round-2. Operational and set-up cost upgraded to cluster-2, and as already mentioned, transportation quantity joined resource need in cluster-1. Although travel distance was a mediocre affecting decision factor, it did not achieve general agreement along with all factors from cluster-3 in the first round. However, all the non-consensus factors in the first round remained unchanged in the second round, except beneficiaries' access cost. It secured its consensus with 84.6% of the general agreement in the final round. Lastly, the rating for penalty cost and transportation cost were unstable (as $CV > 0.5$) in round-1 that became stable in round-2.

Decision Constraints. The decision factors in this category already achieved stability as $CV < 0.5$ for each of them in Delphi round-1, and this stability became higher in round-2 as $CV \leq 0.29$. However, the analysis found no highly important decision factor for cluster-1 in the first round. Seven out of 12 decision-making constraints were considered as mediocre and placed in cluster-2, while the remaining ones were encompassed in cluster-3. The factors constituted this category gained their maximum percentage of general agreement in round-1, which remained the same in round-2 as *road capacity,* and the *number of storehouses* switched their places in achieving consensus. However, five decision constraints (*storehouse capacity, budget availability, demand satisfaction, travel distance, and resource availability*) from cluster-2 gained higher importance in the second round and moved to cluster-1, which was the maximum content of this cluster. 72.3% of the panel members agreed to consider the listed factors as important decision-making constraints in round-1, whereas 23.1% were not convinced, and 4.6% were unable to comment. In round-2, 78.8% voted for enlisting these factors as decision-making constraints in the intended decision support system (DSS), whereas 21.2% voted not to.

Field-Based Decision Factors. While evaluating the decision factors in round-1, the panelists were requested to recommend essential factors missing so far. Out of 23 panelists, 13 contributed to suggesting additional decision factors based on their experiences. After analyzing and refining, three new decision objectives were identified, whereas 13 new decision variables and ten new decision constraints were enlisted for further evaluation in round-2. The panel members were requested to follow similar evaluating procedures as that of in the first round. This evaluation procedure facilitated panel members with a chance to know and verify the new decision factors proposed by other members. Table 4 demonstrates the newly recommended decision factors, along with the results from the analysis that is subsequently discussed.

After analysis, we identified that two decision objectives, six decision variables, and three decision constraints achieved consensus with over 90% vote and hence, prioritized into the list though their mean rank is lower (please consult Table 4 for detail). Although other decision factors did not achieve consensus, their importance in the decision-making process was significant as they scored over 76% vote. For example, what would be the reason for tending to reduce central control on the *financial flow and other decisions*?

Table 4. Field-based decision factors for relief distribution decision-making

SL	Experts preferring new decision factors	Disagreed (1-3) #	%	Agreed (4-6) #	%	Total openion	Consensus (APMC)	Total Point	Mean Point	Standard Deviation	MeanRank (SPSS)	Final Rank (SPSS)	Kendall's W (SPSS)
Objectives													
1	Central influence on financial flow and other decision (minimize)	3	23.08	10	76.92	13	N	52	4	1.08	1.31	3	W=0.644
2	Proper Operational Mgt model by maximizing social capital	0	0	13	100	13	Y	66	5.08	0.86	2.15	2	
3	Proper response plan for minimizing social tension	0	0	13	100	13	Y	72	5.54	0.78	2.54	1	
	Consnesus calculation	0		36		39	92.31						
Variables													
1	Assessing local sources of supplies	0	0	13	100	13	Y	68	5.23	0.73	8.35	3	
2	Relief package standerdization (heavy, lightweight, etc.)	3	23.08	10	76.92	13	N	57	4.38	1.19	5.54	12	
3	Duration of response operation	2	15.38	11	84.62	13	N	58	4.46	1.33	6.27	9	
4	Understanding and assessing the disaster situation (environment, vulnerabilities, and coping mechanisms)	1	7.692	12	92.31	13	Y	67	5.15	1.21	8.77	2	
5	Need assessment for current and future operations (victims' locations, items' and victims' categorization, prioritization, and quantity, difficulties to make the materials available to them)	1	7.692	12	92.31	13	Y	69	5.31	1.44	9.46	1	
6	Synchronization of need and operation: think of the responding capacity (from warehouse to the field) before deployment	2	15.38	11	84.62	13	N	60	4.62	1.12	6.81	7	W =0.184
7	Knowledge acquisition on previous incidents and analysis	2	15.38	11	84.62	13	N	59	4.54	1.2	5.62	11	
8	Digital communicating devices	3	23.08	10	76.92	13	N	59	4.54	1.27	6.42	8	
9	Traffic control plan at distribution points	3	23.08	10	76.92	13	N	61	4.69	1.25	7.42	5	
10	Social capital (support from local leaders, experts or community)	2	15.38	11	84.62	13	N	56	4.31	1.6	5.38	13	
11	Targeted community's cultural knowledge or understanding	1	7.692	12	92.31	13	Y	66	5.08	1.19	8.23	4	
12	Relief distribution plan sharing with the beneficiaries	1	7.692	12	92.31	13	Y	59	4.54	1.13	5.69	10	
13	Knowledge on neighboring regions; geographical, topography and demography knowledge about the targeted point of distribution	1	7.692	12	92.31	13	Y	63	4.85	0.9	7.04	6	
	Consnesus calculation	0		147		169	86.98						
Constraints													
1	Characteristics of disasters	2	15.38	11	84.62	13	N	57	4.38	1.26	5.12	7	
2	Characteristics of affected areas	2	15.38	11	84.62	13	N	62	4.77	1.42	6.15	3	
3	Access to the point of distribution	1	7.692	12	92.31	13	Y	64	4.92	1.12	6.69	2	
4	Civil-military relationship	2	15.38	11	84.62	13	N	60	4.62	1.04	5.23	6	W = 0.166
5	In-country political situations	1	7.692	12	92.31	13	Y	62	4.77	1.17	5.5	5	
6	Safety and security to respondents, relief supply chain, and beneficiaries	1	7.692	12	92.31	13	Y	66	5.08	1.19	7.27	1	
7	Social and communication infrastructure	2	15.38	11	84.62	13	N	54	4.15	0.99	3.73	10	
8	Geographical and environmental (weather) conditions of the disaster area	2	15.38	11	84.62	13	N	60	4.62	1.39	5.12	8	
9	Coordinating with other relief distributing groups (big/small)	3	23.08	10	76.92	13	N	58	4.46	1.45	4.58	9	
10	Trained, committed and technology supported volunteers/supporting staffs	2	15.38	11	84.62	13	N	61	4.69	0.95	5.62	4	
	Consnesus calculation	0		112		130	86.15						

Again, from the general observation, it can be understood that most of the panelists suggested having decision-making flexibility in the field, but we do yet not know the actual reasoning. If the rating for this attribute is analyzed, it seems that participants were, somehow, confused to claim that flexibility because 8 out of 10 agreeing participants rated 4 out of 6, whereas 2 out of 3 disagreeing participants rated 3 and in the Likert scale of 6, rating of 3 and 4 are normally meant as *confusing*. Thus, further study is essential. Additionally, based on experts' ranking, these new decision attributes were finally ranked by using the *mean rank* calculated by SPSS software. Furthermore, the degree of agreement among panel members (Kendall's W) was also measured. The Kendall's W for new decision objectives was measured as 0.644; 0.7 is considered as a higher level of general agreement. Hence, it was decided to conclude the Delphi survey though Kendall's W for the other two categories were not that high – for decision variables W = 0.184 and for decision constraints W = 0.166.

Final Ranking. Over 76% of the panelists in round-1, voted to include all the literature-based decision factors in the relief distribution decision-making; over 81% voted this way in round-2. The field-based decision factors received an overall vote of over 77% to accept them in the decision-making process. Thus, the importance of these comprehensive decision factors in the envisioned DSS for relief distribution was accomplished.

Therefore, combinedly the number of enlisted decision factors became large: 13 decision objectives, 26 decision variables, and 22 decision constraints. This bigger list of decision factors is impractical to suggest to the decision-makers and will be challenging to manage in the crucial responding time. Hence, a comprehensive and prioritized list of decision factors is needed.

We further analyzed the consensus regarding highly ranked decision factors in both lists. To be enlisted as highly influential decision-making attributes, literature-based decision factors must accomplish over 80% vote in both Delphi rounds, whereas decision factors from the practice must ensure over 90% vote in round-2. We, thus, identified and enlisted six decision objectives, eight decision objectives, and eight decision constraints as the most influential decision factors for humanitarian relief distribution. Table 5 presents a comprehensive list of top-ranked decision factors, along with the vote percentage. To present them conveniently, we placed the field-based decision factors just after that of the scientific literature.

Table 5. The most effective decision factors for relief distribution decision-making

	Decision Factors	Vote (%)	Sources
Objectives	1. Travel time (minimize)	93	Scientific literature
	2. Emergency route length (minimize)	85	
	3. Coverage (maximize)	83	
	4. Distribution time (minimize)	81	
	5. Social tension (minimize)	100	Expert preferences
	6. Social capital (maximize)	100	
Variables	1. Transportation quantity	95	Scientific literature
	2. Resource need	88*	
	3. Distribution time	88	
	4. Travel time	83	
	5. Inventory flow and capacity	81	
	6. Assessing the situation and local markets	96	Expert preferences
	7. Knowledge in neighboring regions and culture of the targeted community	92	
	8. Relief distribution planning and sharing	92	
Constraints	1. Budget availability	93*	Scientific literature
	2. Demand satisfaction	93	
	3. Travel distance	88	
	4. Resource availability	81*	
	5. Load flow	81	
	6. Safety and security	92	Experts preferences
	7. Access to the point of distribution	92	
	8. In-country political situations	92	
*also recommended by the experts			

5 Synthesis and Discussion

In this section, we synthesize our findings from the Delphi process and discuss them category-wise. Afterward, by exploiting the result, we draw a correlational matrix and propose a relief distribution process model. Finally, we conclude this section by discussing the challenges and portraying our future research directions.

Firstly, distributing a maximum of relief items within a short period is the main objective of the humanitarian operations undertaken in response to disasters [5]. For successful humanitarian operations, DMs always try a fast response and to meet as many demands as possible [16]. In doing so, the operation must be forecasted with adequate data for need assessment. P12 exemplified the context of the Indonesian Earthquake 2018 to point out that the process should prioritize acquiring and assessing demand data before focusing on serving maximum needs. According to the participant, this is sometimes absent in the process operated in the field. To speed up the process, P44 and P52 suggested focusing on fulfilling the basic needs with quality relief items instead of quantity of relief demand. P24 came with a unique idea of publicly forecasting the need information to serve maximum demand by incorporating the concept of *social capital*. After sudden-onset, initial responses come from the people inhabiting in neighboring communities when organizational support is still unavailable (P41, P42, P57). So, if they can be forecasted with frequently updated need information, more demands can be served to save more lives. By monitoring communal services, national or international responders can avoid allocating funds for relief items that may stay unused or become surpluses (P24, P25). This will provide flexibility to responders for meeting important demands that are still missing. However, P40 recommended to *"...prioritize remote regions for relief operations as small and mediocre organizations keep those regions out of their distribution plans to minimize expenditure"* though *operational cost* and *social tension* may increase. According to P20 and P71, the success of any relief operation largely depends on the instructions from the sourcing organizations (e.g., hosting government, United Nations) and their mission objectives and capacity.

Speed is one of the critical success factors of relief distribution [29]. When a responding team is planning to serve maximum demands, it needs to find its way(s) for faster mobilization of maximum relief items (*transport quantity*) to the affected population [16]. According to P26, *minimizing travel time* would ensure timely relief distribution (*distribution time minimization*) by increasing the potential number of trips of shipments. Although it is important to *shorten travel time*, the access constraints need to be considered during emergencies (P58). For example, extreme weather conditions made the relief operation challenging in the East part of Indonesia, where P12 participated. Hence, P24 suggested placing demand notation into a map so that central DMs can select the *shortest practical length of the emergency route*(s) (hence, *shorter travel distance*) and calculate *minimum travel time* to the demand points from the nearest distribution center(s). However, participants identified that *minimizing travel time* is more important than *coverage maximization*. Thus, the later factor was re-evaluated in round-2 and listed cluster-2. It would make the entire operation unsuccessful if maximum coverage is planned without minimizing travel time. Hence, P41 remarked, *"...do well in one area rather than poorly in all areas"*. Furthermore, the cost-related factors are theoretically important (P58), but practically *"...saving lives and providing basic needs and medical treatment are of paramount importance as compared to the cost involved"* (P3). However, although some participants were in favor of having reasonable (or more) distribution centers for serving affected people, others were not concentrating on this issue as this topic is directed to the central logistics hub.

Secondly, for achieving the objectives of humanitarian assistance and successfully distributing relief items, DMs are required to control some variables [37]. Among the 13 listed decision variables, panel members considered, in the first place, balancing *resource need* and relief *transportation quantity* to meet demands at the targeted point of distribution (POD). In doing so, multiple panel members suggested to categorize and prioritize peoples' needs before dispatching relief vehicles, whereas P24 and P40 emphasized to share the distribution plan beforehand to gain beneficiaries' satisfaction. For example, the relief packages can be standardized by categorizing the recipients by age, gender, location, households, family member, etc. and if they are informed earlier about the package (food/non-food, heavy/lightweight), they can ensure their arrangements *(beneficiaries' access cost)* to receive relief package(s) and return home safely. This will ensure the reduction of *social tension*, which is one of the most critical and complex issues to tackle in the disaster-arisen chaotic field (P40). Furthermore, to face such challenges, it is also necessary to maintain reduced travel and distribution time that can be done by establishing *supply unit(s)* with *sufficient storing capacities* in shorter *travel distance*, accelerating inventory flow for shortening *demand meeting time*.

However, none of the cost related issues *(penalty, transport, operational, and set-up cost)* gained ultimate consensus and hence, rank low. According to the participants, achieving cost-benefit may be important in business logistics, not in HumLog. P3 expressed that *"...importance should be given to the mechanism to transport the relief materials as quickly as possible and not the cost involved"*. Nonetheless, P40 criticized the hidden cost-benefit issue in humanitarian operations that restrict NGOs to support remote communities. The participant suggested prioritizing those communities while planning for deployment as they are not covered in most of the cases, and if necessary, this can be negotiated with the donors for supporting responding operations in better ways.

Thirdly, to operate an effective and efficient relief distribution, DMs need to satisfy limiting constraints that are not directly controlled by them. For example, *budget* and *resource availability, travel distance,* and *storehouse capacity* gained maximum attention. Humanitarian operations largely depend on donors [19], and humanitarian organizations have no line of credit (P40). Although it is expected to have an adequate budget to support the entire relief distribution mechanism (P3), it is always difficult to convince donors to increase the budget, even if it is needed to cover more survivors in remote areas (P19, P41). Additionally, if the required items (resources) are unavailable in the hosting area (e.g., local market), the logistical costs become higher and affect the entire operation (P24). On the other hand, the *number of storehouses* and their *capacities* are centrally controlled and always face space unavailability to the upcoming shipments waiting in the port to be unloaded (P57, P58). Although P71 was mentioning to arrange mobile storages, it would, however, increase *operational cost* and relief *distribution time*. Furthermore, unavailable access points would delay the distribution process by limiting *road capacity* or *traveling longer distances* (P40, P44). This results in an irregular *load flow; inventory holding cost* and *replenishment cost* would increase significantly.

Moreover, geographical location, security, political instability, and weather of the hosting area(s) always bring uncontrollable situations to the operations. Besides, having support from the hosting government and the military, responding teams must be careful while tackling such situations. P19 and P41 suggested to incorporate local informants for continuous situational updates on further sections of a distributing network, and local transport provides as they know the local road-links. Hence, P24 was envisioning a technological system where local communities can post information on certain issues that are further refined by system analysts and graphically presented into a distribution network map. This would help DMs to find alternatives.

Fourthly, after getting a clear understanding of decision factors and their influences on the relief distribution process, it is important to know how each factor in decision objectives is correlated with that of in decision variables and constraints. Table 6 illustrates the positive and negative correlations. For positive correlation, we considered a correlation coefficient of ≥ 0.3; for negative correlation, we notated all of them although some values were insignificant. By doing so, we warn DMs, in case they intend to consider these factors for the process. The presented correlation matrix guides DMs to select appropriate variables and constraints for achieving certain objectives. By consulting the correlational values in the matrix, DMs can rapidly decide on the factors that are necessary for supporting decision-making and can thus produce decision alternatives for efficient and effective relief distribution.

Although most of the cost related topics did not achieve consensus and were ranked low, some of them show high correlational significance. For example, the operational cost has the highest impact when practitioners intend to transport maximum relief items to different PODs. It scored highest in both decision variables (0.78) and decision constraints (0.6) categories. This justifies that DMs working in the down-stream of the humanitarian supply chain are not fully independent while budgeting operational costs. They are controlled (to some extent) by donors and central authorities of respective organizations. They may face similar situations when deciding on transport costs and travel distance. However, DMs must be cautious while deciding on variables and constraints because some factors have high positive impacts to achieve certain objectives, whereas the same factor(s) affect other objectives to be accomplished. For example, *operational cost* and *supply unit* has a great influence on transporting maximum relief items, whereas they impact negatively on covering maximum demands. Hence, DMs should evaluate the applicability and impacts of those factors in their targeted context(s).

Fifthly, according to [26] and [45], instead of studying separately, all DPAs should be dealt with jointly and concurrently for effective disaster response. Therefore, by utilizing findings from this Delphi study and personal experiences, we have proposed an RD process model in Fig. 2. The model encompasses two distinct portions: information flow (denoted in solid arrows) and material flow (denoted in dotted arrows). To demonstrate processes more clearly, we assumed each DPA as an individual operational entity. The process starts by receiving (continuous) need information from the field that DMs analyze in the distribution centers. The assessed demand information is publicly forecasted immediately for informing neighboring communities to meet initial demand

Table 6. Correlational matrix of decision factors

*Please consult **Table 1 & 2** for identifying specific decision variables and constrains

Serial	Source	Rank	Decision Objectives	Cons-ensus	Highly correlated decision variables*		Highly correlated decision constraints*	
					Positive Correlation ≥ 0.3	Negative Corr.	Positive Correlation ≥ 0.3	Negative Corr.
1	Scientific literature	1	Distribution time (minimize)	Yes	rn(0.48), td(0.34), dt(0.29)	pc(0.15), trc(0.01)	ds(0.66), repc(0.53), trc(0.46), shc(0.44), ba(0.35), ihc(0.32), lf(0.29)	
2		2	Travel time (minimize)	Yes	ifc(0.45), td(0.4), tq(0.38), tt(0.38), rn(0.37)		lf(0.5), ra(0.4), trc(0.38), rc(0.3), td(0.3)	
3		3	Practical length of emergency route (minimize)	Yes	oc(0.43), tq(0.34), rn(0.3)	pc(0.13), bac(0.013)	trc(0.5), rc(0.4), shc(0.37), repc(0.35), lf(0.32), ihc(0.32), oc(0.31)	
4		4	Transport quantity (maximize)	Yes	oc(0.78), trc(0.57), ifc(0.45), stc(0.44), dt(0.34), su(0.32), tq(0.3)	det(0.2), rn(0.1), td(0.04), bac(0.002)	oc(0.6), shc(0.57), nsh(0.53), ba(0.53), rc(0.49), trc(0.45), lf(0.38), repc(0.34)	ds(0.12)
5		5	Coverage (maximize)	Yes	det(0.51), tt(0.47), rn(0.4), bac(0.31)	oc(0.06), su(0.01)	td(0.59), ra(0.47)	ba(0.18), shc(0.06), repc(0.03)
6		6	Penalty cost (minimize)	No	su(0.67), pc(0.58), tq(0.56), ifc(0.54), stc(0.49), oc(0.43), td(0.37), bac(0.32)	rn(0.09)	nsh(0.75), shc(0.62), ba(0.61), ihc(0.61), trc(0.52), rc(0.52), oc(0.41)	ds(0.04)
7		7	Total cost (minimize)	No	oc(0.71), trc(0.4), stc(0.4)	det(0.28), tt(0.23), rn(0.2), td(0.03)	trc(0.71), shc(0.6), nsh(0.4), ba(0.55), repc(0.58)	td(0.05), ds(0.002)
8		8	Number of distribution centers (DC) (minimize)	No	tq(0.58), det(0.55), su(0.52), tt(0.45), rn(0.4), pc (0.35), oc(0.34), dt(0.34), bac(0.32), ifc(0.33)		td(0.74), oc(0.58), ra(0.47), nsh(0.47), trc(0.47), ds(0.46), rc(0.43), shc(0.42), ihc(0.3)	
9		9	Travel distance (minimize)	No	pc(0.36), oc(0.36), trc(0.3)	rn(0.03)	ihc(0.5), trc(0.48), repc(0.36), lf(0.31)	
10		10	Resource cost (minimize)	No	trc(0.68), oc(0.67), su(0.6), stc(0.6), tq(0.4), td(0.4), pc(0.38), ifc(0.37)	det(0.23), rn(0.2)	nsh(0.71), oc (0.62), rc(0.62), trc(0.58), ba(0.58), shc(0.55), ihc(0.4), lf(0.35), repc(0.3)	ds(0.2)
11	Expert-preferences	1	Response plan (maximize)	Yes	v1(0.5), v2(0.57), v3(0.47), v4(0.79), v5(0.81), v6(0.55), v7(0.56), v8(0.44), v9(0.53), v10(0.46), v11(0.77), v12(0.59), v13(0.73)		c1(0.71), c2(0.8), c3(0.73), c4(0.79), c5(0.7), c6(0.78), c7(0.75), c8(0.75), c9(0.58), c10(0.47)	
12		2	Operational management (maximize)	Yes	v1(0.77), v2(0.46), v4(0.7), v5(0.59), v7(0.6), v8(0.34), v9(0.33), v11(0.65), v12(0.47), v13(0.66)		c1(0.35), c2(0.63), c3(0.53), c4(0.59), c5(0.6), c6(0.48), c7(0.48), c8(0.65), c9(0.44), c10(0.44)	
13		3	Central influence (minimize)	No	v2(0.45), v7(0.45), v11(0.33), v12(0.69)	v3(0.12), v9(0.19), v10(0.15)	c2(0.33), c5(0.4), c7(0.31), c8(0.5), c9(0.11)	c4(0.22), c10(0.08)

and to maximize coverage. The information on *social capital* is continuously assembled while preparing the responses by exploiting the decision factors evaluated in this research. By understanding the achieving objectives, DMs concentrate on utilizing necessary variables and constraints along with contextual ones. They consult and negotiate with other DPAs (if related) and plan for deployment.

RSC receives initial demand notes and establishes communication with the logistics hub or local market for procuring necessary items. Parallelly, RSC communicates with IM for updates of FL status and Sched for scheduling items to be transported and vehicles to be utilized. Then, Sched contacts with Transp and IM for finalizing the shipment(s) to be stored in FL or sent to the distribution centers (DC). As soon as deploying arrangement(s) is finalized, DC shares the distribution plan with the PODs. After dispatching relief items either directly from the procurement or the selected FLs, DC monitors the entire shipment(s) and continually communicates with responsible ones for updating the safety and security of the selected distribution network. Along with official informants,

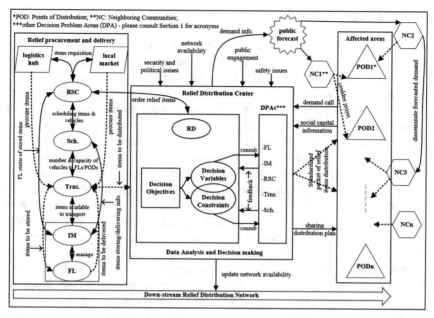

Fig. 2. The proposed relief distribution process model (inspired by [4, 28, 37])

DC may increase public involvement for a faster update on distribution networks (i.e., blocked road, collapsed bridge), political instability in the network, safety, and security.

While considering limitations, our study faced the typical weaknesses summarized by Hsu and Sanford [18]: low response rates and high time consumption. Our study also faced the challenge of participation discontinuing in future rounds despite participants being motivated by providing information about the survey topic, method, rounds, outcomes, and the overall research theme. Since we exploited emails to communicate with geographically dispersed experts, it was difficult to reach them as we got no indicate whether we were using the right addresses until participants replied. The conducted interviews were informative, but it was laborious for us to convert them to a questionnaire-like format.

After tackling all these difficulties, these summarized findings allow us to identify paths for future research. Decision factors learned from our work can be translated as system requirements for developing future IS artifacts (e.g., DSS), where the prioritization by the experts can form the basis of a typical *Must-Should-Could* assessment. The step following this article will be a design-oriented pragmatic approach that will effectively support rapid decision making for efficient relief distribution in large-scale disasters [30]. Our research will focus on proposing an operational ecosystem for RD by examining the influences that it receives from other problem areas introduced in Sect. 1. This operational ecosystem could feedback DSS to produce effective and efficient decision-making support.

6 Conclusion

Relief distribution is the core task of the humanitarian logistics operations. It depends on qualified decision-making in facility location, inventory management, relief supply chain, transportation, and scheduling. Except for a few of them, decision factors in relief distribution are shared by different problem areas. Thus, decision-makers need to know the decision objectives and how and to what extent decision variables and constraints influence them. In this article, we generated and evaluated two generalized sets of decision factors. The first one encompasses decision factors that researchers exploited in their objective functions and models to solve case-specific or scenario-specific relief distribution problems, whereas the latter one incorporates expert-recommended decision factors from the field. To provide decision-makers with manageable and comprehensive advice, we proposed a shortened and prioritized list based on expert ranking. However, for receiving the operational benefit, we still suggest decision-makers to keep tracking all the enlisted decision factors instead of searching the top-ranked ones only. As humanitarian operations are highly contextual and decision-makers face severe uncertainty in information gathering, processing, and implementation [31], we expect that the enlisted decision factors will support them to visualize and understand the changes and quickly identify relevant ones necessary for fast humanitarian relief distribution. We also proposed a correlational matrix to assist decision-makers with an understanding of the influential relationship between decision factors, so that they can select essential decision factors based on their respective contexts.

The findings in this research have various implications. Empirically evaluating the decision factors has extended the current body of knowledge on the RD process in large-scale sudden onsets. Based on our findings, we have contributed to the HumLog literature by extending the existing models to accelerate decision-making in disaster-like deeply uncertain events, where information is infrequent and incomplete. Our research findings, along with the proposed process model, will support field-based decision making in the down-stream of the humanitarian relief supply chain, as well as in the center. Moreover, it serves as an input to information system development to support decision-making. Additional research is needed to refine the findings and extend the process model to prototype and develop a decision support system to assist decision-makers with decision alternatives for actual implementation.

Acknowledgement. The authors acknowledge the cooperation and valuable assistance received from Eli Hustad, Dag Håkon Olsen, and Rania El-Gazzar on the Delphi process. At the same time, the authors are grateful to all panel members, who provided insightful information, and evaluations and valuable comments for this research on relief distribution decision making.

References

1. Afshar, A., Haghani, A.: Modeling integrated supply chain logistics in real-time large-scale disaster relief operations. Socio-Economic Plan. Sci. **46**(4), 327–338 (2012)
2. Aljamal, M.S., Ashcroft, D., Tully, M.P.: Development of indicators to assess the quality of medicines reconciliation at hospital admission: an e-Delphi study. Int. J. Pharm. Pract. **24**(3), 209–216 (2016)

3. Avery, A., Savelyich, B., Sheikh, A., Cantrill, J., Morris, C., Fernando, B., Bainbridge, M., Horsfield, P., Teasdale, S.: Identifying and establishing consensus on the most important safety features of GP computer systems: e-Delphi study. J. Innov. Health Inform. **13**(1), 3–11 (2005)
4. Balcik, B., Beamon, B.M., Krejci, C.C., Muramatsu, K.M., Ramirez, M.: Coordination in humanitarian relief chains: practices, challenges and opportunities. Int. J. Prod. Econ. **126**(1), 22–34 (2010)
5. Barahona, F., Ettl, M., Petrik, M., Rimshnick, P.M.: Agile logistics simulation and optimization for managing disaster responses. In: Proceedings 2013 Winter Simulation Conference: Simulation: Making Decisions in a Complex World, pp. 3340–3351. IEEE Press (2013)
6. Chunguang, C., Dongwen, C., Xiaoyu, S., Bo, G.: Logistics routes optimization model under large scale emergency incident. In: 2010 International Conference on Logistics Systems and Intelligent Management, Harbin, pp. 1471–1475 (2010)
7. Comes, T., Schätter, F., Schultmann, F.: Building robust supply networks for effective and efficient disaster response. In: ISCRAM Conference, Baden-Baden, pp. 230–240 (2013)
8. Cottam, H., Roe, M., Challacombe, J.: Outsourcing of trucking activities by relief organisations. J. Humanitarian Assistance **1**(1), 1–26 (2004)
9. Dajani, J.S., Sincoff, M.Z., Talley, W.K.: Stability and agreement criteria for the termination of Delphi studies. TFSC **13**(1), 83–90 (1979)
10. El-Gazzar, R., Hustad, E., Olsen, D.H.: Understanding cloud computing adoption issues: A Delphi study approach. J. Syst. Softw. **118**, 64–84 (2016)
11. English, J.M., Kernan, G.L.: The prediction of air travel and aircraft technology to the year 2000 using the Delphi method. Transp. Res. **10**(1), 1–8 (1976)
12. Gralla, E., Goentzel, J., Fine, C.: Assessing trade-offs among multiple objectives for humanitarian aid delivery using expert preferences. Prod. Oper. Ma. **23**, 978–989 (2014)
13. Grime, M.M., Wright, G.: Delphi method. Wiley StatsRef, 1–6 (2014)
14. Gutjahr, W.J., Nolz, P.C.: Multicriteria optimization in humanitarian aid. Eur. J. Oper. Res. **252**(2), 351–366 (2016)
15. MacCarthy, B.L., Atthirawong, W.: Factors affecting location decisions in international operations–a Delphi study. IJOPM **23**(7), 794–818 (2003)
16. Han, Y., Guan, X., Shi, L.: Optimal supply location selection and routing for emergency material delivery with uncertain demands. In: 2010 International Conference on Information, Networking and Automation (ICINA), pp. V1-87–V1-92. IEEE (2010)
17. Hasson, F., Keeney, S., McKenna, H.: Research guidelines for the Delphi survey technique. J. Adv. Nurs. **32**(4), 1008–1015 (2000)
18. Hsu, C.C., Sandford, B.A.: The Delphi technique: making sense of consensus. Pract. assess. Res. Eval. **12**(10), 1–8 (2007)
19. Humanitarian assistance from Non-State donors (2015). http://www.devinit.org/wp-content/uploads/2015/05/Private-Funding-2015_May2015.pdf. Accessed 30 Mar 2019
20. Kapoor, P.: Systems approach to documentary maritime fraud. University of Plymouth (1987)
21. Kobus, J., Westner, M.: Ranking-type Delphi studies in IS research: step-by-step guide and analytical extension. In: 9th IADIS IS, pp. 28–38. IADIS, Vilamoura (2016)
22. Li, Y., Hu, Y., Zhang, X., Deng, Y., Mahadevan, S.: An evidential DEMATEL method to identify critical success factors in emergency management. A. Soft C. **22**, 504–510 (2014)
23. Liberatore, F., Ortuño, M.T., Tirado, G., Vitoriano, B., Scaparra, M.P.: A hierarchical compromise model for the joint optimization of recovery operations and distribution of emergency goods in humanitarian logistics. Comput. Oper. Res. **42**, 3–13 (2014)
24. Linstone, H., Turoff, M.: The Delphi Method: Techniques and Applications. Addison-Wesley, Reading (2002)
25. McMillan, S.S., King, M., Tully, M.P.: How to use the nominal group and Delphi techniques. Int. J. Clin. Pharm. **38**(3), 655–662 (2016)

26. Okoli, C., Pawlowski, S.D.: The Delphi method as a research tool: an example, design considerations and applications. Inform. Manag. **42**(1), 15–29 (2004)
27. Peres, E.Q., Brito Jr., I., Leiras, A., Yoshizaki, H.: Humanitarian logistics and disaster relief research: trends, applications, and future research directions. In: 4th International Conference Information Systems, Logistics and Supply Chain, Quebec, pp. 26–29 (2012)
28. Pettit, S.J., Beresford, A.K.: Emergency relief logistics: an evaluation of military, non-military and composite response models. Int. J. Logistics Res. Appl. **8**(4), 313–331 (2005)
29. Pettit, S., Beresford, A.: Critical success factors in the context of humanitarian aid supply chains. IJPDLM **39**(6), 450–468 (2009)
30. Rahman, M.T., Comes, T., Majchrzak, T.A.: Understanding decision support in large-scale disasters: challenges in humanitarian logistics distribution. In: International ISCRAM-MED Conference, Xanthi, pp. 106–121 (2017)
31. Rahman, M.T., Majchrzak, T.A., Comes, T.: Deep uncertainty in humanitarian logistics operations: decision-making challenges in responding to large-scale natural disasters. Int. J. Emerg. Manag. **15**(3), 276–297 (2019)
32. Rancourt, M.È., Cordeau, J.F., Laporte, G., Watkins, B.: Tactical network planning for food aid distribution in Kenya. Comput. Oper. Res. **56**, 68–83 (2015)
33. Ransikarbum, K., Mason, S.J.: Multiple-objective analysis of integrated relief supply and network restoration in humanitarian logistics operations. Int. J. Prod. Res. **54**(1), 49–68 (2016)
34. Richardson, D.A., de Leeuw, S., Dullaert, W.: Factors affecting global inventory prepositioning locations in humanitarian operations—a Delphi study. J. Bus. Logistics **37**(1), 59–74 (2016)
35. Rottkemper, B., Fischer, K.: Decision making in humanitarian logistics – a multi-objective optimization model for relocating relief goods during disaster recovery operations. In: 10th International ISCRAM Conference, Baden-Baden, pp. 647–657 (2013)
36. Rowe, G.: A guide to Delphi. Foresight **8**, 11–16 (2007)
37. Roy, P., Albores, P., Brewster, C.: Logistical framework for last mile relief distribution in humanitarian supply chains: considerations from the field. In: Proceedings of the International Conference on Manufacturing Research, Birmingham, pp. 11–13 (2012)
38. Safeer, M., Anbuudayasankar, S.P., Balkumar, K., Ganesh, K.: Analyzing transportation and distribution in emergency humanitarian logistics. Pro. Eng. **97**, 2248–2258 (2014)
39. Schmidt, R.C.: Managing Delphi surveys using nonparametric statistical techniques. Decis. Sci. **28**(3), 763–774 (1997)
40. Stewart, D., Gibson-Smith, K., MacLure, K., Mair, A., Alonso, A., Codina, C., et al.: A modified Delphi study to determine the level of consensus across the European Union on the structures, processes and desired outcomes of the management of polypharmacy in older people. PLoS ONE **12**(11), 1–17 (2017)
41. Strasser, A.: Design and evaluation of ranking-type Delphi studies using best-worst-scaling. Technol. Anal. Strateg. Manag. **31**(4), 492–501 (2018)
42. Tofighi, S., Torabi, S.A., Mansouri, S.A.: Humanitarian logistics network design under mixed uncertainty. EJOR **250**(1), 239–250 (2016)
43. Trkman, P.: The critical success factors of business process management. Int. J. Inf. Manage. **30**(2), 125–134 (2010)
44. Varho, V., Tapio, P.: Combining the qualitative and quantitative with the Q2 scenario technique—the case of transport and climate. TFSC **80**(4), 611–630 (2013)
45. Vitoriano, B., Ortuño, M.T., Tirado, G., Montero, J.: A multi-criteria optimization model for humanitarian aid distribution. J. Glob. Optim. **51**(2), 189–208 (2011)
46. Yadav, D.K., Barve, A.: Analysis of critical success factors of humanitarian supply chain: an application of interpretive structural modeling. IJDRR **12**, 213–225 (2015)
47. Özdamar, L., Ertem, M.A.: Models, solutions and enabling technologies in humanitarian logistics. Eur. J. Oper. Res. **244**(1), 55–65 (2015)

Smart Grid Challenges Through the Lens of the European General Data Protection Regulation

Jabier Martinez[1]([✉]), Alejandra Ruiz[1], Javier Puelles[1], Ibon Arechalde[2],
and Yuliya Miadzvetskaya[3]

[1] Trustech - Tecnalia, Basque Research and Technology Alliance (BRTA), Derio, Spain
{jabier.martinez,alejandra.ruiz,javier.puelles}@tecnalia.com
[2] Digital Lab Services - Tecnalia, Derio, Spain
ibon.arechalde@tecnalia.com
[3] KU Leuven Centre for IT & IP Law – Imec, Louvain, Belgium
c.author@uni.edu

Abstract. The General Data Protection Regulation (GDPR) was conceived to remove the obstacles to the free movement of personal data while ensuring the protection of natural persons with regard to the processing of such data. The Smart Grid has similar features as any privacy-critical system but, in comparison to the engineering of other architectures, has the peculiarity of being the source of energy consumption data. Electricity consumption constitutes an indirect means to infer personal information. This work looks at the Smart Grid from the perspective of the GDPR, which is especially relevant now given the current growth and diversification of the Smart Grid ecosystem. We provide a review of existing works highlighting the importance of energy consumption as valuable personal data as well as an analysis of the established Smart Grid Architecture Model and its main challenges from a legal viewpoint, in particular the challenge of sharing data with third parties.

Keywords: Smart Grid · Privacy · Data protection · Personal data · GDPR

1 Introduction

The General Data Protection Regulation (GDPR) came into force on the 25th of May 2018. The GDPR ensures the protection of natural persons with regard to the processing of their personal data and guarantees the free movement of such data provided that the appropriate safeguards are applied. The GDPR finds its legal basis in Article 16 of the Treaty on the Functioning of the European Union (TFEU), which reads as follows: "Everyone has the right to the protection of personal data concerning them". The definition of personal data has always been an issue of controversy and includes factors related

A prior version of this paper has been published in the ISD2019 Proceedings (http://aisel.aisnet.org/isd2014/proceedings2019).

© The Author(s) 2020
A. Siarheyeva et al. (Eds.): ISD 2019, LNISO 39, pp. 113–130, 2020.
https://doi.org/10.1007/978-3-030-49644-9_7

to the "physical, physiological, genetic, mental, economic, cultural or social identity of natural persons" (Art. 4(1) of the GDPR).

In the present paper, we focus on the Smart Grid, an ecosystem of hardware- and software-intensive systems with a large diversity of stakeholders. The Smart Grid is a world-wide solution towards a more reliable, efficient and sustainable electrical grid [12]. Electricity distributors and suppliers are experiencing profound changes in their business where manually reading or reconfiguring electricity meters is no longer valid. Smart Meters automatically register and transmit the data through the Power Line Carrier (PLC) or wireless connections to data concentrators and central systems using Meter Data Management (MDM) Systems. Also, several services can be remotely applied such as changing the pricing policy or activating or deactivating the electrical service.

All the stakeholders in the value chain can benefit from the Smart Grid: End users are empowered through near real-time information (24 h per day, 7 days a week) that they can use to adjust their consumption or to identify a more appropriate pricing policy. Suppliers can perform profiling and provide innovative and personalized pricing policies that can be beneficial to avoid consumption peaks or waste of energy [47]. Distributors have an effective tool to better monitor and manage their networks. In addition, smart metering promises to enable "prosumers" (both producers and consumers of energy) to be more easily rewarded for their contribution. The market around the Smart Grid includes big companies but also SMEs acting as distributors or suppliers as well as a dynamic ecosystem of third-parties providing value-added services.

Data processed in a Smart Meter includes more than one thousand parameters and metrics such as the quality of the signal, but the main one is the electricity consumption which is transmitted at very small intervals of time. That was not the case before the establishment of the Smart Grid, where the electricity consumption was measured with low frequency (e.g., on a monthly basis). The privacy-related issues mainly arise now when instantaneous data can be taken. Energy consumption can be used for guessing the data subject habits, creating a personal behaviour profile, deducing personal and socioeconomic information, listing the existing electrical equipment and monitoring their usage, or guessing the presence, absence or current activity of the residents [5, 45]. Therefore, energy consumption measurements can be considered personal data in the meaning of Art. 4 (1) of the GDPR with great potential to be processed, solely or in combination with other data, for "professional or commercial activities" (Recital (18) of the GDPR). Actually, the EU Electricity Directive (amended in 2019) explicitly mention the requirement that smart meters must comply with the EU's data protection rules [12], and the Supreme Court of an EU state member (Spain) recognized electricity consumption data as personal data [6]. Exploiting behavioral data through the Smart Grid can be motivated mainly by financial or political reasons [30] and a list and categories of privacy harms is available [23].

Other personal data such as the address, contact details, bank accounts etc. can be found in the Smart Grid context. However, these data mainly appear in administrative or organizational processes such as the billing process of distributors, suppliers and third parties. These cases fall in the general category of privacy issues for information technology services. The aspect that makes the Smart Grid special regarding privacy concerns is the energy consumption, the possibility to associate it with a data subject, and the consequences of disclosing these personal data or its usage without explicit consent.

The methodology of this work consisted on several iterations to create and refine the content with Smart Grid and GDPR experts (both researchers and practitioners) from the European PDP4E project consortium (Methods and tools for GDPR compliance through Privacy and Data Protection Engineering) [38], the Digital Lab, the Digital Energy, and the Digital Trust Technologies area at Tecnalia, as well as legal experts from the KU Leuven Centre for IT & IP Law, along with a literature review using the snowballing approach [46].

This paper is structured as follows: Sect. 2 presents background information. Then, Sect. 3 provides our analysis of the Smart Grid Architecture Model regarding the GDPR. Section 4 elaborates on the legal and technical challenges. Finally, Sect. 5 concludes this work and outlines future research objectives.

2   Background on the Smart Grid

In this section, we provide background information on electricity consumption data (Sect. 2.1), widely accepted conceptual frameworks (Sect. 2.2), and the normative spaces governing the Smart Grid context (Sect. 2.3).

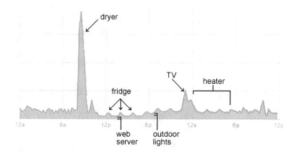

Fig. 1. Illustration of a time series of electricity consumption (Source: [16])

2.1   Electricity Consumption Data

Electricity consumption is usually represented as a time series where time is presented in the horizontal axis and the energy consumption (in watts) is presented in the vertical axis. The shape of the time series will be then defined based on the appliances used or not used in the daily lives of residents. Several techniques for time series analysis can be performed such as time series classification or forecasting [29]. For more examples on time series analyses, a taxonomy of Smart Meter data analytics is available [45]. Figure 1 is an illustrative example of a time series from the Google Power Meter project (discontinued in 2011) [16] which, once integrated with Smart Meters and with the appropriate consent, allowed users to record and visualise their own electricity consumption. We can observe how load signatures (e.g., consumption pattern of the dryer, fridge etc.) can be identified.

The simultaneous use of several appliances can make it difficult to automatically analyse time series (e.g., accumulative effect of energy consumption). However, this effect can be minimized if the load signatures were isolated at some point in time or through approximation techniques. A review by Wang et al. [45] of Smart Meter Data Analytics presents different applications of this data, and ten open data sets of Smart Meter data.

2.2 The Smart Grid Architecture Model

The Smart Grid Architecture Model (SGAM) [4] is a reference framework widely adopted by the Smart Grid community. Figure 2 is the representation of the SGAM that helps to position Smart Grid actors and use cases in a three-dimensional space of:

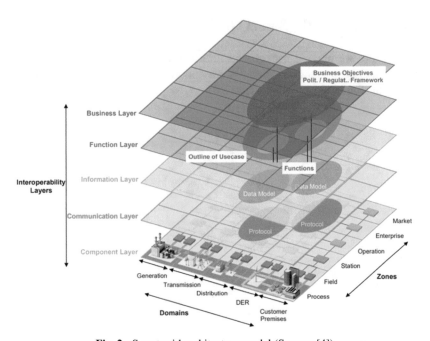

Fig. 2. Smart grid architecture model (Source: [4])

- Domains (Generation, Transmission, Distribution, Distributed Electrical Resources (DER) and Customer Premises),
- Zones (Process, Field, Station, Operation, Enterprise and Market), and
- Interoperability layers (Component, Communication, Information, Function and Business).

As mentioned in Sect. 1, Smart Meters have drastically changed the electric power industry, notably the SGAM Information and Communication layers have now much more importance compared to the era when the meters were not highly and continuously connected. Compared to the other layers, these two layers are not yet completely mature, so crosscutting concerns such as security have inevitably gained relevance.

2.3 Normative Spaces

The International Electrotechnical Commission created and maintains a standards map [22] using the SGAM as the reference conceptual framework. It currently contains information about 512 standards categorized in 16 component-related clusters. In addition, for each component, several use cases and examples are included. The standards map identifies 4 crosscutting functions: Telecommunication, Security, Electromagnetic Compatibility (EMC), and Power Quality. Another crosscutting aspect related to security is privacy which is the focus of this work.

The European Smart Grids Task Force Expert Group for Standards and Interoperability produced an interim report on My Energy Data [15], where Energy Data services were identified as subject to the GDPR. They also analysed the diversity of Smart Grid setups in different countries with respect to privacy. Our aim is to provide a general view without a special focus on country specificity. The Smart Grid Task Force also provides guidance for conducting Privacy Impact Assessment (PIA) and prepared Data Protection Impact Assessment Templates for Smart Grid and Smart Metering systems [14]. Regarding standards, a survey identified ten standards related to privacy in the Smart Grid [28]. The two of high relevance are NISTIR 7628 [36, 37], and NIST SP 800-53 [34]. NISTIR 7628 is also mentioned as the reference for security requirements for device access control and message protection in the Task Force of Privacy and Security approach at the Smart Meters Co-ordination Group.

3 Natural Persons Identifiers and Energy Consumption Through the SGAM Layers

This section presents an analysis of how the identifier of the data subject and its energy consumption is used through the technical infrastructure and stakeholders of the Smart Grid.

3.1 Component and Communication Layers

Figure 3 illustrates the Component and Communication layers of the SGAM. The Smart Meter device (bottom right) usually transfers data through the Power Line Carrier (PLC) to a Distribution Data Collector (DDC). PLC is used in some countries such as France, Spain or Italy. Others like UK or USA use wireless communications or DDCs. These DDC concentrators installed in the secondary substations, usually one per neighbourhood, are the intermediary points in the transmission to the distributor Head End System (HES) for around three hundred smart meters.

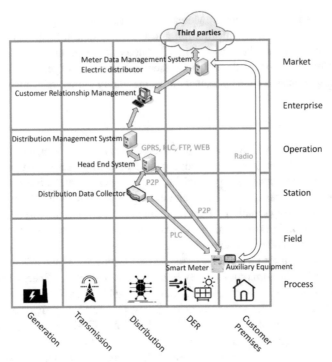

Fig. 3. Component and communication layers of the smart grid architecture

PLC does not perform well in data transmission for long distances, thus, in case of remote locations, more expensive solutions should be put in place such as Point-to-Point (P2P) protocols to send the data directly to the HES without the need of DDCs. To communicate with the HES, the DDC might use PLC, General Packet Radio Service (GPRS), other radio protocols, Digital Subscriber Lines (xDSL) or Fiber Optics. The HES communicates with the Distribution Management System (DMS) to receive the aggregated reports. Approximately, a DMS exists at national scale for each distributor. Then, already in the Enterprise SGAM zone, the DMS communicates with the Customer Relationship Management (CRM) system. The CRM system is responsible to manage and analyze the interactions with customers. The CRM communicates with the Meter Data Management System (MDMS) of the electric distributor. This MDMS is responsible to store, manage, and analyse the vast amount of data generated in the Smart Grid. For more details we refer to a survey on Advanced Metering infrastructures [33]. A huge variety of other systems, that do not belong to the traditional distributor and supplier actors of the SGAM, appear as third parties completing the ecosystem. The MDMS can communicate with these third parties to enable or complement third-party services.

Regarding the communication, the data is encrypted (e.g., AES 128 [32]) and Smart Meter devices that transmit unencrypted data are being replaced. Privacy-preserving data aggregation schemes are also being investigated to prevent the inference of electricity consumption information of specific customers when the data is aggregated [21]. The arrows in Fig. 3 are bidirectional because central systems can remotely monitor and operate in the Smart Meter through these protocols (e.g., to respond to customer requests in real-time, to change date/hour, to modify the tariff or power demand threshold). In Fig. 3, close to the Smart Meter device, the auxiliary equipment is another possible component which might directly communicate with the MDMS or with third parties. For instance, in the UK, the communication from the Smart Meter auxiliary equipment with the supplier is direct through radio, replacing the need of DDCs, HES etc. Also, electricity users can decide and consent to add auxiliary equipment to enable third-party services. This way, third parties can obtain the data without the electric distributor.

3.2 Information Layer

Figure 4 illustrates the SGAM Information layer. The Smart Meter contains the customer's supply identifier. Several identifiers can be used to link a data subject with its electrical consumption, the Smart Meter serial number (unique identifier assigned to the individual piece of hardware), MAC address (Media Access Control address, a unique identifier used as a network address for the data link layer), and the CUPs (Universal Supply Point Code) which is a unique identifier for each home or business electricity supply point which does not change in case of selecting a different supplier or energy consumption tariff.

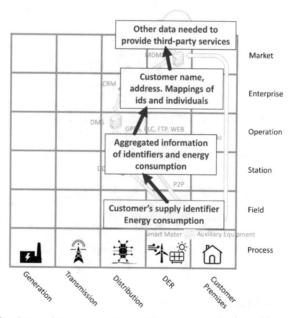

Fig. 4. Information layer of the smart grid architecture focused on the supply identifier and the energy consumption

From the Field SGAM zone where the Smart Meter is located, the information moves to the Station and Operation zones where the identifiers and energy consumption data is aggregated with those of other users. Then, at the Enterprise zone, as part of the billing process, both the distributor and the supplier have the customers' physical address, the energy consumption metrics, and the smart meter identifier. Distributors and suppliers process personal data and they might transmit this information to third parties. As we can observe, the information transverses several SGAM zones, complicating the data lineage (term used to designate the management and traceability of the data life-cycle). Figure 4 shows a coarse granularity of the information flow. The presented steps could be largely expanded using more detailed Data Flow Diagrams (DFD) with privacy-related information (e.g., [7]) on specific organizational and technological settings. However, the presented information is sufficient for the understanding of the challenges.

3.3 Function and Business Layers

Figure 5 illustrates the Function and Business layers, showing only an excerpt of all the possible functions. The data processing by the distributor or the supplier is a function related to business purposes or to improve the quality of service. The customer examining his or her consumption is also an example of function from the Customer Premises domain. Then, the data processing by third parties is a generic function referring to the diversity of current and future functions that will be available using Smart Grid information beyond distributors and suppliers.

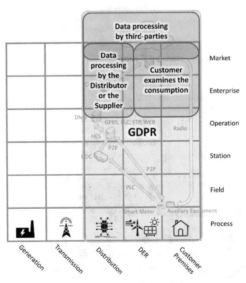

Fig. 5. Functional and business layers of the smart grid architecture showing an excerpt of the possible functions and the GDPR as business normative space

A Spanish study on the access to the electric power consumption of Smart Meters and its access and usage by third parties [40], lists more than forty companies offering services from power consumption data. Some of them use the Smart Meter from the distributor/supplier, while others offer submetering, which means the use of their own auxiliary equipment as mentioned in Sect. 3.1.

Other third parties can be related to the Internet of Things (IoT) [1]. The IoT paradigm extends physical devices and traditional real-life objects with Internet connectivity, sensors to get information about their context, and with the capacity to communicate and interact with other devices and objects to provide services. These dynamic IoT networks and the use of power consumption data are intended to unleash the promises of the Smart House [12] or the Smart City [48]. IoT also complicates the data lineage and the use of privacy technologies, given the heterogeneity, potential mobility, and usually limited resources of IoT devices and objects [1].

As we have explained in Sect. 2.3, several normative spaces are placed in the different SGAM domains and zones [22] and privacy is a prevalent topic among them. The SGAM business layer also includes normative spaces [4], so we included the GDPR as a legal act impacting all zones and domains, except the electricity generation and transmission domains, as they are unrelated to individuals. Other privacy-related normative spaces [28] will be similarly positioned.

4 Challenges

We classified GDPR related Smart Grid challenges based on different the concepts stemming from the GDPR chapters. These concepts are summarized in Table 1. Section 4.1 refers to the principles relating to processing of personal data, Sect. 4.2 elaborates on the rights of the data subject and finally, Sect. 4.3 presents the challenges linked with the obligations of controllers and processors. The controller is the GDPR entity determining the purposes for which and the means by which personal data is processed.

Table 1. Categories of challenges based on GDPR concepts

GDPR concept	
Principles relating to the processing of personal data	Section 4.1
- Lawfulness, fairness and transparency	
- Data minimisation and purpose limitation	
- Special categories of data	
Rights of the data subject	Section 4.2
- Right to information about processing operations	
- Right to access by the data subject and right to erasure	
- Right to data portability	
- The right not to be subject to a decision based solely on automated processing	
Obligations of controllers and processors	Section 4.3
- Data protection by design and by default and the security of processing	
- Data breach management	

4.1 Principles Relating to the Processing of Personal Data

Lawfulness, Fairness and Transparency The GDPR requires controllers to process personal data in a lawful manner. It entails the need for an appropriate legal basis. Art. 6 of the GDPR provides an exhaustive list of criteria for fulfilling the conditions of lawfulness. In the Smart Grid scenario two potential legal grounds for the data processing stand out as the most relevant ones: consent and contract. The performance of a contract could, for instance, be relied upon for processing electricity consumption data for billing purposes, whereas the consent might be required for conducting marketing campaigns. In all those cases the data should be collected and processed for a specific purpose and, prior to the processing, the controller should opt for the most suitable lawful ground. If there are any additional purposes of processing, a controller should obtain a separate specific and informed consent from a data subject for each of them, where the processing is consent based.

Smart Meter users can currently subscribe by giving their consent to be monitored to receive marketing offers from suppliers or be informed about the pricing policy. Even though the transmission of the personal data to third parties can contribute to the provision of extended services or to more targeted marketing offers, the data subject shall be informed of all the recipients of his or her personal data and, where required, explicitly give their consent. Such consent can be considered freely given only if it can be as easily withdrawn as it was granted. While the Smart Grid was conceived as a new field for the launch of innovative value-added services and improvement of the sustainability of our environment, the management of the consent and handling of its withdrawal, where data is transmitted across the SGAM actors and to third parties, might encounter certain technical difficulties.

Data Minimisation and Purpose Limitation
Since data minimisation and purpose limitation constitute the core GDPR principles, the personal data provided should be limited to what is strictly necessary in relation to the purposes for which they are processed, for instance for the performance of the contract, and for the supply and billing purposes. Thus, the controller must guarantee that third-party processors have the minimal amount of data to perform their intended processing. In contrast to other scenarios where this usually consists in not transmitting some columns from a database, the data minimisation of the energy consumption is different and requires manipulating the time series in different ways. A usual technique is to modify the resolution of the data. For example, the data with a time interval of seconds might not be needed and may be limited to each hour or be collected for the whole day or week. Some works suggest that a half-an-hour frequency is sufficiently reliable for most purposes and hides the operation states of most of the appliances [17]. However, in 2012, the European Commission recommended keeping a frequency under 15 min to "allow the information to be used to achieve energy savings" [12]. Several works explore the trade-offs between privacy and the operational needs of Smart Grid data mainly by investigating different data resolution schemes and load shaping [2, 8, 26, 42, 43], but this research field is still considered to have many open challenges. In fact, the Smart Grid data minimisation is a well-studied case study for the more general problem of time series compression [9].

Data minimisation could be also performed in early phases (e.g., in the Smart Meter) considering the needs of processing in the whole chain for which the data subject gave his or her consent. Failing to guarantee data minimisation can expose the controllers to fines as it is non-compliant with the GDPR. In addition, it could have the consequence that users start adopting techniques to preserve their privacy. Known techniques are charging and discharging batteries [41] or the use of load shaping with storage and distributed renewable energy sources [26].

Special Categories of Data

While weather conditions stay a typical influential factor in predicting energy consumption, data fusion can contribute to more effective Smart Grid data analysis. For example, personal energy consumption prediction and forecasting can be enhanced if other data sources are combined with energy consumption histograms. The cumulative analysis of other data sources, containing various information about a data subject (location, age, gender, socio-economic parameters like the income level, employment status, educational level, whether they are property owners, the number and type of appliances) can help to establish a correlation between electricity consumption and personal habits. On the basis of precise energy consumption details some further assumptions can be made with regard to more sensitive aspects of personal life, such as religious beliefs and practices [12]. According to Art. 9 of the GDPR, the processing of personal data revealing racial or ethnic origin, political opinions, religious or philosophical beliefs etc. is prohibited (with specific exceptions). Whereas the intense analysis of multiple data sources can improve the quality of energy services, it is crucial to strike the right balance between legitimate interests of controllers and the fundamental right to protection of personal data. Several studies are trying to identify which are the relevant variables that are worthy to use for the different analyses [19, 25, 31]. While some of these data sources might be discarded, others might be highly valuable for providing better or new services.

As mentioned before, energy consumption is a relevant information to satisfy the promises of the IoT. This way, the devices can decide when to charge, operate, or shut down, to be more cost and energy efficient. The automatic and unsupervised use of this data by the inter-connected devices can be problematic. The Smart Meter can be an inter-connected actor providing energy consumption measurements as well as other data such as the current pricing policy to other actors. Though coordination mechanisms between machines can be established, devices might disclose data or transfer data without consent (e.g., to the manufacturers). IoT manufacturers are very diverse and it is not possible to control which devices will be part of this configurable or self-configurable network at the design stage. Still they might need to transfer data between them (e.g., to accomplish their mission or to provide better and more efficient services), with the consequence of complicating the consent management for the data subjects each time a new device is added. The interconnected devices should be able to negotiate, preferably without human intervention, to make these networks efficient and self-managed. In addition, while the Smart Meter might be related to the controller for the energy consumption and the energy pricing policies, other IoT devices might be related to the controllers of other type of personal data, which will need to be aggregated to provide new or enhanced services.

4.2 Rights of the Data Subject

Right to Information About Processing Operations

The right to information about processing operations is crucial for the exercise of all other data subject's rights. If customers of the Smart Grid are not informed about processing operations over their data at the time of its collection, they will never be aware of the use of their personal data. The lack of information will prevent them from eventually taking further decisions and actions (e.g., ask for its erasure). The GDPR stipulates that the controller shall take all the appropriate measures to inform the data subject about processing related to his or her personal data. This information shall include all the contact information about the controller, the purposes of processing operations, their legal basis and also recipients of this personal data, if any. The data subject shall be also informed if there are any intentions to transfer personal data to third parties. This information shall be provided free of charge and without undue delay. Since not all SGAM actors are known in advance, especially because of the dynamic ecosystem of third parties, it might be difficult to manage the information obligation under the GDPR.

Right to Access by the Data Subject and Right to Erasure

Upon a data subject's request, it is technically challenging to guarantee the access to (Art. 15 of the GDPR) and removal (Art. 17) of the energy consumption information from all the Smart Grid actors. As in many other scenarios, the processing chain is complex and coordinating the processing actors and validating a complete access or removal might require complex operations. While there is a legal permission to keep consumption data for the billing purposes, there might be difficulties with managing and separating different data sets. Therefore, the removal will have to take into account when, how and which data should be removed from each processing party. In the context of third parties related to the IoT, there might be connectivity issues that disconnect the controller from a device for long periods of time, making difficult the actual and timely access and removal of the personal data.

Right to Data Portability

Art. 20 of the GDPR provides for the right to data portability. When a data subject wants to change his or her electricity provider, the data portability must allow personal data to be transferred directly to a new company in a practical and simple way for the end user. This might include the historic of energy consumption. Also, prior to the selection of a new company as a supplier (initiated by the user), the new potential supplier might require to perform an analysis of the personal data to identify the best personalised offer. There is a risk that companies may try to hide the access to personal data from competitors. To overcome this issue, a typification of consumption profiles (e.g., standardizing a predefined list of profiles) would contribute to data portability and provide certain degree of data minimisation.

The Right Not to be Subject to a Decision Based Solely on Automated Processing

As set out in Art. 22(1) of the GDPR, the data subject shall have the right not to be subject to a decision based solely on automated processing, including profiling, which produces legal effects concerning him or her. The wording of this provision is not straightforward and may be subject to divergent interpretations, for instance, with regard to its scope of application. The application of this provision to the Smart Grid scenario requires a detailed analysis of all the uses of personal data for profiling considerations. Moreover, there is a need to check whether a data subject might be legally affected by any decisions taken without human intervention and based solely on automated processing.

Profiling is probably the most direct use of the personal data regarding energy data consumption, and highly-personalized marketing is one of its most obvious commercial uses. One of the main objectives of customized advertisement is to create personal profiles and cluster the profiles to maximize the profitability of commercial actions. Apart from that, profiling and monitoring could leave the door open to other kind of uses such as deriving sensitive personal data or targeted monitoring. All these examples interfere with the right to privacy and the right to self-determination. In the Smart Grid scenario profiling can meet the requirement of lawfulness if it is necessary for the performance of a contract between the data subject and an electricity provider, or if it is based on the data subject's explicit consent as provided in Art. 22(2) of the GDPR.

Manufacturers are interested in knowing how people use their appliances. Each appliance has an electricity load signature which can be used to differentiate its shape from other appliances. For example, in Fig. 1 we observed a peak corresponding to a dryer, and smaller and periodic peaks corresponding to a fridge. If the appliance can be configured by the user or if the circumstances change, this signature can be modified to some extent. Thus, it is possible not only to know the existing appliances, but also how the residents use them. Newborough and Augood [35] illustrated this fact by showing the difference in the load signatures of the same washing machine using a 40 °C cycle and a 85 °C cycle.

This practice of using energy consumption and appliance load signatures for nonintrusive load monitoring (NILM), or nonintrusive appliance load monitoring (NIALM) was already identified as problematic regarding privacy when the technologies enabling it started to appear [20]. As another example of how personal preferences can be obtained, automatic analysis of time series was used by Greveler et al. [18] to show how the information about which TV channel is being watched can be disclosed through Smart Meter power usage profiles. Given the brightness of the TV screen, a consumption prediction model can be defined and used for each channel and compared with the actual consumption. This research concluded that a sample taken each 0.5 s during five minutes is in many cases sufficient to identify the viewed content. Thus, the interests of a person can be inferred through the viewed contents and used for professional or commercial purposes.

4.3   Obligations of Controllers and Processors

Data Protection by Design and by Default and Security of Processing
According to Art. 24 and 32 of the GDPR, the controller and processor should implement all the necessary technical and organisational measures in order to ensure the protection of personal data and appropriate level of security. Moreover, in its Art. 25, the GDPR emphasises the principle of data protection by design and transforms it in a cornerstone

obligation of the software development process. However, it is difficult to translate the legal rules into effective technical safeguards. Despite of this, the security of energy networks is closely intertwined with risks to the fundamental rights to data protection and privacy. Principles for privacy by design in the Smart Grid context, and aspects that Smart Grid technologies should consider regarding privacy, has been a subject of study [3]. The Smart Meters constitute a part of a massive "attack surface" and are exposed to security failures [12]. The TACIT project [44] studied the different cyber-attacks that can take place in a Smart Grid scenario. As electricity supply impacts other critical infrastructures, the cybersecurity threat to the energy sector has an effect on the whole society. Addressing data protection considerations from the design of the meters, and from all the SGAM levels, can contribute to a stronger cybersecurity.

Cyber-attacks have caused important problems for the energy sector, and the European Union has tried to address the issue with the Network and Information Security (NIS) Directive [13] that increases the harmonization of national laws of Member states. However, since the directive requires the transposition into national laws, some discrepancies across the EU might still remain. While the directive also applies to the energy sector and contains in its annex a list of energy sector organisations that could be considered as operators of essential services, it does not specify the appropriate measures and risk mitigation strategies that should be taken in order to reinforce security. According to Art. 4(1) of the NIS Directive, a risk is "any reasonably identifiable circumstance or event having a potential adverse effect on the security of network and information systems". Therefore, energy providers should implement a threat and risk management system, establish an effective incident response network, improve resilience to cyber-attacks and ensure technical and human intervention in order to address such issues [10]. Moreover, the European Commission has provided the Smart Grid industry with recommendations on how to perform such data protection impact assessments [14].

Convergent security analysis (physical and digital) is needed to guarantee the security of processing of personal data as referred to in Art. 32 of the GDPR. NIST [36] refers to it as combined cyber-physical attacks, and they can affect also privacy concerns. Smart Meters are usually located in a shared place for several apartments. As examples of security threats on a Smart Grid scenario, we can mention physically accessing the Smart Meter, watching the visible display with the counter, observing the residence or identifying the names in the post boxes. These are actions that can reveal the mapping between energy consumption and the associated person. Less populated areas present more technical problems regarding these threats. Smart Meters do not need visible displays, but they are equipped with them. They usually include a LED which blinks more when the power consumption is higher. This could be used, not only to guess the power consumption, but also to associate a Smart Meter with a person if we can link the physical observation of the residence with the visible displays or the blinking of the LED for singling out an apartment. While this kind of activity seems to be more related to sophisticated preparation of criminal activities, their usage for professional or commercial purposes might not be discarded. Also, the operators from the distributor or the supplier have access to various personal information, so privacy adherence by operating personnel must be guaranteed.

Even if the Smart Meters themselves are fully compliant with the law, their connection to other devices makes them more vulnerable. Vulnerability is exacerbated by the low security standards implemented on some IoT devices [1], so manufacturers should provide for stronger safeguards from the design stage. Recall that controllers are obliged to choose manufacturers that provide for privacy-friendly solutions. Personal data within IoT devices can be available to persons that are not authorized for it, and without the consent of the data subject. Also, Cyber-Physical Systems (CPS) [39] are highly present in the Smart Grid, and it is considered that security and privacy are hindering the development of CPS in the Smart Grid context since user actions can be monitored or devised from the data that CPS manage [24].

Data Breach Management

Cybersecurity risks include data breaches that can happen in any information system dealing with personal data. However, there is a special aspect regarding the Smart Grid, which is related to the fact that data subject privacy might have less priority than energy availability. Provided that such measures are proportionate and transparent, public safety will often overrule protection of personal data. For example, Denial-of-Service (DoS) attacks (e.g., sending large amounts of data so that the device is overloaded and it is incapable of answering legitimate requests) have more priority than Man in the middle/Sniffing and intrusion to the servers [44]. DoS has higher priority because the availability of electricity is safety-critical. Safety-critical systems are those whose failure can cause injury or death to people or harm to the environment in which they operate [27]. In other scenarios such as a non-critical web page providing some services, a data breach can be stopped by shutting down the service until the security patch is in place. In the Smart Grid, shutting down the availability of electricity can have uncontrolled or catastrophic consequences (e.g., hospitals or other critical infrastructures connected to the Smart Grid might be affected).

The trade-offs between disclosing personal data or cutting off the electricity should be investigated with appropriate risk assessments (e.g., the Data Protection Impact Assessment mentioned in the GDPR). In a hypothetical case of a data breach, a higher priority may be given to the availability of the service. Microgrid operations or islanding (autonomously providing power to a location without being connected to the main electrical grid) is being investigated to mitigate cyber-attacks and cascading effects [3, 11, 36]. Additionally, operators are asked to report incidents that affect the security, integrity and confidentiality of the service, if such incidents have a significant disruptive effect on the provision of an essential service. Regarding personal data disclosure, the impact on data subjects will need to be assessed, and data subjects or authorities will need to be informed depending on the risk assessment and the severity of the risk.

5 Conclusions

We analysed the General Data Protection Regulation (GDPR) compliance challenges of the Smart Grid and presented a characterization of the Smart Grid Model Architecture layers with respect to the GDPR. We also categorized and described Smart Grid challenges with respect to GDPR concepts and principles. The GDPR is not only limited to distributors' and suppliers' operations, but also covers the growing and diverse ecosystem of third parties providing extra services. The challenges include the large amounts of information that can be obtained from the Smart Meter via personalized profiles, the assurance and minimization of the data flows as well as the consent management before transmitting personal data to third parties. In the Smart Grid, profiling represents substantial risks to the right to data protection since one can single out what the person is doing every hour of the day. This is an important interference to the right to data protection, the right to privacy and the right to self-determination. As future plans, Smart Grid challenges will be addressed at technical level, by providing tools and methods that can help in GDPR compliance.

Acknowledgments. This work is funded by the PDP4E project, H2020 European Project Number: 787034. We would like to thank all PDP4E project partners for their valuable inputs and comments, and Marta Castro and Mikel Vergara for their discussions.

References

1. Bandyopadhyay, D., Sen, J.: Internet of Things: applications and challenges in technology and standardization. Wirel. Pers. Commun. **58**(1), 49–69 (2011)
2. Cárdenas, A.A., Amin, S., Schwartz, G., Dong, R., Sastry, S.: A game theory model for electricity theft detection and privacy-aware control in AMI systems. In: Allerton Conference on Communication, Control, and Computing, pp. 1830–1837. IEEE (2012)
3. Cavoukian, A., Polonetsky, J., Wolf, C.: SmartPrivacy for the smart grid: embedding privacy into the design of electricity conservation. IDIS **3**, 275–294 (2010)
4. CEN-CENELEC-ETSI Smart Grid Coordination Group: Smart Grid Reference Architecture (2012)
5. Chicco, G.: Customer behaviour and data analytics. In: 2016 International Conference and Exposition on Electrical and Power Engineering (EPE), pp. 771–779 (2016)
6. Consejo General del Poder Judicial: Electricity consumption data recognized as personal data by the Spanish Supreme Court (2019). http://www.poderjudicial.es/search/openDocum ent/36f4171fa1525d61/20190723. Accessed 3 Mar 2020
7. Deng, M., Wuyts, K., Scandariato, R., Preneel, B., Joosen, W.: A privacy threat analysis framework: supporting the elicitation and fulfillment of privacy requirements. Requirements Eng. **16**(1), 3–32 (2011)
8. Eibl, G., Engel, D.: Influence of data granularity on smart meter privacy. IEEE Trans. Smart Grid. **6**(2), 930–939 (2015)
9. Eichinger, F., Efros, P., Karnouskos, S., Böhm, K.: A time-series compression technique and its application to the smart grid. VLDB J. **24**(2), 193–218 (2015)
10. Energy Expert Cyber Security Platform: Cyber Security in the Energy Sector, Recommendations for the European Commission on a European Strategic Framework and Potential Future Legislative Acts for the Energy Sector (2017)
11. EU H2020: EU funding for energy beyond the "Secure, Clean and Efficient Energy" challenge (2017)
12. European Data Protection Supervisor: TechDispatch #2: Smart Meters in Smart Homes (2019)
13. European Parliament and Council: NIS Directive (EU) 2016/1148 of the European Parliament and of the Council of 6 July 2016 (2016)

14. European Smart Grids Task Force: Data protection Impact assessment template for smart grid and smart metering environment (2014)
15. European Smart Grids Task Force: My Energy Data (2016)
16. Google: Google PowerMeter (2011). https://en.wikipedia.org/wiki/Google_PowerMeter. Accessed 3 Mar 2020
17. Granell, R., Axon, C.J., Wallom, D.C.H.: Impacts of raw data temporal resolution using selected clustering methods on residential electricity load profiles. IEEE Trans. Power Syst. **30**(6), 3217–3224 (2015)
18. Greveler, U., Justus, B., Loehr, D.: Multimedia content identification through smart meter power usage profiles. In: Computers, Privacy and Data Protection (CPDP) (2012)
19. Han, Y., Sha, X., Grover-Silva, E., Michiardi, P.: On the impact of socio-economic factors on power load forecasting. In: 2014 IEEE International Conference on Big Data, pp. 742–747 (2014)
20. Hart, G.W.: Residential energy monitoring and computerized surveillance via utility power flows. IEEE Technol. Soc. Mag. **8**(2), 12–16 (1989)
21. He, D., Kumar, N., Zeadally, S., Vinel, A., Yang, L.T.: Efficient and privacy-preserving data aggregation scheme for smart grid against internal adversaries. IEEE Trans. Smart Grid **8**(5), 2411–2419 (2017)
22. International Electrotechnical Commission: Smart Grid Standards map. http://smartgridstandardsmap.com. Accessed 3 Mar 2020
23. Joyee De, S., Le Métayer D.: Privacy harm analysis: a case study on smart grids. In: IEEE Security and Privacy Workshops (SPW), pp. 58–65 (2016)
24. Karnouskos, S.: Cyber-physical systems in the smartgrid. In: 2011 9th IEEE International Conference on Industrial Informatics, pp. 20–23 (2011)
25. Kavousian, A., Rajagopal, R., Fischer, M.: Determinants of residential electricity consumption: using smart meter data to examine the effect of climate, building characteristics, appliance stock, and occupants' behavior. Energy **55**, 184–194 (2013)
26. Kement, C.E., Gultekin, H., Tavli, B., Girici, T., Uludag, S.: Comparative analysis of load-shaping-based privacy preservation strategies in a smart grid. IEEE Trans. Ind. Inf. **13**(6), 3226–3235 (2017)
27. Laprie, J.C.C., Avizienis, A., Kopetz, H. (eds.): Dependability: basic concepts and terminology. Springer, Heidelberg (1992)
28. Leszczyna, R.: Cybersecurity and privacy in standards for smart grids - a comprehensive survey. Comput. Stand. Interfaces **56**, 62–73 (2018)
29. Liao, T.W.: Clustering of time series data - a survey. Pattern Recogn. **38**(11), 1857–1874 (2005)
30. McDaniel, P., McLaughlin, S.: Security and privacy challenges in the smart grid. IEEE Secur. Priv. **7**(3), 75–77 (2009)
31. McLoughlin, F., Duffy, A., Conlon, M.: Characterising domestic electricity consumption patterns by dwelling and occupant socio-economic variables: an Irish case study. Energy Build. **48**, 240–248 (2012)
32. Miller, F.P., Vandome, A.F., McBrewster, J.: Advanced Encryption Standard (2009)
33. Mohassel, R.R., Fung, A., Mohammadi, F., Raahemifar, K.: A survey on advanced metering infrastructure. Electr. Power Energy Syst. **63**, 473–484 (2014)
34. National Institute of Standards and Technology (NIST): NIST SP 80053 Rev.4 Recommended Security Controls for Federal Information Systems and Organizations (2013)
35. Newborough, M., Augood, P.: Demand-side management opportunities for the UK domestic sector. IEE Gener. Transm. Distrib. **146**(3), 283–293 (1999)
36. NIST: NISTIR 7628: Guidelines for Smart Grid Cyber Security: Volume 2, Privacy and the Smart Grid (2014)

37. NIST: NISTIR 7628: Guidelines for Smart Grid Cybersecurity: Volume 1 - Smart Grid Cybersecurity Strategy, Architecture, and High-Level Requirements (2014)
38. PDP4E Project: Methods and Tools for GDPR Compliance through Privacy and Data Protection Engineering (2018). https://www.pdp4e-project.eu. Accessed 28 June 2019
39. Rajkumar, R., Lee, I., Sha, L., Stankovic, J.A.: Cyber-physical systems: the next computing revolution. In: DAC, pp. 731–736. ACM (2010)
40. Salas, P.: Acceso a los datos de consumo eléctrico de los contadores digitales y su uso. Estudio del caso en España y propuestas de mejora para hacer posible el acceso a los datos a terceras partes (2017). https://tinyurl.com/y4gwvrud. Accessed 3 Mar 2020
41. Salehkalaibar, S., Aminifar, F., Shahidehpour, M.: Hypothesis testing for privacy of smart meters with side information. IEEE Trans. Smart Grid **10**(2), 2059–2067 (2018)
42. Sankar, L., Rajagopalan, S.R., Mohajer, S., Poor, H.V.: Smart meter privacy: a theoretical framework. IEEE Trans. Smart Grid. **4**(2), 837–846 (2013)
43. Savi, M., Rottondi, C., Verticale, G.: Evaluation of the precision-privacy tradeoff of data perturbation for smart metering. IEEE Trans. Smart Grid. **6**(5), 2409–2416 (2015)
44. TACIT Project: Threat Assessment framework for Critical Infrastructures proTection (2016). https://www.tacit-project.eu. Accessed 3 Mar 2020
45. Wang, Y., Chen, Q., Hong, T., Kang, C.: Review of smart meter data analytics: applications, methodologies, and challenges. IEEE Trans. Smart Grid **10**(3), 3125–3148 (2018)
46. Wohlin, C.: Guidelines for snowballing in systematic literature studies and a replication in software engineering. In: EASE 2014, pp. 38:1–38:10. ACM (2014)
47. Yang, J., Zhao, J.H., Luo, F., Wen, F., Dong, Z.Y.: Decision-making for electricity retailers: a brief survey. IEEE Trans. Smart Grid. **9**(5), 4140–4153 (2018)
48. Zanella, A., Bui, N., Castellani, A., Vangelista, L., Zorzi, M.: Internet of Things for smart cities. IEEE Internet Things J. **1**(1), 22–32 (2014)

Swedish Undergraduate Information Systems Curricula: A Comparative Study

Odd Steen[✉] and Paul Pierce

Department of Informatics, Lund School of Economics and Management, Lund University, Lund, Sweden
{odd.steen,paul.pierce}@ics.lu.se

Abstract. The authors do a comprehensive comparison of the Swedish Information Systems undergraduate programs in order to on the one hand get a better understanding of how the Swedish curriculum compares to the Australian and US counter parts and on the other hand also get an understanding of where the IS field has changed over time. This change is debated to get a clearer view of what courses should be core in a post 2020 curriculum. The study points to some significant overlaps where Foundations of Information Systems, Data and Information Management, and Systems Analysis and Design are important for both Swedish, Australian, and US undergraduate IS programs. The study also shows differences in focus in the different countries' curricula, where the Swedish programs have a clear focus towards enterprise architecture and application development in comparison to both the Australian and US counterparts.

Keywords: Curriculum design · IS education · IS curriculum classification · Information systems curricula · Information system education

1 Introduction

Information Systems (IS) and the use of IS could be argued to be one of the most important, if not the most important, emblematic and ubiquitous technologies in our modern society. This implies that teaching and understanding of how IS interacts with business and society as a whole should be of central importance to all governments. Even though academic programs catering to IS knowledge started to appear in the late 1960's, the major professional body, i.e. the Association of Information Systems (AIS), was not established until the mid 1990's[1].

This indicates that the field is still young and one representation of this can be seen in the fact that we find academic programs centred around IS in many different faculties as well as different departments within the faculties. IS permeates everything in our everyday life, and the way we interact with different systems and technology increases

---

A prior version of this paper has been published in the ISD2019 Proceedings (http://aisel.aisnet.org/isd2014/proceedings2019).

[1] https://history.aisnet.org/images/Docs/Association_for_Information_Systems.pdf.

A. Siarheyeva et al. (Eds.): ISD 2019, LNISO 39, pp. 131–145, 2020.
https://doi.org/10.1007/978-3-030-49644-9_8

every day and, in that capacity, it should be apparent that an up to date and functioning IS curriculum is of vital importance. The latest guideline for IS curriculum [21] is now 10 years old and it is uncertain if it still represents the sought after curriculum for universities around the world. A few studies have been done in order to verify to what degree academic programs adhere to the IS 2010 guidelines, most notably [14] did a comprehensive study on the Australian undergraduate Information System curricula as a comparative study towards other studies done in a similar fashion. This study was envisioned to be a comparative study of [14] set in a Swedish context.

2 IS Curricula

Over the decades it has been argued that Information Systems is not a mature field and that it even exhibits some uncertainty about its own identity e.g. [17]. The IS field in itself is built on rapidly changing technologies, which would inherently suggest that the field as such must change with the evolving technologies. [20, p. 731] argues that: "the professional context in which our graduates do their work has changed considerably over the past decade, and this change should be reflected in the curriculum."

One strong factor behind this article and the mayor revision of the IS curricula that became IS2010 was a rapid decline in the study of IS as a field among student. In hindsight it could be argued that some of this decline could be attributed to the dot come bubble bursting, but this does not take away from the fact that the IS curriculum needs constant change due to the very nature of the subject being studied. This has led us to present times where we find criticism against the lack of programming in the IS 2010 Curriculum Guidelines, e.g. [1, 2, 15]. Even a program specifically designed after the IS2010 Curriculum Guidelines [4] still put quite an emphasis on programming and program design.

Furthermore, there has also been discussion on the flattened curriculum structure e.g. [13] who argue that students who work from IS 2002 will have a greater depth of knowledge in specific areas compared to students who have gone through a program which models its curriculum after IS 2010. One change from the IS 2002 curriculum compared to the IS 2010 curriculum is the inclusion of Enterprise Architecture (EA) as a core module. EA is often considered to be one of the better ways to understand how information systems align with business needs [16].

Even though we have these discussions, or criticisms, it is interesting to note that, during his 2016 study of the IS curricula in US AACSB-accredited colleges, Yang by using his current as well as 2012 work on IS curricula, concludes that IS has become a mature discipline from the perspective of academic institutions [22]. Could it be that IS as a field needs to always have an ongoing discussion, but that we now have reached some form of maturity so this doesn't imply that we are in a crisis, or that we don't have an identity but rather that it is inherent in the subject matter that we need to constantly reinvent ourselves and the field in which we are working?

3   Method

The term Information Systems (IS) is typically translated into the terms "systemveten-skap" or "informatik" in Swedish. In order to find the undergraduate IS education programs given in Sweden, we therefore searched the web using search strings for "systemvetenskap&program" and "informatik&program." This search gave us a first list of potential undergraduate IS programs. Since we know most of the other universities and IS education programs in Sweden, we first checked the generated list to see that it contained these. We then checked the intake statistics for undergraduate education programs[2] for the fall of 2018 published on the web by the Swedish Council for Higher Education to further confirm the list of institutions and programs. Through this method we found 19 programs that are either explicitly called an IS program (including Swedish derivatives of the IS term) or, by checking the curricula with expected learning outcomes, program layout and structure, etc. we deemed to be IS programs.

The kinds of program we were interested in are three years long education programs comprising 180 HEC (Higher Education Credits) according to the Bologna accord for higher education in Europe. We excluded programs that were designed as 90 HEC IS and 90 HEC of non-IS content and learning, since we do not consider such programs to be pure IS programs (the Y shape of programs in the study by [14]) in a Swedish context. An example of such a program could be 90 HEC IS and 90 HEC BA forming an IT-BA program. Other types of program that were not considered in this study, are programs that instead of a BA focus have a more technical and computer science kind of focus, which we also deemed to be outside of the scope of this study.

Each curriculum was downloaded and stored locally. Following that every syllabus for the courses offered in the programs according to the curricula were downloaded and stored locally. The curricula, syllabi, the programs, and course websites were then checked for consistency.

In order to hold the data collected for the study, we built a relational database in MySql Server 8.0 to persist the data in a structured model that made it possible to do different kinds of queries and analysis. This database was loaded with the facts about the institutions (university, faculty, and department), programs, courses, and modules found in the downloaded documents. We again ran checks against the websites and education portals of the institutions giving the IS education programs to confirm that the curricula matched the information published on the web. When it differed, we chose the information published online as this would more likely be up to date.

We retrieved the fourteen IS 2010 modules (courses) from [21, p. 35] and entered them into the database. Seven of the modules are considered as core and have assigned codes (IS2010.1 to IS2010.7)[3] while the remaining seven are example elective modules and thus lack codes. To uniquely identify all the modules, they were stored with a numerical identification index of 1 to 14.

---

[2] https://www.uhr.se/studier-och-antagning/Antagningsstatistik/soka-antagningsstatistik/.

[3] We discovered that [1] are inconsistent and that IS2010.4 is IS Project Management on page 35 but is IT Infrastructure on page 45. In our study, we have used the labels from page 35.

3.1 Coding and Analysis

The typical size in HEC of a course in a Swedish IS education program is 7.5, meaning five full-time study weeks. However, some programs have courses that are more than 7.5 HECs and thus may comprise distinct modules with name and amount of HECs specified in the syllabi. In such a case, it was treated as an identifiable module and entered into the database. If there were distinctively identifiable course exams clearly indicating course modules, they were also treated as identifiable modules and entered into the database.

The courses investigated are worth between 1 HEC and 30 HECs, where 30 HEC is equivalent to a full semester of full-time studies. 257 (73.8%) of the courses are worth 7.5 HECs, 63 (18.1%) are worth 15.0 HECs, 18 (5.2%) are worth 30.0 HECs, 5 (1.4%) are worth 6.0 HECs, 3 (0.9%) are worth between 1.0 and 4.0 HECs, and 2 (0.6%) are worth between 12.0 and 14.0 HECs.

A further analysis of bigger courses (>7.5 HECs) that were not designed with distinct modules (55 courses) revealed that 30 were degree project courses, placement courses (real-world projects), project work courses, and research methodology courses, without rationales for separate modules. This leaves 25 courses that could have associations with more than one IS 2010 module. A review of these courses' syllabi resulted in 11 courses (3.2% of all the courses) that in e.g. the expected learning outcomes clearly showed that they involved more than one IS 2010 module, for instance IS Project Management, Systems Analysis and Design, and Application Development. If it was possible to infer identifiable modules through e.g. name of exams and if it was possible to infer or guess the size of these in HEC we divided the course into distinct modules. Otherwise, we coded the course as one IS 2010 module based on the main topics and learning outcomes of the course.

In the database, courses without modules were treated as modules in themselves. Courses that had some form of modules were assigned modules identified by the course code plus an index (course code plus "-n", e.g. TIG015-1) and were associated with these modules in the database. In total, this procedure resulted in 348 distinct courses and 392 distinct modules. Hence, we inferred 44 modules from the syllabi. Each such module was then analysed by scrutinizing the module name, expected learning outcomes, content, etc. This was compared with the IS 2010 modules from [21] and the modules were either coded with 1 to 14, or, if we did not see a distinct match, with 'null'. The results of the coding were stored in the database.

In order to improve the validity of the analysis the comparison between the identified modules in our data and the IS 2010 modules was first done by the first author of the paper. This list was then checked by the second author and the differences in coding was discussed to form a joint opinion and one code. This procedure resulted in 287 modules associated with IS 2010 modules (coded 1 to 14) and 105 modules not associated with IS 2010 modules (coded 'null').

4 Findings

In Sweden, there are 36 government funded higher education institutions. Through the procedure described above we concluded that 17 of these offer 19 undergraduate IS programs that had an intake during 2018. In the text, tables, and figures we use the

ISO3366-1 alpha-2 two-letter country codes for Sweden (SE), Australia (AU), USA (US), and UK (GB).

4.1 Program Placement in Academic Division

Different to the discussion in [14], the type of academic division where the Swedish programs are placed is less straight forward. In [14] two types of divisions account for 28 out of 32 programs, namely Science, Engineering & Technology (SET) and Business divisions. The typical organization of higher education in Swedish universities and university colleges is Institution -> Faculty -> Department. There are also Business Schools that are faculties (Lund University) or departments (Örebro University). The Department of Computer and Systems Sciences (DSV) of Stockholm University is part of the Faculty of Social Sciences. At the University of Gothenburg, the department, Applied Information Technology, involved in the education program is part of the IT Faculty, which also has the department of Computer Science and Information Technology. Most of the 19 programs involve more than one faculty and at most three faculties.

Table 1. The main type of division of program placement

Main academic division type	Count
Social Science	3
Social Science and Technology	6
Technology	4
Business	4
	17

A further analysis revealed that the academic divisions where the majority of the courses of the programs were given were distributed as in Table 1. Historically, business administration has been part of Social Science divisions and hence it is fair to say that the IS undergraduate education programs in this study largely reside under the Social Science umbrella of subjects and divisions. Under this umbrella, four departments could be classified as Business.

4.2 Subject Areas Compared to the IS 2010 Curriculum Guidelines

In Table 2 the IS 2010 Curriculum Guidelines modules that we determined to be covered by the education programs are listed and the coverage calculated in percent. We added a column showing the matching figures from Table 1 in [14] rounded to one decimal.

As can be seen, two IS 2010 modules are covered by all the investigated programs (Foundations of Information Systems and Application Development) while five of the IS 2010 core modules are covered by at least close to 60% of the programs in Sweden (SE). In the Australian study (AU) by [14] four core IS 2010 modules are covered by at least close to 70% of the programs. In Table 1 in [14] only IS 2010 modules covered by

Table 2. IS 2010 modules required in Swedish (SE) and Australian (AU) undergraduate IS programs (modules with assigned IS 2010 codes are core modules)

IS 2010 code	IS 2010 subject category	SE % (n = 19)	AU % (n = 33) [14]
IS2010.1	Foundations of Information Systems	100.0%	75.7%
	Application Development	100.0%	18.2%
IS2010.2	Data and Information Management	94.7%	94.0%
IS2010.6	Systems Analysis and Design	89.5%	97.0%
	Introduction to Human-Computer Interaction	78.9%	27.3%
IS2010.4	IS Project Management	68.4%	69.7%
IS2010.3	Enterprise Architecture	57.9%	n.a.
	Enterprise Systems	47.4%	18.2%
	Business Process Management	42.1%	21.2%
IS2010.7	IS Strategy, Management and Acquisition	31.6%	30.3%
	IT Security and Risk Management	31.6%	15.2%
IS2010.5	IT Infrastructure	26.3%	45.5%
	IS Innovation and New Technologies	15.8%	n.a.
	IT Audit and Controls	0,0%	n.a.

at least five programs are listed, which might explain the "n.a." that we needed to insert in the AU column in Table 2.

There are both similarities and differences between the Swedish and Australian figures that might reflect different traditions and foci. As can be seen in Table 3, four core IS 2010 modules differ less than 10% between Sweden and Australia and thus seem to form a set of common core subjects between these countries' undergraduate IS education programs.

Table 3. Similarities between SE and AU programs with reference to IS 2010 modules

IS 2010 code	IS 2010 subject category	SE % (n = 19)	AU % (n = 33) [14]
IS2010.2	Data and Information Management	94.7%	94.0%
IS2010.6	Systems Analysis and Design	89.5%	97.0%
IS2010.4	IS Project Management	68.4%	69.7%
IS2010.7	IS Strategy, Management and Acquisition	31.6%	30.3%

The differences are shown in Table 4, where eight subject categories differ more than 10% (including the "n.a." values). Substantial differences are evident in the Application Development subject category, where 100% of the Swedish programs cover this subject while only 18.2% of the programs in the Australian study do that.

However, in Table 1 in [14] there is a non-IS 2010 subject category called Fundamentals of Programming that 78.8% of the programs in the Australian study covers. This subject could be subsumed under the IS 2010 Application Development module. If we then compare to Table 2 we still find a relatively big difference of more than 20%. Hence, one clear difference between Sweden and Australia concerning undergraduate IS education programs is that programming fundamentals is a required subject in Sweden but not in Australia.

Table 4. Major differences between SE and AU program with reference to IS 2010 modules

IS 2010 code	IS 2010 subject category	SE % (n = 19)	AU % (n = 33) [14]
IS2010.1	Foundations of Information Systems	100.0%	75.7%
	Application Development	100.0%	18.2%
	Introduction to Human-Computer Interaction	78.9%	27.3%
IS2010.3	Enterprise Architecture	57.9%	n.a.
	Enterprise Systems	47.4%	18.2%
	Business Process Management	42.1%	21.2%
	IT Security and Risk Management	31.6%	15.2%
	IS Innovation and New Technologies	15.8%	n.a.

Other important differences relate to Enterprise Architecture, Enterprise Systems, Business Process Management, and IT Infrastructure. The three former subjects are quite important in the Swedish programs since at least 40% cover them and especially Enterprise Architecture, which is close to 60%. This might have to do with coding, since the ACM/AIS IS 2010 Curriculum Guidelines [21] is a bit imprecise (necessarily so) and also more technical aspects of architecture could be coded as Enterprise Architecture, for instance a more technical level of Information Architecture or Software Oriented Architecture (SOA) with implementations using e.g. Web Services. Enterprise Architecture however did not make it to Table 1 in [14] and according to the authors, Enterprise Architecture was a distinct unit in only two Australian programs.

Finally, and what surprised us, was the low coverage of IT Infrastructure and IT Audit and Controls in Sweden with only 26.3% and 0% respectively of the programs devoting space to these subjects. Very few modules in the 19 programs concern themselves with computer and systems architecture. Rather, the fact that just over a fourth had this subject in the program has to do with the communication network part of IT Infrastructure. The

IS 2010 subject category of IT Audit and Controls is totally absent in the Swedish 19 programs and also did not make it to Table 1 in [14].

4.3 A Comparison Between Swedish, Australian, US, and GB Studies

In Table 5 this study, the Australian study [Table 1 in ref. 14] and the two US studies [22, p. 262] (US$_1$), [Table 1 in ref. 9] (US$_3$) referenced in [14] and a third US study [Table 5 in ref. 3] (US$_2$) are compared. The rows with medium blue background (darker grey in black and white) represent less than 20% difference (e.g., 80% differs 20% from 100%) between the Swedish values and the average. Rows marked with a light red background (lighter grey in black and white) represents bigger than 20% difference between Swedish values and the average.

Based on the table, it is evident that three core IS 2010 Modules (IS2010.2, IS2010.6, and IS2010.1) are very important to all the studied programs and are common to IS undergraduate programs in Sweden, Australia and USA. We also see quite similar values for IS2010.7 (except for US$_3$). Big differences exist for IS2010.5, which is quite important in the three US studies, medium important in the Australian study, and less important in the Swedish study. Another big difference is IS2010.4, which is quite important in both the Swedish and Australian studies, but less so in the three US studies. The Introduction to Human-Computer Interaction IS 2010 subject category seems to be very important in Sweden with 78.9% of the studied programs covering this kind of module compared to 27.3% in the Australian study [14] and 0.0% in the US$_1$ study [22]. Also, for IS2010.3, there is a big difference between Sweden and the other countries. At the same time is it evident in Table 5 that IS undergraduate programs in Sweden and Australia have more in common than they have with IS undergraduate programs in USA.

The study by [14] also references a similar UK study [17]. The major difference in the UK study is that they use the IS 2002 Model Curriculum and Guidelines [7] and the QAA SBSC for classification of modules and not the IS 2010 Curriculum Guidelines [21]. Hence, it is not possible to add that study to Table 5. However, the authors of the UK study [17, p. 402] conclude that "Traditional IS subjects such as systems analysis, IS theory, IS practice, programming, databases and project management were confirmed as the most popular across the 228 IS courses identified." It therefore feels safe to conclude that the UK study in [11] corresponds well with the SE findings in Table 5.

Table 5. Comparison of IS 2010 module coverage between SE, AU and three US studies (US$_2$ and US$_3$ did not provide any figures for non-core IS 2010 modules).

IS 2010 code	Subject category	SE % (n = 19)	AU % (n = 33)	US$_1$ % (n = 234)	US$_2$ % (n = 127)	US$_3$ % (n = 394)	Avg.
IS2010.2	Data and Information Management	94.7%	94.0%	94.0%	97.0%	87.3%	93,4%
IS2010.6	Systems Analysis and Design	89.5%	97.0%	90.0%	84.0%	79.7%	88,0%

(continued)

Table 5. (*continued*)

IS 2010 code	Subject category	SE % (n = 19)	AU % (n = 33)	US₁ % (n = 234)	US₂ % (n = 127)	US₃ % (n = 394)	Avg.
IS2010.1	Foundations of Information Systems	100.0%	75.7%	84.0%	87.0%	62.7%	81,9%
	Application Development	100.0%	18.2%	84.0%	n.a.	n.a.	67,4%
IS2010.5	IT Infrastructure	26.3%	45.5%	68.0%	70.0%	66.2%	55,2%
IS2010.4	IS Project Management	68.4%	69.7%	28.0%	38.0%	32.2%	47,3%
	Introduction to Human-Computer Interaction	78.9%	27.3%	0.0%	n.a.	n.a.	35,4%
IS2010.7	IS Strategy, Management and Acquisition	31.6%	30.3%	30.0%	29.0%	15.5%	27,3%
	Enterprise Systems	47.4%	18.2%	9.0%	n.a.	n.a.	24,9%
	Business Process Management	42.1%	21.2%	6.0%	n.a.	n.a.	23,1%
IS2010.3	Enterprise Architecture	57.9%	n.a.	3.0%	17.0%	13.5%	22,9%
	IT Security and Risk Management	31.6%	15.2%	9.0%	n.a.	n.a.	18,6%
	IS Innovation and New Technologies	15.8%	n.a.	5.0%	n.a.	n.a.	10,4%
	IT Audit and Controls	0.0%	n.a.	0.0%	n.a.	n.a.	0,0%

4.4 Programs Placement in Academic Division and IS 2010 Module Coverage

According to [14] the placement of the program within a SET (Science, Engineering and Technology) or a Business academic division had an impact on the size of the IS core in their study. The SET-based programs had on average 12.3 core IS units per program while Business-based programs on average had nine core IS units per program. The differences between SET-based and Business-based programs were, according to the authors, not so marked for the non-core IS units.

One program in our study covers all IS 2010 core modules and is placed in a Technology academic division. Two programs cover six IS 2010 core modules with one program residing in a Social Science and Technology division and the other in a Business division. At the other end of this scale we find four Social Science and Technology placed programs and two Technology placed programs covering four IS 2010 core modules and two Business placed programs covering three IS 2010 core modules.

The coverage of the non-core IS 2010 modules show a similar non-systematic distribution. Four programs cover five non-core IS 2010 modules. Three of these are Business type and one is Social Science and Technology type. At the other end of this scale are a Business placed program covering three non-core IS 2010 modules, two Technology and one Social Science placed programs covering two non-core IS 2010 modules, and two Social Science and Technology placed programs covering one non-core IS 2010 module. When it comes to all IS 2010 modules we also see no real differences as shown in Table 6.

Table 6. Program placement according to academic division type

IS 2010 modules	Academic division types
5	Social Science and Technology
6	Technology and Business
7	Social Science and Technology
8	Social Science and Technology
9	Technology
10	Social Science, Business, and Technology

4.5 Swedish IS Modules Compared to IS 2010 Modules

Leaving the comparison between Sweden, Australia and US programs to concentrate on the details of the Swedish programs investigated in this study, we see in Table 7 a clear relation to Table 2. In our analysis, the number of modules in the programs that we coded as associated with IS 2010 modules is consistent with the IS 2010 modules coverage by the programs. Two IS 2010 Subject Categories count for close to a fourth of the modules in our study, showing that these two represent real core modules and subjects in the studied programs. In Table 2 these two subject categories are also associated with all the 19 programs.

Table 7. IS 2010 module coverage in Swedish undergraduate IS programs (Core modules are assigned with IS 2010 codes)

IS 2010 code	IS 2010 subject category	Count	%
IS2010.1	Foundations of Information Systems	66	23,0%
	Application Development	65	22,6%
IS2010.6	Systems Analysis and Design	33	11,5%
	Introduction to Human-Computer Interaction	23	8,0%
IS2010.2	Data and Information Management	21	7,3%
IS2010.4	IS Project Management	19	6,6%
IS2010.3	Enterprise Architecture	17	5,9%
	Enterprise Systems	10	3,5%
IS2010.5	IT Infrastructure	8	2,8%
IS2010.7	IS Strategy, Management and Acquisition	8	2,8%
	Business Process Management	7	2,4%
	IT Security and Risk Management	6	2,1%
	IS Innovation and New Technologies	4	1,4%
		287	**100,0%**

In Fig. 1 the coverage of IS 2010 core and non-core modules in the Swedish programs is shown. Minimum three and maximum seven IS 2010 core modules are associated with the programs, with an average of 4.7. For the IS 2010 non-core modules the corresponding figures are between one and five with an average of 3.2.

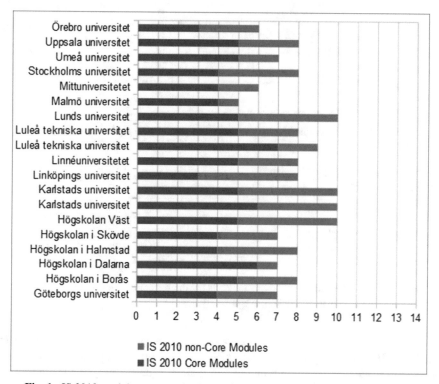

Fig. 1. IS 2010 module coverage by Swedish IS undergraduate education programs

There are a number of modules in the studied programs that we could not match with any IS 2010 module. The inferred subject categories of these are shown in Table 8.

Compulsory for undergraduate education programs in Sweden is they must include a degree project and in the case of three years long programs (180 HEC) for a general degree (not vocational programs like nursing programs) this means a bachelor's thesis. Since the IS programs in this study have their traditional base in Social Science and are of a general degree type, the degree project is a bachelor's thesis. Even though the tradition stem from Social Science is the degree normally a BSc. All the programs in this study have a thesis module and therefore several programs have distinct modules for research methods.

Table 8 shows the subject categories for the modules that we did not associate with any IS 2010 modules. As evident, research methods and degree project (BSc thesis) are in the top three non-IS 2010 module list together with modules in the Business Administration (BA) subject category. Under this subject category, we find typical BA modules of

Table 8. Subject categories for modules not associated with any IS 2010 modules in Swedish undergraduate IS programs

Subject category	Count	Percent
Business Administration	25	6.4%
Research Methods	21	5.4%
Degree Project/Bachelor's thesis[a]	20	5.1%
Placement/Real-world project	8	2.0%
Computer Science	7	1.8%
Mathematics	6	1.5%
Geographical Information Systems	4	1.0%
IT Service Management	2	0.5%
IT Law	2	0.5%
Cognitive Science	1	0.3%
Neuroscience	1	0.3%
Semiotics	1	0.3%
Language	1	0.3%
Learning Portfolio	1	0.3%
	100	**25.51%**

[a]We did not find any syllabus for the bachelor's thesis course at Stockholm University

accounting, marketing, organization and leadership, management accounting, etc. Seven programs offer the students a possibility placement or real-world projects. The subject category of Computer Science has modules of logics and data structures and algorithms. The Mathematics subject category comprises statistics, logics and discrete mathematics.

5 Conclusions

This study has mainly compared IS undergraduate programs in Sweden with a similar study done in Australia [14]. When analyzed through the lens of IS 2010 Curriculum Guidelines [21] we find that four core IS 2010 subject categories differ less than ten percentages in coverage between Swedish and Australian IS undergraduate programs: Data and Information Management, Systems Analysis and Design, IS Project Management, and IS Strategy, Management and Acquisition. Four IS 2010 core and non-core subject categories coverage that show big differences between Sweden (from relatively high to high coverage) and Australia (relatively low coverage) are: Foundations of Information Systems, Application Development, Introduction to Human-Computer Interaction, and Enterprise Architecture. The strong importance of academic division type and placement of the programs found in the Australian study is not found in this study. There seems to be no systematic variation in IS 2010 module coverage attributed to academic division type program placement in this study.

We also compared to three US studies of IS 2010 Curriculum Guidelines module coverage and found that Foundations of Information Systems, Data and Information Management, and Systems Analysis and Design are important for both Swedish, Australian, and US undergraduate IS programs. A big difference between on the one hand Sweden and Australia and on the other hand USA are IT Infrastructure which has more than 65% coverage in the US, circa 45% coverage in Australia, and just circa 26% coverage in Sweden. Another big difference is IS Project Management, which has close to 70% coverage in both Sweden and Australia, but under 40% in the US studies. Therefore, there seems to be a common core in Swedish, Australian, and US undergraduate IS programs. However, there are also important differences in e.g. the high importance of IT Infrastructure and low importance of IS Project Management in the US programs. In this respect, Swedish and Australian IS undergraduate programs have more in common than what they have with similar programs in USA.

We see that Application Development (including programming fundamentals) is still very important in all the Swedish programs, reflecting the discussions in [1, 2, 15] about the omission of this from the core of IS 2010 Curriculum Guidelines modules. One of the differences between the IS 2002 Model Curriculum [5] and the IS 2010 Curriculum Guidelines [21] is the inclusion of Enterprise Architecture as core and the problems of this as discussed in e.g. [16]. The Swedish programs have, totally different to the programs in the referenced Australian and US studies, implemented this change to a high degree with close to 60% coverage in programs and counting for close to 6% of all modules in the programs. This is not as much as e.g. Foundations of Information Systems, but far more than the closest coverage value of 17% in one of the US studies.

It is interesting to note that [19] has, at least partially, incorporated a few of the subjects we could not associate with any IS 2010 modules as discussed under Sect. 4.5. Noteworthy are Ethics and Sustainability, which are both core parts of the research methods module as well as the actual Bachelor thesis. Furthermore, Strategy and Governance could fall under IT Law. In [18] Topi discusses how the modern curricula is shaped by competencies, as also described in [19], where the knowledge, skills and human characteristics become important guideposts. This is something that we would refer to as falling under learning portfolio, cognitive science as well as real world projects.

In the IS 2010 Curriculum Guidelines a core module is Enterprise Architecture, which Table 5 shows to be more important in Sweden than in both Australia and US. Interestingly, in the MSIS 2016 global competency model for graduate degree programs in information systems [19], Enterprise Architecture (EA) is an important competence area in IS with a minimum expected competence level of at least novice. Hence, EA seems to be quite important to the curriculum and competency models authors in IS for both undergraduate and graduate level, as well as to Swedish undergraduate curriculum designers.

We have not studied graduate IS programs in Sweden and have no information about the presence of EA in those programs. The undergraduate programs in Sweden are targeted on a Swedish context and are normally taught in Swedish. The development of what was to become IS in Sweden was early on focused on application of computing in business, processes and workflows, historically marked by the difference between Börje Langefors's datalogical and infological interests in 1966 [10], his idea of using computer systems to steer and control companies [11], and the development of higher education in the area [12]. We would say that in Sweden the kinds of issues that EA addresses were already from the beginning important. EA therefore, despite its machine-like engineering view on organizations evident in e.g. the Zachman EA framework [e.g. 6, 23] as opposed to the more prevalent systems and socio-technical Swedish view rooted in the Scandinavian School [e.g. 5, 8], fits well in our tradition.

As a final reflection upon the value of IS 2010 and similar guidelines, we find they have a value in construing and aligning IS as a concept and education in various parts of the world while still giving headroom for national and/or historical differences. Without them, the field would probably be much more diverse and conceptually confusing, making it hard to compare education and curriculum designs, not least the important learning outcomes. Therefore, our view is that the work is important and needs to reflect changes in IS: Increased digitization, world shaping Digital Transformation and Automation with AI and Decisioning, IoT and Data Analytics, Social Media, etc. As we probably all experience, the pace is ever faster and there is hardly any part or aspect of society that is not affected and now also cognitive tasks in workflows are automated. Hence, IS has become one of the most powerful concepts for change and education in this area is thus central, making modernization of guidelines such as IS 2010 highly important.

6   Future Work

Looking to the findings in this study it would be interesting to extend the study to other European countries to see if European undergraduate IS programs are similar to each other and how they compare to Australian and US counterparts. Is there e.g. a European and/or Nordic IS "style"? Furthering this question would be to try to both understand why the Swedish IS curriculum has been designed to overlap IS 2010 to a greater extent than other countries. On the other end of this spectrum is how the students have perceived the education as well as curriculum, i.e. did the curriculum offered play into their choice of university? Furthering the question around how students have chosen their educational track would be to try to understand if the offered curriculum helps to fill job "voids". This could be done by comparing curriculum designs in Sweden with IS/IT job listings. We have a database that has been collecting such job postings published by The Swedish Public Employment Service between April 2018 and November 2019 and, at the time of writing this paper, is holding 45 000 postings. Analyzing that would give us an employer perspective that could be compared to the collected undergraduate IS curricula. Furthermore, potential employers could be e.g. interviewed to see the relation between job postings, interview data, and curriculum data.

In conclusion, on one hand this comparative study gave us new insights into our own IS curriculum in comparison to curricula at other Swedish as well as international institutions. On the other hand, we also identified a gap in our understanding of why students choose specific educational institutions as well as a gap in our understanding in and around how the IS curriculum in general measures up to the market needs. Fair to say, these two questions were not part of the original research question, but rather grew as new questions based on the current findings.

References

1. Babb, J.S., et al.: Confronting the issues of programming in information systems curricula: the goal is success. Inf. Syst. Educ. J. **12**(1), 42–72 (2014)
2. Baugh, J.M., Kovacs, P.J.: Programing not required? Did the is-model curriculum get it right? Issues Inf. Syst. **15**(1), 399–408 (2014)
3. Bell, C., Mills, R., Fadel, K.J.: An analysis of undergraduate information systems curricula: adoption of the IS 2010 curriculum guidelines. Commun. Assoc. Inf. Syst. **32**(2), 73–94 (2013)
4. Carlsson, S., Hedman, J., Steen, O.: Integrated curriculum for a bachelor of science in business information systems design (BISD 2010). Commun. Assoc. Inf. Syst. **26**, 525–546 (2010)
5. Ehn, P.: Work-oriented design of computer artifacts. Almqvist & Wiksell International, Stockholm (1988)
6. Finkelstein, C.: Enterprise Architecture for Integration: Rapid Delivery Methods and Technologies, 3rd edn. Information Engineering Services Pty Ltd., Perth (2015)
7. Gorgone, J., et al.: IS 2002: model curriculum and guidelines for undergraduate degree programs in information systems. Commun. Assoc. Inf. Syst. **11**(1), 1–53 (2003)
8. Greenbaum, J., Kyng, M. (eds.): Design at Work: Cooperative Design of Computer Systems. Lawrence Erlbaum, Hillsdale (1991). 294 s.
9. Hwang, D., Ma, Z., Wang, M.: The information systems core: a study from the perspective of IS core curricula in the US. Inf. Syst. Educ. J. **13**(6), 27–34 (2015)
10. Langefors, B.: Theoretical Analysis of Information Systems. Studentlittiteratur, Lund (1966)
11. Langefors, B.: System för företagsstyrning. Studentlitteratur, Lund (1968)
12. Langefors, B.: Behovet och framväxten av universitetsämnet Administrativ Databehandling. SSIaren, (2) (1979)
13. Reynolds, J.H., Ferguson, R.C., Leidig, P.M.: A tale of two curricula: the case for pre-requisites in the IS model curriculum. In: Proceedings of the EDSIG Conference (2015)
14. Richardson, J., et al.: Australian undergraduate information systems curricula: a comparative study. In: The 27th International Conference on Information Systems Development (ISD 2018). Lund University, Sweden (2018)
15. Rosenthal, P., Dhariwal, K., Whitehouse, J.: IS'15-a model curriculum reflecting the emerging IS profession. In: Proceedings of the Information Systems Educators Conference ISSN. Citeseer (2013)
16. Schell, G.: Early results-including an enterprise architecture course in information systems curricula. In: SAIS 2014 Proceedings, 35 (2014)
17. Stefanidis, A., Fitzgerald, G.: Mapping the information systems curricula in UK universities. J. Inf. Syst. Educ. **21**(4), 391–410 (2010)
18. Topi, H.: Reflections on the current state and future of information systems education. J. Inf. Syst. Educ. **30**(1), 1–9 (2019)
19. Topi, H., et al.: MSIS 2016 global competency model for graduate degree programs in information systems. Commun. Assoc. Inf. Syst. **40**(1), MSIS-i-MSIS-107 (2017)
20. Topi, H., et al.: Revising the IS model curriculum: rethinking the approach and the process. Commun. Assoc. Inf. Syst. **20**(1), 728–740 (2007)
21. Topi, H., et al.: IS 2010: curriculum guidelines for undergraduate degree programs in information systems. Commun. Assoc. Inf. Syst. **26**(1), 1–88 (2010)
22. Yang, S.C.: The core curricula of information systems undergraduate programs: a survey of AACSB-accredited colleges in the United States. J. Educ. Bus. **91**(5), 258–266 (2016)
23. Zachman, J.A.: A framework for information systems architecture. IBM Syst. J. **38**(2&3), 454–470 (1999)

Temporal Analysis in Massive Open Online Courses – Towards Identifying at-Risk Students Through Analyzing Demographical Changes

Lei Shi[1(✉)], Bokuan Yang[2], and Armando Toda[3]

[1] Durham University, Durham, UK
lei.shi@durham.ac.uk
[2] University of Liverpool, Liverpool, UK
b.yang12@student.liverpool.ac.uk
[3] University of Sao Paulo, Sao Carlos, Brazil
armando.toda@usp.br

Abstract. This chapter demonstrates a temporal analysis in Massive Open Online Courses (MOOCs), towards identifying at-risk students through analyzing their demographical changes. At-risk students are those who tend to drop out from the MOOCs. Previous studies have shown that how students interact in MOOCs could be used to identify at-risk students. Some studies considered student diversity by looking into subgroup behavior. However, most of them lack consideration of students' demographical changes. Towards bridging the gap, this study clusters students based on both their interaction with the MOOCs (activity logs) and their characteristics and explores their demographical changes along the MOOCs progress. The result shows students' demographical characteristics (membership of subgroups) changed significantly in the first half of the course and stabilized in the second half. Our findings provide insight into how students may be engaged in MOOCs and suggest the improvement of identifying at-risk students based on the temporal data.

Keywords: MOOCs · Clustering · Behavior patterns · Temporal analysis · Unsupervised machine learning · Learning analytics · Demographical characteristics

1 Introduction

Massive Open Online Courses (MOOCs) are a unique form of educational information systems offering free access to the intellectual holding of universities [35]. It has been spreading in both domestic and international education sectors. Many world-class universities have joined in the MOOC movement. A number of MOOC platforms have been launched across the globe in many subjects [21]. Despite the potential and hype

---

A prior version of this paper has been published in the ISD2019 Proceedings (http://aisel.aisnet.org/isd2014/proceedings2019).

A. Siarheyeva et al. (Eds.): ISD 2019, LNISO 39, pp. 146–163, 2020.
https://doi.org/10.1007/978-3-030-49644-9_9

associated with MOOCs, the persistence or completion rates overall are astonishingly low. Some studies reported that the completion rate could reach as low as 5% [34]. This challenge has catalyzed considerable studies on identifying dropout possibilities of MOOC students [1, 17, 27, 45], as well as how to increase persistence or completion [16, 36, 44]. The ultimate goal of this research is thus to identify the at-risk students as early as possible; such that early interventions can be injected to prevent them from dropping off from the MOOCs.

In comparison to traditional educational methods, MOOCs allow for prediction of whether a student may dropout off from a course using their prior voluntary actions logged in the database – so called "educational big data", since the dataset is normally diverse, complex and of a massive scale. Most existing studies of predicting or identifying at-risk students in MOOCs (those students who are likely to drop out from a MOOC) heavily rely on the "average/overall" analyses, lacking adequate examination of the potential differences amongst subgroups of students. This approach may produce result with potential pitfalls [5, 8, 18]. Thus, our study, presented in this chapter, aims at addressing this concern by exploring the diversity of students and their behavioral changes (the percentage of students falling into each subgroup and the subgroup transitional patterns) along the MOOCs progress.

In this study, we combine the previous study on identifying student subgroups, using both students' interaction data (behavioral) with the MOOCs and their characteristics (demographical) to allow for a more accurate clustering [11, 23, 38]. This chapter presents the student subgroups clustered from two MOOCs delivered on the Future-Learn[1] MOOC platform and visualizes demographical pattern changes of these subgroups along the courses progressed to help unmask these changes at different stages of the course. In particular, this study aims to answer the following three research questions:

RQ1. How can we subgroup students in MOOCs?
RQ2. How can demographical characteristics of each subgroup change by weeks?
RQ3. Are there transitional patterns amongst subgroups, on a weekly time scale?

2 Related Work

2.1 Learning Analytics

Learning Analytics (LA) is a rapidly expanding area, especially with the advent of "big data" era, more widely used data-driven analytics techniques, and new extensive educational media and platforms. It is defined as the measurement, collection, analysis and reporting of data about learners and their contexts, for purposes of understanding and optimizing learning and the environments in which it occurs [46]. Using LA, many studies were conducted with the aim of understanding and predicting student behavior in educational information systems.

For example, [42] used machine learning and statistical modelling techniques to explore students' engagement in MOOCs. [33] investigated students' demographical

---

[1] https://www.futurelearn.com.

information in MOOCs, intended behavior and course interactions, to investigate variables indictive of MOOC completion. [41] examined how student demographic indicators might correlated to their activities in MOOCs. [12] used dimension reduction and clustering techniques with affinity propagation to identify clusters and determine students' profiles based on their help-seeking behavior. [9] explored the effects of common MOOC discussion forum activities on peer learning and learner performance. [38] identified three influential parameters to cluster students into subgroups and profiled them by comparing various behavioral and demographical patterns, in order to investigate their engagement in MOOCs.

Most of these studies grouped or clustered learners into subgroups and compared behavioral patterns amongst subgroups allowing for a deeper understanding of how MOOC learners engage and perform. In the currently study presented in this chapter, we also used the learning analytics approach, leveraging various techniques including unsupervised machine learning and statistical modeling.

2.2 Subgroup Clustering in MOOCs

Some previous studies attempted to cluster students based on their interaction with lecture videos and assignments using a variety of methods and approaches, including bottom-up approaches to identify potential subgroups [29, 31, 38] and top-down approaches to partition students into pre-defined groups [1, 32].

For example, [24] demonstrated a clustering technique based on a derivative single variable for engagement, where they labelled all the students either as "on track" (took the assessment on time), "behind" (turned in the assessment late), "auditing" (didn't do the assessment but engaged in watching videos), or "out" (didn't participate in the course at all). [19] extracted four types of engagement trajectories, including 1) "Completing" – the students who completed the majority of the assessments; 2) "Auditing" – the students who did assessment infrequently if at all and engaged instead of watching video lectures; 3) "Disengage" – the students who did assessment at the beginning of the course but then had a marked decrease in engagement; and 4) "Sampling" – the students who watched the lecture video(s) for only one or two assessment periods. While, in their research, the authors used the k-means clustering algorithm to categorical data, to a certain extent, since they simply assigned a numerical value to each of the labels ("on tack" $= 3$, "behind" $= 2$, "auditing" $= 1$, "out" $= 0$). However, converting categorical data into numeric values does not necessarily produce meaningful results in the case where categorical domains are not ordered [20]. Therefore, these approaches have potential problems with converting participation labels, although they still can provide a viable way to cluster students based on the log data from the MOOCs platforms. In our study, to mitigate this issue, we used the one-hot encoding [6] to convert categorical data, thus reducing the impact of the categorical data.

Other studies were focused on different approaches to identifying subgroups, but most of them did not consider behavioral changes over time from the clustering [18, 22, 26, 28]. It is important to explore behavior patterns of subgroups of the students on a specific time scale, since the characteristics of each subgroup, and the proportion of its total interaction, vary along a MOOC progresses. This can also help the platform adjust the content of the course, according to the progress of the course.

In our current study, we apply a bottom-up cluster approach using the k-means++ cluster algorithm with students' log data to identify distinct subgroups as well as observe their characteristics changes on a weekly time frame, thus offering a dynamic perspective for students' subgroups.

2.3 Learning Persistence in MOOCs

Considering the problem of the low completion rates in MOOCs, learning persistence was selected as a critical MOOC outcome, which can provide valuable insights into the interactions between the course design and students factors [13, 14, 19]. Several studies have demonstrated possible ways of using learning analytics on interaction and assessment to meaningfully classify student types or subgroups and visually represent patterns of student engagement in different phases of a MOOC. For example, Coffrin et al. [11] divided weekly participation into three mutually exclusive student subgroups: Auditors – those who watched videos in a particular week instead of participating assessments; Active learners – those who participated in an assessment in a week; and Qualified learners – those who watched a video or participated in an assessment. The study investigated students' temporal engagement along course progressed. It also showed a way of combining the State-Transition diagram with an analysis of student subgroups to illustrate the students' temporal engagement in courses. Their result indicated that different courses might show similar patterns, although they were different in terms of the curriculum and assessment design.

Similar studies have attempted to compute a description for individual students in terms of how they engaged in each assessment period of a course and then applied clustering techniques to find subgroups in these engagement descriptions [15, 18, 24]. While these studies have successfully concluded the proportion of students in different subgroups by week, they did not attempt to analyze the individual subgroup changes on a specific time scale. Student behavior may change along a MOOC progresses, where they may have been labelled into one subgroup and transit to another in subsequent weeks. It is meaningful to evaluate the transitional pattern for each subgroup on a certain time scale. Therefore, in this study, we measured the proportion of students falling into each subgroup and concluded the transitional pattern for each subgroup on a weekly time frame.

3 Method

3.1 MOOCs and Dataset

The two MOOCs under study included "Leadership for Healthcare Improvement and Innovation" and "Supply Chains in Practice: How Things Get to you", delivered on FutureLearn, a MOOC platform that is freely available for everyone. Each MOOC was structured in weekly learning units. A weekly learning unit was composed of a few learning blocks, each of which consisted of a number of steps. Steps were the basic learning items, which contained lecture streams that the students needed to access, during the learning process. Both MOOCs were *synchronous* – having an official starting week, considered as Week 1 in this study, with a duration of six weeks, and an ending week, i.e. Week 6.

Both MOOCs attracted thousands of students. However, only around 7% of them finally completed the courses, reflecting one the of the biggest challenges in MOOC platforms – the low retention/completion rate [10]. According their completion, we categorized the students as the following:

- *Registered students* – have enrolled in the course
- *Participated students* – have attended at least one steps
- *Completed students* – have completed the courses by the end of Week 6
- *Purchased students* – have bought the certificate of the course.

Table 1 shows the statistics for these two courses.

Table 1. Course design and participants.

Course	"Leadership for healthcare improvement and innovation"	"Supply chain in practice: How things get to you"
Duration of the course	6 weeks	6 weeks
Total steps	73	109
Registered students	4,046	5,808
Participated students	2,397	2,924
Completed students	377	318
Purchased students	149	69

The dataset used in this study was from those two MOOCs and included:

- Step record – which student at what time visited which step; when they marked a step as complete.
- Comment record – which student at what time left what comment on which step; how many "likes" a comment received.
- Student record – students' demographical information such as gender, age group, country, highest educational level, employment status, as shown in Table 2.

Students' demographical information was collected using a pre-course survey asking optional questions about their gender, age group, country, and so on, as shown in Table 2, the column on the left. Only 9.5% of the students (506 out of 5,321) answered all the survey questions. As using incomplete student record would affect the result of the analysis, in this study we only used the records of students who answered all the survey questions.

Table 2. Demographic information in student record.

Variable	Description
User ID	The unique identifier for a student
Gender	The gender of the student
Age group	The age group where the student belongs to
Country	The country where the student belongs to
Highest educational level	Student's highest education level
Employment status	Students' employment status
Employment area	Students' employment area

3.2 Subgroup Clustering

In previous studies, watching lecture videos and submitting assignments were used for clustering students [18, 22]. Considering the conversational framework of FutureLearn and the course design, two interactive indicators were generated from the step record and the comment record:

- Steps visited – the proportional of all the steps available visited by a given student in a given week.
- Comments submitted – the number of comments submitted by a given student in a given week) and the gender (of a given student).

Other studies, e.g. [2, 38], used demographical indicators such as gender and age to predict student engagement; [37, 40] focused on the use of learning platform's features in order to analyze learning behavior patterns. Different from these previous studies, in this study, we selected both students' demographical data and their interaction (activity logs) data for the clustering process. We excluded the highly correlated variables with the numbers of steps visited or comments submitted, leaving gender as an extra variable for the clustering process.

The clustering process was based on the k-means++ algorithm [4], which could reduce the influence of randomly assigned initial centroids in the *k-means* algorithm [30]. Similar to previous studies, e.g. [42], we used the "Elbow method" to select the reference k value for the k-means++ algorithm [25]. We used a number of k values around the reference k to cluster subgroups of the students, and then we conducted Kruskal-Wallis H tests and Mann-Whitney U tests to examine whether the k value could differentiate subgroups on every clustering variable. Moreover, different from most existing studies, which used cumulative data from the entire course to cluster subgroups of the students, in this study, we used cumulative data from each week for the subgroups clustering.

3.3   Transitional Pattern for Subgroups

We clustered students into subgroups based on their temporary behavioral data (how they interact with the MOOCs including how they visited steps and submitted comments, from one week to another). We used State-Transition diagrams to visualize the weekly transitional patterns amongst the subgroups, where the dropped-out students were marked into a different subgroup. Similar to the subgroup clustering, two indicators were generated: 1) the number of steps a student visited, and 2) the number of comments a student submitted, as defined in Sect. 3.2. From the State-Transition diagram, we analyzed the proportion for students falling into each of the subgroups by week and generalized the transitional pattern for different subgroups each week.

4   Result

4.1   Subgroup Clustering

In this study, we selected the percentage (instead of the raw number) of the steps visited, and the number of comments submitted, by the students, as prime cluster variables, with additional demographical variables selected from the student record. From the correlation analysis, we excluded highly correlated variables. More specifically, we used the η (eta) statistics to measure the degree of association between categorical and numeric variables – the independent variable Y, i.e. Steps and Comments, and the dependent variable X, i.e. Gender, Country, Age range, Educational level, Employment area and Employment status, as Table 2 shows.

For the association between the categorical variables, we used the Chi-square test with the significant level $= 0.05$. The result suggested a strong association between the variables of Gender and Employment area ($\chi^2(23) = 39.9, p < 0.05$). Therefore, only one of these two variables might be selected as a clustering variable. Considering the fact that the MOOCs analyzed in this study were specialized in certain subjects thus maybe resulting in special employment distribution, the gender variable was selected for a general conclusion. Therefore, our absolute selection of variables included:

- Steps – the percentage of steps visited by a student.
- Comments – the number of comments submitted by a student.
- Gender – the gender of a student.

Although the FutureLearn MOOC platform provides multiple gender options in the pre-course survey, we only considered two options – *female* and *male*, as the other options were very underrepresented. Therefore, we considered the gender variable as a dummy variable and we used 0 to represent the option of *female* and 1 to represent the option of *male*.

Using the "elbow method", Mann-Whitney U tests and the K-means++ clustering algorithm, we successfully clustered those 506 students into three distinct subgroups based on the cumulative data. More specifically, we used the "elbow method" to estimate the optimal k value for the k-means++ algorithm processed in this study – the result can be seen below in Fig. 1.

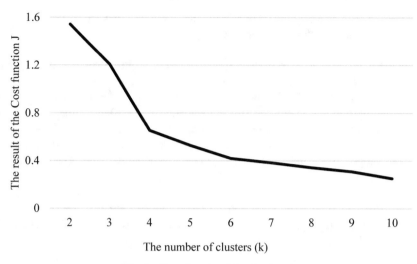

Fig. 1. Cost function J for the dataset

The "elbow method" believes that one should choose a number of clusters so that adding another cluster does not offer much better modelling of the data. As shown in Fig. 1, the result of *cost function J* experienced the most significant decrease in $k = 4$ (where the "elbow" appears). Therefore, the $k = 4$ was chosen as a reference k value candidate in the subsequent analysis. Based on this reference k value, we used several k values, ranging from 2 to 5, in order to cluster student into subgroups. In this case, the Mann-Whitney U test with significant level $= 0.05$ was chosen to validate whether there was a significant difference among these subgroups of the students, and the results suggested that neither $k = 4$ nor $k = 5$ could differentiate subgroups. Therefore, we chose $k = 3$ in this study and the cluster results can be seen below in Table 3 below.

Table 3. Subgroup cluster centroids.

	Steps	Comments	Gender	N
Cluster 1 – Samplers	.926	7.16	.360	113
Cluster 2 – Viewers	.107	.91	.353	369
Cluster 3 – All-rounders	.990	67.54	.550	24

Based on the previous work [3], where the authors labelled students into three subgroups, based on lecture video watching and assignment submission: Viewer (primary watching lecture videos, handing in few if any assignments), Solvers (primary handing in assignments, viewing few if any lecture videos) and All-rounders (balancing between watching lecture videos and handing in assignments). On the basis of this work, we further clustered students by their positivity. In this study, we did not choose assignment submission as one of the clustering variables, but we chose the number of comments submitted, to replace assignment submission, as in the previous work. We labelled all those 506 students into the following subgroups:

- **Viewers** (Cluster 1; 22.33% of the total population): overall, they visited a very high percentage (92.6%) of the steps but submitted very few comments (Mean = 7.16).
- **Samplers** (Cluster 2; 72.92% of the whole population): they made up the largest student subgroup, but they were also the least engaged students – they visited only 10.7% of the steps and on average they left only 0.91 comments.
- **All-rounders** (Cluster 3; 4.74% of the total population). They made up the smallest student subgroup, yet they were the most engaged students – they visited 99.0% of the steps and on average they left 67.54 comments.

From this subgrouping method and its result, we can see that the least engaged students occupied the largest percentage of the total population. This is consistent with many previous studies, e.g., [7, 43], and has been one of the biggest challenged in the field of MOOCs.

4.2   Weekly Changes of Cluster Centroid

In order to explore the temporal changes of subgroup memberships, we further divided the students into two categories based on the number of steps they have visited and the number of comments they have submitted. The students who had partially participated (i.e. they have submitted at least one comment or visited at least one step) the courses in a given week were selected and clustered into 3 subgroups, based on the k-means++ algorithm. Steps, comments and gender were selected as the input variables for the clustering process. As shown in Table 4, the cluster centroids stabilized at a certain level across weeks, which suggests that the same subgroup had a similar behavior pattern at different stages of the MOOCs.

4.3   Weekly Changes of Subgroup

To investigate how the subgroups changed along the MOOCs, the percentage of the students labelled in each subgroup per week were also retrieved from the dataset. From Fig. 2 and Table 5 we can see that the first half of the MOOC and the second half of the MOOC had very different demographical characteristics, where the percentage of the students in each subgroup changed significantly in the first half of the courses (between Week 1 and Week 3). More specifically, the percentage of Samplers decreased from 50.4% to 17%, which may be caused by a large number of dropout students in the first two weeks. The proportion of Viewers increased significantly from 42.8% in Week 1 to 68.8% in Week 3 and kept stable at a certain level in the rest of the weeks. The proportion of All-rounders kept at a relatively stable level, i.e. around 10.0%, which suggests that these students were relatively stable, even in the beginning weeks when many students dropped out, and that this type of students had more chance to complete the MOOCs.

Here, we use the State-Transition Diagram to present in detail how the students shifted between subgroups, i.e. the changes of the students' memberships of the subgroups. We assumed possible student subgroups, i.e. Sampler, Viewer, All-rounder and

Table 4. Centroids for weekly subgroups.

		Steps	Comments	Gender
Viewer	Week 1	0.964	1.300	0.544
	Week 2	0.979	0.934	0.610
	Week 3	0.988	0.792	0.625
	Week 4	0.936	0.624	0.624
	Week 5	0.986	0.784	0.589
	Week 6	0.971	1.490	0.640
Sampler	Week 1	0.214	0.300	0.428
	Week 2	0.229	0.195	0.507
	Week 3	0.207	0.000	0.467
	Week 4	0.206	0.035	0.517
	Week 5	0.259	0.105	0.526
	Week 6	0.180	0.133	0.467
All-rounder	Week 1	0.986	11.886	0.571
	Week 2	0.998	12.138	0.483
	Week 3	0.990	10.880	0.560
	Week 4	1.000	10.583	0.625
	Week 5	0.998	12.320	0.640
	Week 6	0.952	14.875	0.687

Drop-out, as four possible states each week, and the transitions from one subgroup to another was indicated by the arcs between two states. Figure 3 provides a legend to understand the State-Transition Diagram used in the analysis. The legend shows two sub-groups, A and B; the arcs between circles represent the students transited their subgroup from A to B in a subsequent week. In order to better visualize the number of students in each subgroup in each transition, the circle areas and arc's weight are linearly related to the number of students in the subgroups and the transitions respectively.

Figure 4 demonstrates the demographical changes for the Sampler subgroup – a very large proportion of the Samplers dropped out from the courses in the following weeks, while only a small percentage of them maintained their behavior or transited to become Viewers. This means that, the Samplers are definitely the "at-risk" students, who need immediate interventions to prevent them from drooping out from the MOOCs. Apart from the first week, no student had transited from the Sampler subgroup to the All-rounder subgroup (the most active and engaged group) in the following weeks, which suggests that, without any intervention, it is very unlikely for a highly inactive student to become highly active in a short period. Therefore, it is crucial that, early intervention is injected, once a student is detected or identified as being inactive or less engaged.

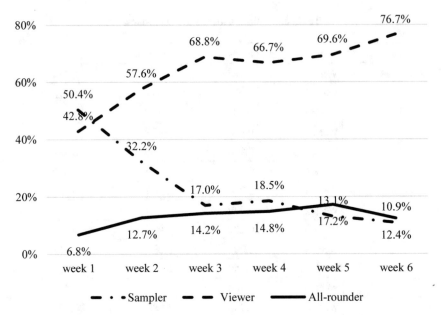

Fig. 2. The percentage of students each subgroup across weeks

Table 5. The number of students each subgroup across weeks.

	Sampler	Viewer	All-rounder
Week 1	252	214	34
Week 2	76	136	30
Week 3	30	121	25
Week 4	30	108	24
Week 5	19	101	25
Week 6	14	99	16

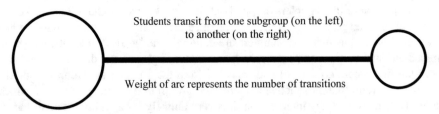

Fig. 3. State-transition diagram legend

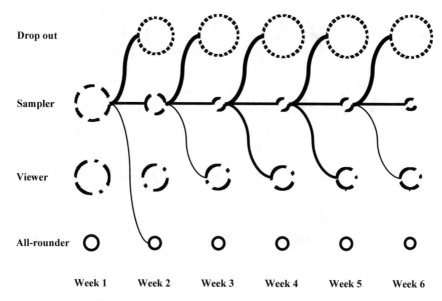

Fig. 4. Samplers' demographical changes across weeks

For example, a reminder email could be sent to them, emphasizing the importance of keeping up with the MOOC.

Figure 5 focuses on the demographical changes for the Viewer subgroup, which also indicates that each subgroup had a similar behavioral pattern transition each week. However, different from the Sampler subgroup, most students belong to the Viewer subgroup maintained their behavior patterns in the following week with only a very small percentage of them dropped out from the courses or transited to another subgroups. As it was unlikely that these students would drop out from the MOOCs, they were not clearly not as "at-risk" as those Sampler students. Nevertheless, according to the definition of Viewer (as per Sect. 4.2), although these students were focused on accessing learning materials, they did not tend to interact with peers. Previous studies, e.g. [39], have demonstrated that social interactions might be very helpful for the students to have better learning result in MOOCs. Therefore, some mild interventions, such as an email promoting participation in the discussion forum, may be very useful to be provided with.

Similarly, Fig. 6 shows that while All-rounders represented the smallest proportion of the students, they were the most stable subgroup – there was no significant demographical fluctuation event in the first half of the MOOCs, where the number of Samplers and the number of Viewers decreased from 250 to 30 and from 215 to 120, respectively. Students belong to this subgroup are clearly the least "at-risk" students. This means that it may be not necessary to provide them with any interventions; and on the contrary, unnecessary interventions may cause these students being interrupted thus becoming less active or engaged. In another word, when providing interventions, it is crucial to have a clear target group of students, as well as to avoid interrupt the students who do not need any intervention.

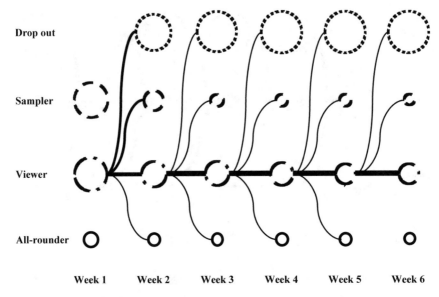

Fig. 5. Viewers' demographical changes across weeks

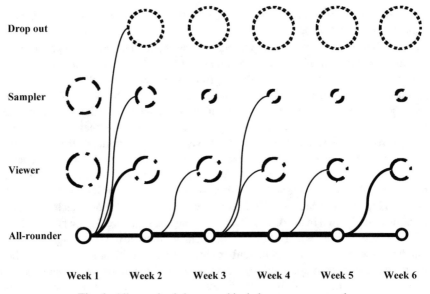

Fig. 6. All-rounders' demographical changes across weeks

5   Discussions

This chapter demonstrates a temporal analysis in Massive Open Online Courses (MOOCs), towards identifying at-risk students through analyzing their demographical changes. At-risk students are those who tend to drop out from the MOOCs. In this study, we have examined how students' memberships of subgroups changed on a weekly time scale. Different from previous studies that used behavioral data to pre-define or cluster student subgroups, our study used both interaction log data and students' characteristics (gender, in particular).

In particular, to answer the first research question, **RQ1**, we clustered students into three distinct subgroups using the K-means++ algorithm and the "elbow method", as well as the Mann-Whitney test. Three subgroups, including *Sampler*, *Viewer* and *All-rounder*, were generalized. We have analyzed the differences amongst these subgroups and measured the proportion of students in different subgroups by week. To answer the second research question, **RQ2**, we examined the demographical changes for students labelled in each subgroup where we found that using similar cluster approaches on weekly accumulated data could generate similar subgroups as the overall clustering result. Most of the subgroup's centroid remained stable within a certain range except All-rounders with the number of comments continuously rising in the second half of the course. To answer the third research question, **RQ3**, we visualized the demographical changes of subgroups across weeks. Our result suggests that the first half of the course, i.e. Week 1 to Week 3, and the second half of the course, i.e. Week 4 to Week 6, had different demographical characteristic. The demographics of these subgroups changed significantly from the first half of the former and maintained a certain degree of stability in the second half. More specifically, our study suggests that the less active subgroups took up most of the participants in the early courses, and as the course progressed, the proportion of those subgroups continued shrinking to around 10% (see Fig. 2). This result is opposite to those from previous studies which assume proportion of participants falling into each category keep stable to some extent along courses progress.

For the transition of each subgroup, our result demonstrates that each of them had similar transitional pattern along the MOOCs progressed – most of the Samplers dropped out in the subsequent week with only a small percentage of them kept Sampler's behavior unchanged or transited into the Viewer subgroup. A large proportion of the Viewers maintained the same behavior pattern to a subsequent week, and a relatively small percentage of these students transited to the Sampler or All-rounder subgroups, or simply dropped out. The All-rounder was the most stable subgroup – the demographical characteristics stabled from the beginning to the end of the MOOCs, i.e. from Week 1 to Week 6. Interestingly, the result in Sect. 4.3 suggests that it was almost impossible for the students to switch from being highly inactive (Sampler, as in this study) to being highly active (All-rounder, as in this study) in a short period of time, and vice-versa. Therefore, once being detected or identified as inactive, these students should be strongly intervened, and as early as possible, in order to prevent them from dropping out from the MOOC; whereas for the active students, strong intervention may be not necessary, but mild interventions may be still useful to keep them active, as discussed in Sect. 4.3.

6   Conclusions

To conclude, in this study we have analyzed students' data from two MOOCs offered by the FutureLearn platform. The result suggests that the first half and second half of both MOOCs had different demographical characteristics and each student subgroup had their unique behavior and transitional pattern along the MOOCs progressed. Given the fact that MOOC students have various study behavior, with a very different interaction patterns with the course materials and their peers, when designing MOOCs, there is a strong need for providing personalized support to students that can be labelled into different subgroup at different stages of the MOOC. This means that the MOOC platforms should personalize the way their users learn, such as adapting learning paths and supporting adaptive intervention for different subgroups of students. Moreover, the subgroups identified in this study and the weekly demographical changes of those clusters may help inform a range of strategies for the intervention and improvement of MOOCs and MOOC platforms. For example, providing more previews of learning materials allows Sampler students to make a more informed decision about whether to participate in the first place. Offering more reminders for students who labelled as Sampler on unfinished steps and reduce the incentives for their comment submissions.

This study contributes to the understanding of subgroup clustering and demographical changes in MOOCs. Empirical evidence from this study supports that students' characteristics can also be used as clustering variables/indicators, and the proportion of different subgroups in the total number of students each week may vary along the MOOCs progress. These results highlight the importance of examining subgroup to improve the effectiveness of the identification of at-risk students.

In future studies, the same research approach could be applied into MOOCs with more general content where there are more attributes with less association with students' interaction data (the number of steps that a student visited and the number of comments that a student submitted, as in current study). In this study, the course "Leadership for healthcare improvement and innovation" does not contain any assignment, hence the assessment factor was not considered in subgroup clustering. In a future study, the assignment submission and grade could also be considered as clustering variables/indicators.

In terms of limitations, first, the dataset available was limited – after removing students with incomplete information, only 506 students' data was retained, and those students might share different characteristics with eliminated students. Second, the filed involved in the MOOCs used in this study were highly targeted. Third, the MOOCs that we were focused on were unique in duration and structure in which students needed to access both a large number of steps and tools supporting reflection, comment and response. Therefore, the conclusion drawn from the analysis of the dataset may be not universally applicable to a MOOC in the other fields.

References

1. Alamri, A., et al.: Predicting MOOCs dropout using only two easily obtainable features from the first week's activities. In: Coy, A., et al. (eds.) Intelligent Tutoring Systems, pp. 163–173. Springer International Publishing, Cham (2019). https://doi.org/10.1007/978-3-030-22244-4_20
2. Alshehri, M., et al.: On the Need for fine-grained analysis of gender versus commenting behaviour in MOOCs. In: Proceedings of the 2018 the 3rd International Conference on Information and Education Innovations - ICIEI 2018, pp. 73–77. ACM Press, London (2018). https://doi.org/10.1145/3234825.3234833

3. Anderson, A., et al.: Engaging with massive online courses. In: Proceedings of the 23rd International Conference on World Wide Web - WWW 2014, Seoul, Korea, pp. 687–698. ACM Press (2014). https://doi.org/10.1145/2566486.2568042

4. Arthur, D., Vassilvitskii, S.: k-means++: the advantages of careful seeding. http://ilpubs.sta nford.edu:8090/778/. Accessed 05 Mar 2020

5. de Barba, P.G., et al.: The Role of students' motivation and participation in predicting performance in a MOOC: motivation and participation in MOOCs. J. Comput. Assist. Learn. **32**(3), 218–231 (2016). https://doi.org/10.1111/jcal.12130

6. Beck, J.E., Woolf, B.P.: High-level student modeling with machine learning. In: Gauthier, G., et al. (eds.) Intelligent Tutoring Systems, pp. 584–593. Springer, Heidelberg (2000). https://doi.org/10.1007/3-540-45108-0_62

7. Bote-Lorenzo, M.L., Gómez-Sánchez, E.: Predicting the decrease of engagement indicators in a MOOC. In: Proceedings of the Seventh International Learning Analytics & Knowledge Conference on - LAK 2017, Vancouver, British Columbia, Canada, pp. 143–147. ACM Press (2017). https://doi.org/10.1145/3027385.3027387

8. Brinton, C.G., et al.: Mining MOOC clickstreams: on the relationship between learner behavior and performance. arXiv preprint arXiv:1503.06489 (2015)

9. Chiu, T.K.F., Hew, T.K.F.: Factors influencing peer learning and performance in MOOC asynchronous online discussion forum. Australas. J. Educ. Technol. (2017). https://doi.org/10.14742/ajet.3240

10. Clow, D.: MOOCs and the funnel of participation. In: Proceedings of the Third International Conference on Learning Analytics and Knowledge - LAK 2013, Leuven, Belgium, p. 185. ACM Press (2013). https://doi.org/10.1145/2460296.2460332

11. Coffrin, C., et al.: Visualizing patterns of student engagement and performance in MOOCs. In: Proceedings of the Fourth International Conference on Learning Analytics and Knowledge - LAK 2014, Indianapolis, Indiana, pp. 83–92. ACM Press (2014). https://doi.org/10.1145/2567574.2567586

12. Corrin, L., et al.: Using learning analytics to explore help-seeking learner profiles in MOOCs. In: Proceedings of the Seventh International Learning Analytics & Knowledge Conference on - LAK 2017, Vancouver, British Columbia, Canada, pp. 424–428. ACM Press (2017). https://doi.org/10.1145/3027385.3027448

13. Cristea, A.I., et al.: Can learner characteristics predict their behaviour on MOOCs? In: Proceedings of the 10th International Conference on Education Technology and Computers - ICETC 2018, pp. 119–128, Tokyo, Japan. ACM Press (2018). https://doi.org/10.1145/3290511.3290568

14. Cristea, A.I., et al.: Earliest predictor of dropout in MOOCs: a longitudinal study of FutureLearn courses. In: Presented at the 27th International Conference on Information Systems Development (ISD2018), Lund, Sweden, 22 August 2018

15. Cristea, A.I., et al.: How is learning fluctuating? FutureLearn MOOCs fine-grained temporal analysis and feedback to teachers and designers. In: 27th International Conference on Information Systems Development (ISD2018), Lund, Sweden. Association for Information Systems (2018)

16. Evans, B.J., et al.: Persistence patterns in massive open online courses (MOOCs). J. High. Educ. **87**(2), 206–242 (2016). https://doi.org/10.1353/jhe.2016.0006

17. Feng, W., et al.: Understanding dropouts in MOOCs. In: AAAI, vol. 33, pp. 517–524 (2019). https://doi.org/10.1609/aaai.v33i01.3301517

18. Ferguson, R., Clow, D.: Examining engagement: analysing learner subpopulations in massive open online courses (MOOCs). In: Proceedings of the Fifth International Conference on Learning Analytics And Knowledge - LAK 2015, Poughkeepsie, New York, pp. 51–58 ACM Press (2015). https://doi.org/10.1145/2723576.2723606

19. Halawa, S., et al.: Dropout prediction in MOOCs using learner activity features. In: Proceedings of the Second European MOOC Stakeholder Summit, vol. 37, no. 1, pp. 58–65 (2014)
20. Huang, Z.: Extensions to the k-Means algorithm for clustering large data sets with categorical values. Data Min. Knowl. Discov. **2**(3), 283–304 (1998). https://doi.org/10.1023/A:100976 9707641
21. Jung, Y., Lee, J.: Learning engagement and persistence in massive open online courses (MOOCS). Comput. Educ. **122**, 9–22 (2018). https://doi.org/10.1016/j.compedu.2018.02.013
22. Khalil, M., Ebner, M.: Clustering patterns of engagement in massive open online courses (MOOCs): the use of learning analytics to reveal student categories. J. Comput. High. Educ. **29**(1), 114–132 (2017). https://doi.org/10.1007/s12528-016-9126-9
23. Khalil, M., Ebner, M.: What massive open online course (MOOC) stakeholders can learn from learning analytics? arXiv:1606.02911 [cs], pp. 1–30 (2016). https://doi.org/10.1007/978-3-319-17727-4_3-1
24. Kizilcec, R.F., et al.: Deconstructing disengagement: analyzing learner subpopulations in massive open online courses. In: Proceedings of the Third International Conference on Learning Analytics and Knowledge, pp. 170–179. ACM (2013)
25. Kodinariya, T.M., Makwana, P.R.: Review on determining number of cluster in K-Means clustering. Int. J. **1**(6), 90–95 (2013)
26. Kovanović, V., et al.: Profiling MOOC course returners: how does student behavior change between two course enrollments? In: Proceedings of the Third (2016) ACM Conference on Learning @ Scale - L@S 2016, Edinburgh, Scotland, UK, pp. 269–272. ACM Press (2016). https://doi.org/10.1145/2876034.2893431
27. Li, B., et al.: What makes MOOC users persist in completing MOOCs? a perspective from network externalities and human factors. Comput. Hum. Behav. **85**, 385–395 (2018). https://doi.org/10.1016/j.chb.2018.04.028
28. Li, Q., Baker, R.: The different relationships between engagement and outcomes across participant subgroups in massive open online courses. Comput. Educ. **127**, 41–65 (2018). https://doi.org/10.1016/j.compedu.2018.08.005
29. Liao, J., et al.: Course drop-out prediction on MOOC platform via clustering and tensor completion. Tinshhua Sci. Technol. **24**(4), 412–422 (2019). https://doi.org/10.26599/TST.2018.9010110
30. Likas, A., et al.: The global k-means clustering algorithm. Pattern Recogn. **36**(2), 451–461 (2003). https://doi.org/10.1016/S0031-3203(02)00060-2
31. Maldonado-Mahauad, J., et al.: Predicting learners' success in a self-paced MOOC through sequence patterns of self-regulated learning. In: Pammer-Schindler, V., et al. (eds.) Lifelong Technology-Enhanced Learning, pp. 355–369. Springer International Publishing, Cham (2018). https://doi.org/10.1007/978-3-319-98572-5_27
32. Peng, X., Xu, Q.: Investigating learners' behaviors and discourse content in MOOC course reviews. Comput. Educ. **143**, 103673 (2020). https://doi.org/10.1016/j.compedu.2019.103673
33. Pursel, B.K., et al.: Understanding MOOC students: motivations and behaviours indicative of MOOC completion: MOOC student motivations and behaviors. J. Comput. Assist. Learn. **32**(3), 202–217 (2016). https://doi.org/10.1111/jcal.12131
34. Reich, J., Ruipérez-Valiente, J.A.: The MOOC pivot. Science **363**(6423), 130–131 (2019). https://doi.org/10.1126/science.aav7958
35. Rieber, L.P.: Participation patterns in a massive open online course (MOOC) about statistics: MOOC participation. Br. J. Educ. Technol. **48**(6), 1295–1304 (2017). https://doi.org/10.1111/bjet.12504
36. Salmon, G., et al.: Designing massive open online courses to take account of participant motivations and expectations: designing MOOCs. Br. J. Educ. Technol. **48**(6), 1284–1294 (2017). https://doi.org/10.1111/bjet.12497

37. Sanz-Martínez, L., et al.: Creating collaborative groups in a MOOC: a homogeneous engagement grouping approach. Behav. Inform. Technol. **38**(11), 1107–1121 (2019). https://doi.org/10.1080/0144929X.2019.1571109

38. Shi, L., et al.: Revealing the hidden patterns: a comparative study on profiling subpopulations of MOOC Students. In: The 28th International Conference on Information Systems Development (ISD2019), Toulon, France. Association for Information Systems (2019)

39. Shi, L., et al.: Social engagement versus learning engagement - an exploratory study of FutureLearn Learners. In: Presented at the 14th IEEE International Conference on Intelligent Systems and Knowledge Engineering (ISKE 2019), Dalian, China November (2019)

40. Shi, L., et al.: Towards understanding learning behavior patterns in social adaptive personalized e-learning systems. In: The 19th Americas Conference on Information Systems, Chicago, Illinois, USA, pp. 1–10 Association for Information Systems (2013)

41. Shi, L., Cristea, A.I.: Demographic indicators influencing learning activities in MOOCs: learning analytics of FutureLearn courses. In: Presented at the 27th International Conference on Information Systems Development (ISD2018), Lund, Sweden, 22 August 2018

42. Shi, L., Cristea, A.I.: In-depth exploration of engagement patterns in MOOCs. In: Hacid, H., et al. (eds.) Web Information Systems Engineering – WISE 2018, pp. 395–409. Springer International Publishing, Cham (2018). https://doi.org/10.1007/978-3-030-02925-8_28

43. Sunar, A.S., et al.: How learners' interactions sustain engagement: a MOOC case study. IEEE Trans. Learning Technol. **10**(4), 475–487 (2017). https://doi.org/10.1109/TLT.2016.2633268

44. Tsai, Y., et al.: The effects of metacognition on online learning interest and continuance to learn with MOOCs. Comput. Educ. **121**, 18–29 (2018). https://doi.org/10.1016/j.compedu.2018.02.011

45. Xing, W., Du, D.: Dropout prediction in MOOCs: using deep learning for personalized intervention. J. Educ. Comput. Res. **57**(3), 547–570 (2019). https://doi.org/10.1177/0735633118757015

46. 1st International Conference on Learning Analytics and Knowledge 2011|Connecting the Technical, Pedagogical, and Social Dimensions of Learning Analytics. https://tekri.athabascau.ca/analytics/. Accessed 01 Mar 2020

The Quest for Usable Usability Heuristics for Game Developers

Sami Mylly$^{(\boxtimes)}$, Mikko Rajanen, and Netta Iivari

University of Oulu, Oulu, Finland
noxious_productions@hotmail.com,
{mikko.rajanen,netta.iivari}@oulu.fi

Abstract. Human Computer Interaction (HCI) research has provided many processes and methods for ensuring good usability during software development. The importance of usability in games has been acknowledged. However, there is a lack of research examining usability activities during actual game development and the suitability of different usability methods for different phases of game development. Game development industry, although growing fast and already including certain large and successful companies, consists of a huge number of small-to-medium-sized enterprises and start-ups. For these companies, practical, developer-oriented tools for ensuring game usability are needed, as these companies do not have resources for hiring usability specialists for taking care of usability. This paper reviews the concept of game usability and existing research on usability methods for game development. In addition, the paper proposes a set of usable usability heuristics as a practical, developer-oriented tool to be used during the game development process as well as reports on a small-scale survey study on game usability, heuristic evaluation and usability of usability heuristics in game development.

Keywords: Games · Usability · Heuristic evaluation · Game development · Game design

1 Introduction

Computer and video games have extensively entered our everyday life. Game development industry is growing rapidly and has become very competitive. During the last twenty years games and their development have changed a lot in scope and in requirements [5]. Game development ranges from an enthusiastic individual creating a simple game as a spare time hobby to large software projects costing hundreds of millions and having hundreds of personnel. The estimated global sales of the game industry has surpassed 100 billion US dollars [49]. Game industry has also grown rapidly. For example, in Finland there were 150 game companies in 2012, 40% of those started within the last two years [25], which has grown to 250 active studios in 2016 [26]. Digital distribution and mobile games have made entering the field a lot easier. New funding possibilities

© The Editor(s) (if applicable) and The Author(s), under exclusive license to Springer Nature Switzerland AG 2020
A. Siarheyeva et al. (Eds.): ISD 2019, LNISO 39, pp. 164–181, 2020.
https://doi.org/10.1007/978-3-030-49644-9_10

such as crowdsourcing through Kickstarter (www.kickstarter.com) or Indiegogo (www.indiegogo.com) have made it even more flexible for nearly anyone to start a game project. Game jams also grow larger each year; Global Game Jam (www.globalgamejam.org) for example has grown from 53 sites, 23 countries, 1650 participants and 370 games in 2009 to 804 sites, 108 countries, 42800 participants and 8606 games in 2018 [20]. It is estimated that one out of five games that reach the marketplace make profit [30]. Therefore, this one profitable game should pay for the development of the other four games.

This paper examines usability in the context of games and game development. Usability has become an important competitive edge in software markets long ago [21, 35, 62]. Users and user organizations benefit from better usability through higher user satisfaction and productivity when the most frequent tasks take less time and users make fewer errors. The development company, then again, benefits from better usability through reduction in time and resources needed for development due to reduced need for changes in late phases. Furthermore, the development company can use improved usability as a competitive edge and potentially increase sales. Better usability can also reduce the number of contacts made to customer support and reduce support costs [4, 14, 35, 44]. As can be seen, there are numerous motivations to invest in usability, even if it is also acknowledged that in the context of game development, these motivations may not all be relevant anymore.

Games are under research activity in Human Computer Interaction (HCI) research, among other disciplines. HCI has addressed games and their development in many respects. One research stream has particularly concentrated on usability in games, concerning either the relationship between usability and games or the process of ensuring usability of games. Usability intuitively is not the most relevant characteristic of good games, but it has still been argued as a relevant aspect, although in need of slight redefinition, as traditional usability concepts such as efficiency may not be particularly important in games [13, 58]. In game play and game development, motivations for investing in usability have still been found (e.g. [56, 58, 59]).

HCI research has already provided plenty of processes and methods for ensuring good usability during software development. Although game development shares many features with software development in general, there are also many specific features in games that pose differing requirements for the development. Especially this study is interested in initially supporting the integration of usability into game development, i.e. there is an assumption that usability has not been institutionalized [65] in game development but instead measures are needed for initially experimenting with usability methods in practice. In game development industry with small start-ups, it is assumed that simple, cheap and fast to use methods are particularly welcomed. In such a context, there may not be resources for hiring usability specialists to take care of usability, but instead developers may have to take care of it among other duties. In such a situation, developers need to be supported in initiating usability work and the methods recommended for them need to be usable for them. There already is HCI research on educating and supporting developers in taking responsibility of usability during development [17, 23, 28, 66, 71]. Although developers' effort is not seen as replacing the need of professional usability specialists, it is still considered as a valuable contribution towards increased usability.

Along these lines, in this paper the particular interest will be in supporting game developers to initiate usability work in game development with the support of usable usability methods.

Hence, this paper explores the relationship between usability and games and identifies ways for initially introducing usability activities into game development without professional usability specialists. In such a situation, it is recommended to begin with usability evaluations, which can act as a wake-up call [65] and which, overall, are widely used, successful and efficient usability methods [28, 69]. Of usability evaluation methods, usability inspection methods, such as heuristic evaluation, are less resource intensive and expensive to adopt; hence, they can be relatively easily and quickly adopted in development [28, 38, 50], which is very valuable in game development industry with small start-ups. Additional value of heuristics is that they can also easily be used as guidelines or rules of thumb for design and development. Like Hodent [27] says: "... the earlier UX issues are identified, the less it costs to fix them." To introduce usability into game development, some usability methods have already been introduced, including usability inspection methods [13, 19, 34, 52, 55, 64]. There, however, is a research gap relating to the appropriateness of the developed usability methods in game development, particularly relating to suitability of the methods for game developer use. Some recent studies have alarmingly indicated that heuristic evaluation is not a common usability evaluation method in the game development industry [61] and that game developers rather develop their own usability heuristic lists for each of their games than use existing lists, which they consider too difficult to use [60]. Hence, there is a need to better understand developer experience in game usability – HCI and games related research should examine how usable the existing usability methods are for the game developer as well as develop more usable methods. This paper contributes by taking initial steps along this path.

This paper is structured as follows. The next section presents related HCI literature on usability and its development. The third section discusses game development describing the core concepts, processes and methods. The fourth section reviews research specifically on games and usability. The fifth section presents the research method utilized in this study as well as proposes a set of usable usability heuristics for games, organized through the analytical lenses of game development process phases. The sixth section describes a small-scale survey study conducted on game usability, heuristic evaluation and usability of usability heuristics in game development. The final section summarizes the results of the paper, discusses their implications for theory and practice, presents the limitations of the research and identifies paths for future research.

2   Defining and Designing Usability

Usability is a central concept in the field of HCI. The most common definitions are certain ISO standard definitions as well as Nielsen's definition. Usability is identified as one of the main software product and system quality attributes in the international standard ISO 9126. It refers to the capability of the product to be understood, learned, and used by users, as well as to appeal to users when used under specified conditions [32]. Standard ISO 9241-11 provides another common definition for usability: "The extent to which a product can be used by specified users to achieve specified goals with effectiveness, efficiency and satisfaction in a specified context of use" [33]. Nielsen, furthermore, defines usability to consist of learnability, efficiency, memorability, errors and satisfaction – the system should be easy to learn to use, the use should be efficient, it should be easy to remember how to use the system, users should not make errors or they should easily recover from them, and the system use should be satisfactory [50].

Usability can be designed and improved through different kinds of usability engineering (UE) and user-centered design (UCD) methods (see e.g. [11, 42, 43, 50, 63]). For example, usability engineering (e.g. [42, 43, 50], scenario-based design (e.g., [63]) and goal-based interaction design (e.g. [11]) have been developed for ensuring usability (and sometimes also usefulness) of the system under development. These methods all contain general phases first relating to understanding users, their needs and tasks and the context of use, to redesigning users' tasks, to creating various kinds of design solutions and to evaluating the design solutions in an iterative manner.

Thus, evaluation of design solutions is an essential step in UE and UCD. It should be carried out at all stages in the system life cycle. Evaluations should be started as early as possible to iteratively improve the design and to generate new ideas. Early evaluations enable fast and cheap improvement of the design. Later, evaluations should be carried out to validate that the requirements have been met and to identify requirements for the next version. Usability evaluation can be either empirical, meaning that actual or representative users take part in the evaluations, or they can be inspections that do not involve users, but usability specialists carry out the evaluations relying on some sorts of guidelines, heuristics or standards [33, 38, 50]. Empirical usability testing is the most widely used, the most successful, and the most efficient method for improving usability, while also usability inspection methods are widely utilized [28, 65]. Usability inspections are less resource intensive than empirical usability testing; consequently, they can be more easily and quickly adopted in development [28, 38, 50], also by developers [28, 38].

The most common usability inspection method is heuristic evaluation, in which evaluators check whether the system conforms to the given usability heuristics. It is relatively easy to learn to use as well as a quick and cost-beneficial method [38, 50]. Heuristic evaluation is usually performed by a small group of usability specialists by comparing the system against a certain set of good usability principles or rules of thumb called heuristics. Heuristic evaluation involves usability specialists first individually going through the user interface several times, inspecting the general flow and then more specific elements, comparing those with the heuristics. Afterwards, they combine their findings and estimate the severity of the problems. Heuristic evaluation results in the list of usability problems that are connected with the usability principles that they violate. Also fixes to the usability problems should be identified [50]. One of the most recognized and used set of heuristics is the ten heuristics by Nielsen [50], though more precise heuristics have been tailored to serve different areas (e.g. user experience heuristics) and products (e.g. mobile device [29], web development [37] and game usability heuristics [36, 52, 56]).

3   Defining and Designing Games

Games are natural to humans, driven by our desire to play and made possible by our ability to pretend [1]. Game is "a type of play activity, conducted in the context of a pretended reality, in which the participant(s) try to achieve at least one arbitrary, nontrivial goal by acting in accordance with rules" [1] or "an interactive structure of endogenous meaning that requires players to struggle toward a goal" [10]. Video games are an art form that combines traditional artistic endeavors such as the visual arts, storytelling and music, with more modern technical and engineering achievements [54]. Games is an interactive, goal-oriented and rule-based activity, where players can interfere and interact with each other [12]. Game must have the following characteristics: light-hearted character, circumscribed in time and place, outcome is unforeseeable, non-productiveness, rule-based and awareness of a different reality [7]. Game has three features: 1) Players who are willing to participate in the game (e.g. for enjoyment, diversion or amusement); 2) Rules which define the limits of the game, and; 3) Goals which give arise to conflicts and rivalry among the players [67, 68]. We see game as a voluntary interactive activity for diversion or amusement, with rules, goals and opposition. Rules limit the ways of interaction, goals resolve the winner and opposition either tries to reach the goals first or to prevent the other(s) from reaching them.

Game development process is not that much different from a conventional software development process. There are several process models on how to develop games. The game development process, however, can be divided into three main stages that are pre-production, production and post-production [71] Testing phase can be seen as an independent phase of development that is conducted at the same time with the production phase [8]. Moreover, concept development phase can be seen as another independent stage of the game development process [2, 64]. Therefore, the basic game development process can be divided into following phases (derived from [3, 51]):

Concept: During concept development the main idea of the game is decided and described so clearly that anyone can understand instantly what the game is about [2]. This phase involves high-level design and documentation. Concept development is done after the definition of the initial concept as an iterative cycle consisting of design, development and testing [40]. During this phase, the design team is still small, and errors are easy to fix.

Pre-production: This is possibly the most important phase, during which every aspect of the game is researched, designed, documented and possibly even developed. Pre-production phase is critical to defining what the game is, how long it will take to make it, how many people are needed and how much it will cost to make it [8].

Prototype: The goal is to create a prototype that shows the basic ideas behind the game and what separates it from other similar games. The prototype can be lo-tech, such as a paper or a miniature version, or a more advanced digital demonstration. The built prototype can be used to test the non-functional requirements of the game that are otherwise difficult to evaluate, such as gameplay. This practice can also be referred to as rapid iterative prototyping [2]. The pre-production stage finishes when the developer has provided a "proof of concept" in the form of a prototype [2].

Production: During the actual production of the formerly designed elements, some changes may occur, but those should be kept minimal. This phase is when the most action happens, most people work at the same time and most time is consumed. The production phase can be divided into three release sub-phases: Alpha, Beta and Gold releases [70].

Alpha: The alpha phase has been defined as the point in the production where in the release the game is mostly playable from start to finish [2] and where a particular build of the game is the first playable version [70]. This is where the full arch of the game is playable, even though there may be bugs or the audio-visual elements are not finished. There is a draft version of the manual and every feature is implemented. At this point, no new features are designed or created. Outside help can be introduced to playtest. In the alpha phase of production, the testing efforts focus on reviewing the features of the game separately and only small testing team is required [2].

Beta: When the alpha version of the game has been finalized, the focus of the development shifts from development to finishing the game. In this phase, the goal is to have the game stabilized and remove most of the errors and problems [2]. Therefore, instead of testing the story arch, features and mechanics, beta-tests are all about finding and fixing bugs and fine-tuning the performance on targeted platform(s) and hardware. As the production is nearing its end, the full testing team is brought in [8]. During this phase, everything in the game is finalized or very close to final. Some argue that beta release is the ending point for the production phase, but others consider the production phase to end when the final version – often called gold phase or release phase – has been delivered.

Gold: Gold or release phase can be seen as the climax of the process where the game is ready and waiting to be delivered for the distributors. Development and coding may have stopped for a while, but work has not. There are still distribution channels to work with (playable demos to deliver, trailers to publish etc.) and setting up the support environments.

Post-release: This phase involves patching the bugs and issues that were not found or fixed before the initial release, sorting the public relations and caressing the community, without forgetting the upgrades, additional contents and special holiday hats. These concluding actions may be considered as of only cursory interest or they may not be done at all as the development team moves on to the next project [8].

These phases are not strict but can and will overlap and some activities such as quality assurance run through the process. Moreover, among authors there are divergent understandings of the phases involved. For example, some authors [2, 70] do not mention the post-release phase or its activities in their game development process descriptions at all and some [3] include more phases than those selected here.

4 Usability and Games

Game User Research has been around for a few years now. Usability and/or playability in games as well as techniques such as game analytics have gained a lot of attention recently [13, 15, 16, 48]. Increasing number of players and the variety of players have pushed the developers from developing for themselves to developing for everyone. The average Joe or Jane wants to be able to play the game right after installation and wants to be adequately good from the start, without reading any manuals. Thus, usability may provide a competitive edge [31] also in game development e.g. through increased willingness of players to buy a game that has good usability [57, 58]. Usability may contribute to higher user satisfaction and productivity, even though in a slightly different meaning compared to applications supporting work tasks, as game playing is voluntary [63]. Game usability and the quality of the user interface are still very important for players [64]. As more and more game development companies compete for the attention of players, it can be argued that in game development good usability is becoming less an advantage and more a necessity. It is easy for players to change to different game if they are not satisfied with the usability of a game, and trial versions, professional game reviews and online gamer communities ensure that a game with bad usability gets a bad reputation fast [46, 58].

What is usability in games then? Well, pretty much the same as in any other software, with some differences [34]. Games are not intended to be productive, - yes, there are some productive games too – but games are primarily supposed to entertain [1]. Usability in games, therefore, addresses issues that hamper users' ability to get entertainment and fun out of the game, areas such as controls, heads-up display and menu structures. There are various good examples and unfortunately quite a few examples of things done wrong (the original Final Fantasy XIV and Fable 3 user interfaces and menu systems, to name two, are some of the most criticized single aspects in a game ever, addressed for example by Morton [46]). With the current reformation of games to a wider audience, usability plays even a stronger role, as the variety of players' gaming skills increases, the games have to adjust to this with tutorials and simplicity (in how you learn to play the game, not in the game). Playability is an extension of usability in games [48]. It adds layers specific to games on top of usability - immersion, character development and how well the game in general comes together for example, whereas playability is a lot more than these [64].

To introduce usability activities into game development, some methods have already been proposed [13, 18, 36, 45, 52, 55, 64]. Fernandez and colleagues [19], Mylly [47] and Sánchez and colleagues [64], among others, have discussed the introduction of usability or playability factors to game development and shown the need for playability elements during development. There are different approaches to bringing usability or playability into development, from player-centered design models such as in Charles and colleagues [9] to heuristic evaluation such as in Desurwire and Wiberg [13]. One of the simplest ways to enhance usability is to introduce heuristics that can be used by every team member, without the need of usability professionals [28, 38, 50, 66]: they provide a cheap and flexible tool for finding issues early and to better understand usability and/or playability [53] that can be used by novice evaluators with good results [22]. Usability heuristics for games were first introduced by Malone [39] in 1980. After quite a few years they have become current again. Today, various sets of heuristics have been introduced to address game usability. Researchers such as Federoff [18], Pinelle and colleagues [56], Brown [6], and Desurvire and Wiberg [13] have produced their own sets and some sets have also been revised later. These sets tend to have dozens of heuristics that very easily appear as confusing and difficult to apply for a game developer who is not experienced in usability. Therefore, the problem with the existing models is that they are targeted at usability researchers and professionals rather than for people without former studies in usability. For these non-usability experts, the heuristics are hard to understand and use.

So far, most of the research has been on establishing a base for the research itself, but the time for putting all this to use in practice has clearly came. Brown [6] has taken a more simplified, usability-oriented approach to develop his set of heuristics but we feel that to actually increase usability as well as to help game developers, the heuristics need to support all; design, development and usability; hence too simple a solution does not do it either. The closest approach to ours is that of Desurvire and Wiberg [13], i.e. their PLAY -method, yet the heuristics proposed in this method are again more suitable for usability-oriented people, not for a developer uneducated in usability. In Sect. 5, we will propose some examples of usability heuristics that are devised to suit the game developer, in a manner usable to them, divided into different game development phases.

5 Proposal for Usable Usability Heuristics for Game Developers

The research process of this paper utilizes both conceptual-analytical and constructive research approaches [41]. The literature review relies on the former, while this research also includes development of developer-oriented game heuristics to be used as a practical tool in game development, which relies on the latter, i.e. design science research (DSR). DSR aims to develop new or improved ways to achieve human goals [24, 41] and it consists of two basic activities: building and evaluating. Building is a process for constructing an artefact for a specified purpose, and evaluating is a process of determining how well the constructed artefact performs in that specified purpose [41].

This paper has the goal of building a set of usability heuristics to fit into the game development context and process, especially for developer use. March and Smith [41] differentiate two cases concerning whether the construct already exists in some form or whether the construct has not existed before in any shape or form. In case the construct is totally new, the contribution of the research comes from the novelty of the artefact and the persuasiveness of the claims that it is effective [41]. In case the construct has already existed in some form – as it is the case in this paper, where both heuristic evaluation and game development process exist in their own separate forms – the contribution of the research lies in the construct being, in some sense, better than the old one [41]. This paper contributes by fitting the heuristic evaluation to the phases of game development process and context to suit the developer use.

The following section introduce examples of heuristics that could be introduced and used by everyone involved in game development as guidelines, not just as tools for inspection. The heuristics are kept simple for the best efficiency and divided by the development phase to better integrate them into the game development process. They are based on game usability studies (such as [13, 56, 69]) as well as on game development literature (such as [1, 51, 54, 57]) and on real-life game development experiences in multiple projects and discussions with developers of varying roles and backgrounds. The example heuristics are simple and elemental ones: they were chosen due to their general nature (suitable for most games) and as they are easily explainable to everyone, without extensive knowledge in either usability or game development. The proposed usability heuristics were kept simple for the best efficiency while covering the critical areas of game usability in each of the game development phases. Relating to each phase, the selected heuristics try to convey aspects important for ensuring usability of the games as well as aspects particular to the development of games, not software in general.

5.1 Concept

The Game Has (Several) Clear and Visible Goals. Players play for a reason, and they must know what they can do and have to do to win the game: e.g. the players explore the game world to find the evil zombie king that they must kill to save the world. Both long- and short-term goals should be visible, long term goals before reaching them and short-term goals straight from their introduction.

The Player Has a Clear Role that She Can Absorb. The player needs to know who she is and how she is ranked in the game context so that she can get a better understanding of the overlying situation and her place in the game world. Without having a clear role, the player can remain disconnected from the game and not feel engaged to it.

The Game Has a Clear Audience. Because people are different, not everyone will enjoy the game. One needs to have a clear idea about the audience so that one knows who to develop for. "Everyone" can be an audience, but that does not help the development team, or the actual audience it will have. Designers should know their future players, in order to design and test the concept ideas with appropriate users and to develop the game for them.

5.2 Pre-production

The Game is Consistent Thoroughly. For the game to be believable, the elements in the game need to be consistent. Jumbo-jets in Stone Age are hardly believable but using a pterodactyl as an airplane could work.

Effects and Actions of Artificial Intelligence (AI) are Fair, Visible and Consistent. The AI should not have unfair advantages against the player (i.e. gain resources twice as fast as the player), unless the player chooses so. The actions of the AI should be as visible to the player as her own actions (i.e. troops moving or constructions building). Creating artificial difficulty to the game by "cheating AI" risks alienating the players.

Every Platform is Thought of Independently. Platforms are different, sometimes a lot different (mobile phone vs. personal computer for example) in many ways - from hardware to controllers etc. - therefore the game must be adjusted accordingly to all platforms it is developed for. New technologies and the adaptation levels of these technologies offer possibilities to create something on the side of the real game on other devices (like commanders in Battlefield 3). For example, the original version of Final Fantasy XIV had the PC user interface designed to follow the same conventions and limitations as the forthcoming PS3 version, resulting poor usability on PC, which in turn resulted the original PC version failing in the market.

Controls Can Be Customized and are Designed for Each Platform Separately. Players are different: for example, some are right-handed, some left-handed and some may have only one hand or other limitations. The player should be able to adjust the controls so that she can play the game at best possible way. Different platforms have different controllers and some platforms have a multitude of controller options, which should all be designed for independently (within reason). Some platforms and genres have de-facto standards for controls (e.g. WASD), and the designers should follow these when possible for default controls, while giving the players possibility to customize the controls to their liking.

The Game is Paced to Offer Challenge and Rest. Players are human, the vast majority of humans cannot undergo constant pressure for too long and too long easy periods can get boring. Keep the player engaged in the game by keeping the tension close but allow her to stop to think and breathe every now and then.

5.3 Prototype

The Hook Should Be Obvious. The prototype needs to prove that the game is worth making, selling and most importantly playing. Do not just reinvent the wheel, improve it. Provide the hook of the game in the prototype.

The Theme and Genre are Obvious. The prototype shows what the game is about and in what setting, the level of reality (arcade versus simulator) and the main genre (sports, action, role play etc.). The players set their expectations and use mental models based on their existing experience on themes and genres. If the theme or genre is not obvious, players do not know how to approach the game and may be off put from the start.

The Rules and Opposition are Obvious. The rules define how the game is played and opposition is the challenger for the player. These can be demonstrated at general level at this point. The rules and opposition should be clear, fair, and give the player possibility to learn, develop and progress.

The Over-Arching Goal is Obvious. The Player is aware of what the final goal of the game is, even if not yet able to complete that goal.

5.4 Production

The Player Should Be Able Leave or Quit the Game at Any Point. Players have real lives, therefore they should be able to leave (pause) or quit (save) the game at any point without losing too much of their progress. This may not be applicable in competitive multiplayer games, but a quit or pause should be included in every single player game at least and should be taken into account through whole production phase. The player should not have to abandon a lot of progress in the game because of a sudden real-life need.

Produce for the Player. Adjusting to tight schedules often may lead to cutting corners and reducing features, which is understandable, but these cuts should not affect the general game play. Through whole production phase, leave "cool to have" features out if that means you can perfect the necessary features, save time on places that are optional to finish the mandatory and often visited places.

5.5 Alpha

The Player Knows What to Do and How to Do It. The game clearly shows what the player needs to do - a first goal - and the means to do it, so that the player can start playing meaningfully right from the beginning. The original version of Final Fantasy XIV gained notoriety amongst players for leaving them wander in the game world not knowing what to do, how to do it and why to do it.

The Player Does not Repeatedly Make the Same Mistakes. Repetition can frustrate the player easily and repeated mistakes frustrate even faster. Alpha is the first phase where you can really spot these design flaws through player testing, as the developers play tests are biased (developers know how it should be done).

Basic Controls are Easy to Learn, But Expendable for More Experienced Players. The player learns the basic controls fast and can play the game right from the beginning. Advanced players may require more advanced controls to achieve things faster or with fewer actions (e.g. quick keys for production or building).

Menus are Simple, Self-explained and Intuitive. Menus are part of the game and the overall experience too. The menus should be designed and structured to support the game play. Disguising different options as part of an image for example might seem like a good idea, but if it makes it slower or harder for the player to start the game, it does not support the game play and can potentially drive players away from the game.

5.6 Beta

The Game Provides Accurate, Timely and Adequate Feedback. Players need to know and realize they are progressing towards the goal(s) of the game. Giving them feedback of their progress will encourage them to continue playing (progressive feedback) and feedback about their current situation and future will make it a lot clearer how to proceed onward (informative feedback). Most of the core should at this point work like intended, but it is not too late to increase the amount of information the player receives.

The Challenges are Worth Completing and Give a Positive Feeling. The challenges can be very hard, but if the players are given a feeling of success, they will carry on trying. Having sub-goals in a longer challenge (pacing) to provide constant stream of minor successes can help in reducing player stress. The reward(s) for completing a challenge should be on par with the challenge level, greater challenges should provide greater rewards.

User Interface Has Enough Information But Does not Interfere with Game Play. Different games have different requirements for the user interface. Health indicators, ammunition information, mini-maps, compasses, skill bars and every other thing there may be are supposed to support the player and the game play, not to obstruct her view or ability to play.

Similar Forms Should Have Similar Actions. A sign for example should always be a sign, not sometimes a mere sign and sometimes a button as well to avoid confusion and frustration. Less learning is more playing.

The Game and the Different Elements in the Game are Balanced. In the beta phase of the production it is time to make sure that the different elements in the game are balanced so that the players' skills and abilities define the game outcome, more than (bad) early game decisions or imbalanced mechanics.

5.7 Gold

The Game is Ready to Play Out of the Box. The player does not need to install any updates or patches prior to game play. Notify the player that there are updates available, but do not force her to install unless the updates are critical for the game (i.e. online competitive game, where everyone needs to have the same version). The player experience suffers considerably, if the player starts the new game with high expectations, only to have to wait for a massive update package to be downloaded and installed.

There is an Adequate Manual Shipped with the Game. The manual included in the release (preferably in physical form, electronic manuals are hardly ever even opened) has enough information so that the player can quickly look up basic instructions and well-known issues. The player should not have to search for websites, discussion forums or community sites for information.

All Required Third-Party Software is Included in the Release. If the game requires any third-party software (DirectX, PunkBuster etc.), they are all included in the release to make it as easy as possible for the player to start the game. It may be plausible to add links or web-installers for the requirements these days, as internet is widely available and software updates common.

The Community Building is Supported in Several Ways. Playing games is a social activity and a flourishing community is an important part of a successful game experience. Building and caring the community properly also creates ground for your next release or other games, as word spreads quickly.

5.8 Post-release

There is an Up-to-Date FAQ About Known Issues and Their (Possible) Fixes. The players can find information for problem situations in one, centralized place, so that they can overcome and/or fix issues as easy as possible.

There is a Change Log Available for Every Update and Patch. Provide information about changes to game mechanics and content etc. so that the players can adjust their game play accordingly (if needed) and are well informed about fixed bugs and errors.

New Content is Consistent with the Original Game. The new content should support the existence of the original game and the original game experience, which can be extended and expanded, but not overwritten.

6   Feedback from the Field

A small survey was conducted in February 2020 among Finnish game developers of wide variety among company sizes and roles within the companies on game usability, on the role of heuristic evaluation in the companies and on the usability of the usability heuristics presented in the literature as well as of those proposed in this paper. There were 8 respondents in the survey.

When asked about what usability means to the respondents, one answer is quite close to what we think of (game) usability: "Usability is one of the design goals that should be pursued during development to make the product as accessible, intuitive and transparent as necessary to its core audience.". This gives motivation that usability activities should be incorporated to the development cycle as a whole. Another answer underlines giving space to the players to learn the game and the ability to customize: "Usability in a game is how well a player can use and engage with the game itself. Poor usability is normally bad UX design and no customization for the player to mold the game around how they want to play (such as moving controls to fit left and right handedness), along with no space for the player to learn how the game works.".

As for the results, 75% of the respondents found usability in games to be of high importance (4.6 average out of 5) and majority of companies the respondents worked with valued usability very important in their products (4.1 out of 5). However, 50% of the respondents did not currently use heuristic evaluation as a usability tool, yet 57% would like to use some form of heuristics to support their work and quoting one answer straight from open feedback question rather nicely sums up the general feeling among the respondents: "UX is very important. Every team/game/company should have one person full time on this.". When asked why they were not using heuristics in their projects there was answers such as: "Normally it's based on time constraints. Spending time to design and create a fully heuristic sequence or space for players to learn the game themselves is a very difficult and time consuming task, that also doesn't translate to other projects quite as well as something more structured and conventional. However, that doesn't mean that I would like to have the time to create such a space for players so that they can learn the way the game works in their own way.", which indicates that incorporating heuristics as a development tool as well could be potentially both saving time and money.

The respondents were asked about usability of a variety of different heuristics randomly chosen from Federoff [18], Nielsen [50], Desurvire and Wiberg [13] and usability heuristics proposed in this paper. The respondents were not told from where the heuristics are from, or by whom and no further descriptions were given. The survey inquired how easy to apply would a given heuristic be in a current project(s).

Two heuristics by Federoff [18] gained the highest average points and our three heuristics together with Nielsen's heuristics followed very close behind, leaving the impression that simpler and/or less error-prone heuristics are easier to apply. Open question about what kind of heuristics would help in the respondents area of expertise asked for "Live Ops and service heuristics" along with "More understanding", which we see as need for a wider set of heuristics that includes the whole range of game development from concept to live operations and serving the user base, but also a set that explains what and why the heuristics are. The heuristics proposed in this paper are answering those questions and work as a basis for a more detailed and wider spectrum of coverage across game development as a whole.

7 Concluding Discussion

This paper addressed the topic of usability in game development. Game development industry, although growing fast and already including large and successful companies, consists also of a huge number of small-to-medium-sized enterprises and start-ups. For these companies, practical, usable, developer-oriented tools for ensuring game usability are needed, as these companies do not have resources for hiring usability specialists. This paper reviewed the concept of game usability and existing research on usability methods for game development as well as proposed a set of usability heuristics as a usable, developer-oriented tool during the game development process.

In case the construct has already existed in some form – as it is the case in this paper, where both heuristic evaluation and game development process exist in their own separate forms – the contribution of the research lies in the new form of the construct being, in some sense, better than the old one [41]. We propose that the usability heuristics fitting the game development process and context, as presented in this paper, are more usable [32, 33, 46] than the existing game usability heuristics, which are not being favored by the majority of the game companies [60]. The usability of the heuristics is improved especially in the sense of efficiency and effectiveness [33] that hopefully also lead to improved developer satisfaction [33]. The literature indicates that the game companies view the existing game usability heuristics as being too difficult to use, too expensive, requiring too much resources, unknown to them, and unsuited for their development practice [60]. The proposed usability heuristics were kept simple for efficiency while covering the critical areas of game usability in each of the game development phases to ensure effectiveness. Dividing the game usability heuristics into the different development phases aims to help to integrate them into game development and allows the game developers to concentrate on a smaller number of important game usability heuristics in each phase. We argue that this new approach to game usability heuristics makes it easier for the game developers to use these heuristics in their game development process and context and thus to improve the usability of the games they develop.

A small-scale survey study on game usability, heuristic evaluation in game development and usability of the usability heuristics proposed in the literature as well as in this study was carried out. The results show that the respondents and companies value usability of games high, but they do not necessarily use heuristic evaluation for improving usability in the development. Then again, they indicate interest in using heuristic evaluation in the future. In the survey, simpler and less error-prone heuristics were found easiest to apply, such as we propose in this paper. Question about the need for heuristics in the respondent's area of expertise showed the need for a wider spectrum of heuristics than what can be found in current literature, together with the need to know more about the heuristics (what, why, when to use).

The study has both theoretical and practical implications. First of all, through reviewing the concept of game usability and existing research on usability methods for game development as well as through characterizing the existing game development industry – i.e. there being a huge number of small enterprises and start-ups without much resources to invest in usability – the paper revealed the need for a practical, usable and developer-oriented tool to suit the game development process that has been lacking in the existing research [59–61]. Second, the proposed and evaluated usability heuristics for games aim at meeting this need. Other researchers as well as game developers can benefit from the contribution of this paper by experimenting with the heuristics during game development. Researchers can extend this work by testing the fit of particular heuristics in the respective game development phase as well as by refining or developing new game usability heuristics to fit a particular game development phase.

As a limitation of this paper, the explored usability heuristics for game development have not been comprehensively empirically tested to verify their fit, usefulness and ease of use. We also acknowledge that heuristic evaluation conducted by novice evaluators (i.e. developers) is not a perfect solution for improving game usability, but it is better than nothing (see also [17, 23, 71]). This paper focuses on usability evaluation and practical developer-oriented usability tools, ignoring issues such as usability requirements, usability design and the institutionalization of usability [65] in game development, even if they definitely are significant to consider in game development.

There is still a need for more research on introducing usability activities into the game development context and process. More research also needs to be done related to introducing game usability heuristics into game development. The proposed usability heuristics should be more comprehensively empirically tested in game development to verify the fit and usefulness of these heuristics in their particular game development phase. Moreover, heuristic evaluation is just one particular usability method and usability evaluation is just one particular usability activity. Empirical usability testing, usability design and usability requirements should also be considered in game development (see also [45, 61]). Altogether, more research needs to be done related to institutionalizing usability activities [65] in game development. Finally, the potential costs and benefits of usability activities in game development context could be researched further [59].

References

1. Adams, E.: Fundamentals of Game Design, 2nd edn. New Riders, Berkeley (2010)
2. Bates, B.: Game Design, 2nd edn. Course Technology, Boston (2004)
3. Bernhaupt, R.: Game User Experience Evaluation, pp. 4–5. Springer, Cham (2015)
4. Bevan, N.: Cost Benefit Analysis version 1.1. Trial Usability Maturity. Serco (2000)
5. Blow, J.: Game development: harder than you think. Queue 1(10), 28–37 (2004)
6. Brown, M.: Evaluating computer game usability: developing heuristics based on user experience. In: The 2nd Annual Human Computer Interaction Conference (2008)

7. Callois, R.: Les jeux et les homes. Gallimard, Paris (1957)
8. Chandler, H.: The Game Production Handbook, 2nd edn. J. & Bartlett, Burlington (2008)
9. Charles, D., McNeill, M., McAlister, M., Black, M., Moore, A., Stringer, K., Kücklich, J., Kerr, A.: Changing views - worlds in play. In: Proceedings of the DiGRA (2005)
10. Costikyan, G.: I have no words & I must design: toward a critical vocabulary for games. In: Proceedings of Computer Games and Digital Cultures Conference, Tampere, Finland (2002)
11. Cooper, A., Reimann, R.: About Face 2.0: The Essentials of Interaction Design. Wiley, Indianapolis (2003)
12. Crawford, C.: Chris Crawford on Game Design. New Riders, Berkeley (2003)
13. Desurvire, H., Wiberg, C.: Game usability heuristics (PLAY) for evaluating and designing better games: the next iteration. In: Ozok, A.A., Zaphiris, P. (eds.) Online Communities and Social Computing. Springer, Heidelberg (2009)
14. Ehrlich, K., Rohn, J.: Cost justification of usability engineering. In: Bias, R., Mayhew, D. (eds.) Cost- Justifying Usability, pp. 73–110. Academic Press, Cambridge (1994)
15. El-Nasr, M.S, Desurvire, H., Nacke, L., Drachen, A., Calvi, L., Isbister, K., Bernhaupt, R.: Game user research. In: Proceedings of CHI EA, NY, pp. 2679–2682 (2012)
16. El-Nasr, M.S., Drachen, A., Canossa, A.: Game Analytics. Maximizing the Value of Player Data. Springer-Verlag, London (2013)
17. Eriksson, E., Cajander, Å., Gulliksen, J.: Hello World! - experiencing usability methods without usability expertise. In: INTERACT 2009, pp. 550–565 (2009)
18. Federoff, M.: Heuristics and usability guidelines for the creation and evaluation of fun in video games. Thesis, University of Indiana (2002)
19. Fernandez, A., Insfran, E., Abrahão, S., Carsí, J.Á., Montero, E.: Integrating usability evaluation into model-driven video game development. In: Winckler, M., Forbrig, P., Bernhaupt, R. (eds.) Human-Centered Software Engineering, pp. 307–314. Springer, Heidelberg (2012)
20. Global Game Jam (2019). http://globalgamejam.org/history. Accessed 27 June 2019
21. Grudin, J.: Interactive systems: bridging the gaps between developers and users. Computer **24**(4), 59–69 (1991)
22. Hearst, M.A., Laskowski, P., Silva, L.: Evaluating information visualization via the interplay of heuristic evaluation and question-based scoring. In: Proceedings of the 2016 CHI Conference, pp. 5028–5033 (2016)
23. Hertzum, M., Jacobsen, N.E.: The evaluator effect: a chilling fact about usability evaluation methods. Int. J. HCI **13**(4), 421–443 (2001)
24. Hevner, A.R., March, S.T., Park, J.: Design research in information systems research. MIS Q. **28**(1), 75–105 (2004)
25. Hiltunen, K., Latva, S., Kaleva, J.-P.: Peliteollisuus – kehityspolku. Tekes (2013)
26. Hiltunen, K., Latva, S., Kaleva, J.-P.: Finnish Game Industry Report. Neogames (2017)
27. Hodent, C.: The Gamer's Brain: How Neuroscience and UX Can Impact Video Game Design. CRC Press, Boca Raton (2018)
28. Holzinger, A.: Usability engineering methods for software developers. Commun. ACM **48**(1), 71–74 (2005)
29. Inostroza, R., Rusu, C., Roncagliolo, S., Jimenez, C., Rusu, V.: Usability heuristics for touchscreen-based mobile devices. In: Proceedings of ITNG 2012, pp. 662–667 (2012)
30. Irwin, M.J.: Cooking Up a Blockbuster Game. Forbes (2008)
31. Isbister, K., Schaffer, N.: Game Usability: Advice from the Experts for Advancing the Player Experience. CRC Press, Boca Raton (2008)
32. ISO 9126: International standard (2001)
33. ISO 9241-11: International standard (1998)
34. Jørgensen, A.H.: Marrying HCI/usability and computer games: a preliminary look. In: Proceedings of the Third Nordic Conference on Human-Computer Interaction, pp. 393–396. ACM, New York (2004)

35. Karat, C.-M.: A business case approach to usability cost justification. In: Bias, R., Mayhew, D. (eds.) Cost-Justifying Usability, pp. 45–70. Academic Press, Cambridge (1994)
36. Korhonen, H., Koivisto, E.M.I.: Playability heuristics for mobile multi-player games. In: Proceedings of the 2nd International Conference on Digital Interactive Media in Entertainment and Arts, pp. 28–35. ACM (2007)
37. Levi, M.D., Conrad, F.G.: A heuristic evaluation of a World Wide Web prototype. Interactions 3(4), 50–61 (1996)
38. Mack, R., Nielsen, J.: Executive summary. In: Nielsen, J., Mack, R. (eds.) Usability Inspection Methods, pp. 1–23. Wiley, Hoboken (1994)
39. Malone, T.W.: What makes things fun to learn? Heuristics for designing instructional computer games. In: SIGSMALL 1980 Proceedings of the 3rd ACM SIGSMALL Symposium and the First SIGPC Symposium on Small Systems, pp. 162–169. ACM, New York (1980)
40. Manninen, T.: Pelisuunnittelijan käsikirja - Ideasta eteenpäin. Rajalla, Oulu (2007)
41. March, S.T., Smith, G.F.: Design and natural science research on information technology. Decis. Support Syst. 15(4), 251–266 (1995)
42. Mayhew, D.: Strategic development of usability engineering function. Interactions 6(5), 27–34 (1999)
43. Mayhew, D.: The Usability Engineering Lifecycle: A Practitioner's Handbook for User Interface Design. Morgan Kaufmann Publishers, San Francisco (1999)
44. Mayhew, D., Mantei, M.: A basic framework for cost- justifying usability engineering. In: Bias, R., Mayhew, D. (eds.) Cost-Justifying Usability, pp. 9–43. Academic Press, Cambridge (1994)
45. Medlock, M.C., Wixon, D., Terrano, M., Romero, R., Fulton, B.: Using the RITE method to improve products: a definition and a case study. Usability Prof. Assoc. 51, 1–7 (2002)
46. Morton, P.: Learning from Fable III's UX Mistakes, UX booth (2011). http://www.uxbooth.com/articles/learning-from-fable-iiis-ux-mistakes/
47. Mylly, S.: Genre-Based Modular Heuristic Models for Improving Usability During Game Development. Oulun yliopisto, Oulu (2011)
48. Nacke, L.: From playability to a hierarchical game usability model. In: Proceedings of Future Play 2009, pp. 11–12. ACM, New York (2009)
49. Newzoo: Global Games Market Report. Q2 2016 Update (2016)
50. Nielsen, J.: Usability Engineering. Academic Press, Boston (1993)
51. Novak, J.: Game Development Essentials: An Introduction. Delmar, Boston (2012)
52. Paavilainen, J.: Critical review on video game evaluation heuristics: social games perspective. In: Proceedings of the International Academic Conference on the Future of Game Design and Technology, pp. 56–65 (2010)
53. Paavilainen, J., Korhonen, H., Koskinen, E., Alha, K.: Heuristic evaluation of playability: examples from social games research and free-to-play heuristics. In: Drachen, A., Mirza-Babaei, P., Nacke, L. (eds.) Games User Research, pp. 257–280. Oxford University Press, Oxford (2018)
54. Pagulayan, R., Steury, K.: Beyond usability in games. Interactions 11(5), 70–71 (2004)
55. Phan, M.H., Keebler, J.R., Chaparro, B.S.: The development and validation of the game user experience satisfaction scale (GUESS). Hum. Factors 58(8), 1217–1247 (2016)
56. Pinelle, D., Wong, N., Stach, T.: Heuristic evaluation for games: usability principles for video game design. In: Proceedings of CHI 2008, New York, pp. 1453–1462 (2008)
57. Rabin, S.: Introduction to Game Development, 2nd edn. Course Technology, Boston (2010)
58. Rajanen, M., Marghescu, D.: The impact of game usability to player attitude. In: Proceedings of 29th Information Systems Research Seminar in Scandinavia, pp. 1–17 (2006)
59. Rajanen, M., Rajanen, D.: Usability benefits in gamification. In: Proceedings of the 1st GamiFin Conference, Pori, Finland, pp. 87–95 (2017)

60. Rajanen M., Rajanen, D.: Heuristic evaluation in game and gamification development. In: Proceedings of the 2nd GamiFin Conference, Pori, Finland (2018)
61. Rajanen, M., Tapani, J.: A survey of game usability practices in North American game companies. In: Proceedings ISD 2018, Lund, Sweden (2018)
62. Rosenbaum, S., Rohn, J., Humburg, J.: A toolkit for strategic usability: results from workshops, panels, and surveys. In: Proceedings CHI, NY, pp. 337–344 (2000)
63. Rosson, M., Carroll, J.: Usability Engineering: Scenario-Based Development of Human-Computer Interaction. Morgan-Kaufman, San Francisco (2002)
64. Sánchez, J.L., Zea, N.P., Gutiérrez, F.L.: From usability to playability: introduction to player-centered video game development process. In: Human Centered Design, HCII 2009, pp. 65–74 (2009)
65. Schaffer, E.: Institutionalization of Usability: A Step-by-Step Guide. Addison-Wesley Professional, Boston (2004)
66. Seffah, A., Metzker, E.: The obstacles and myths of usability and software engineering. Commun. ACM **47**(12), 71–76 (2004)
67. Smed, J., Hakonen, H.: Towards a definition of a computer game. Technical report 553, Turku Centre for Computer Science (2003)
68. Suits, B.: The Grasshopper: Games, Life and Utopia. Broadview Press, Peterborough (2005). with a new introduction by Thomas Hurka
69. Sykes, J., Federoff, M.: Player-centered game design. In: Proceeding CHI 2006 Extended Abstracts on Human Factors in Computing Systems, pp. 1731–1734 (2006)
70. Vuorela, V.: Pelintekijän käsikirja. BTJ Finland Oy, Helsinki (2007)
71. Øvad, T., Larsen, L.B.: How to reduce the UX bottleneck–train your software developers. Behav. Inf. Technol. **35**(12), 1080–1090 (2016)

Towards a Human-Centered Approach for VRET Systems: Case Study for Acrophobia

Oana Bălan[1]([envelope]), Ștefania Cristea[1], Alin Moldoveanu[1], Gabriela Moise[2],
Marius Leordeanu[1], and Florica Moldoveanu[1]

[1] University POLITEHNICA of Bucharest, Bucharest, Romania
{oana.balan,alin.moldoveanu,marius.leordeanu,
florica.moldoveanu}@cs.pub.ro, stefania.cristea@gmail.com
[2] Petroleum-Gas University of Ploiești, Ploiesti, Romania
gmoise@upg-ploiesti.ro

Abstract. This paper presents a human-centered methodology for designing and developing Virtual Reality Exposure Therapy (VRET) systems. By following the steps proposed by the methodology – Users analysis, Domain Analysis, Task Analysis and Representational Analysis, we developed a system for acrophobia therapy composed of 9 functional, interrelated modules which are responsible for patients, scenes, audio and graphics management, as well as for physiological monitoring and events triggering. The therapist visualizes in real time the patient's biophysical signals and adapts the exposure scenario accordingly, as he can lower or increase the level of exposure. There are 3 scenes in the game, containing a ride by cable car, one by ski lift and a walk by foot in a mountain landscape. A reward system is implemented and emotion dimension ratings are collected at predefined points in the scenario. They will be stored and later used for constructing an automatic machine learning emotion recognition and exposure adaptation module.

Keywords: Virtual reality · Exposure therapy · Human-centered · Acrophobia · Phobia

1 Introduction

Phobia is a prevalent anxiety disorder of our times, affecting 13% of the world's population. They are characterized by an extreme fear of objects or situations, distressing panic attacks and physical symptoms such as sweating, trembling, rapid heartbeat, headaches, dizziness, confusion and disorientation. In severe situations, some people experience psychological symptoms such as fear of losing control or even fear of dying. Phobias are divided into 3 categories – social phobias (fear of meeting people of higher authority, using a telephone or speaking before a large crowd), agoraphobia (fear of open spaces)

A prior version of this paper has been published in the ISD2019 Proceedings (http://aisel.aisnet.org/isd2014/proceedings2019).

A. Siarheyeva et al. (Eds.): ISD 2019, LNISO 39, pp. 182–197, 2020.
https://doi.org/10.1007/978-3-030-49644-9_11

and specific phobias, which are generated by specific objects or situations. In what concerns social phobias, they affect people of all ages, but usually appear in adolescence. 45% of people with social phobias develop agoraphobia and the fear of having an anxiety attack in public or embarrassing themselves, while 17% develop depression [1]. 15–20% of the world's population experience specific phobias at least once in the lifetime [2]. At world level, specific phobias have the following prevalence: acrophobia (fear of height) – 7.5%, arachnophobia (fear of spiders) – 3.5%, aerophobia (fear of flying) – 2.6%, astraphobia (fear of lightning and thunder) – 2.1%, dentophobia (fear of dentist) – 2.1% [3]. The annual total costs of social phobia were 11.952 euros in the Netherlands, higher than the total costs for people with no mental disorder, of 2957 euros [4]. As concerns the European Union, the direct (diagnosis and treatment) and indirect (invisible costs associated with income losses due to mortality and disability) costs were estimated at 798 billion euros. They are expected to double by 2030 [5].

Of the people suffering from social phobias, only 23% seek specialized help. 80% of the patients turn to medicines and Cognitive Behavior Therapy (CBT), a method of gradual in-vivo exposure to stimuli and thought control. Unfortunately, only 50% of the persons suffering from social phobias and 20% of those affected by specific phobias recover completely [1].

Besides CBT and in-vivo exposure, a new therapy has emerged, namely VRET (Virtual Reality Exposure Therapy). The user is presented a computer-generated virtual environment, either on a desktop or mobile platform, via a Head Mounted Display (HMD). Virtual environments can be easily controlled by the therapist, customized and adapted to the condition of each patient. They are immersive, appealing, cheap and most importantly, safe. Over 80% of the patients prefer virtual exposure therapy over the classical in-vivo exposure [6]. VRET has a strong stability of results in time, equal to that obtained by CBT therapy [7]. However, it is appropriate for people who do not possess high imaginative skills such as those required for CBT. It also provides a more comfortable sensation than in-vivo exposure, knowing that it is only a virtual immersion from which you can abscond as soon as you feel like losing control.

In this paper we propose a methodology inspired from the HCDID model proposed by Zhang et al. in [8] and from the NADI model of van der Bijl-Brouwer and Dorst [9] for designing and developing a VRET system. It is quite a difficult task to provide a proper methodology for medical software development because it needs to take into account the complexity of human biology.

In addition, we provide a case study for acrophobia therapy. Such, we designed a virtual environment illustrating a mountain scenario where the user can ride by cable car, ski lift and walk by foot. The therapist can manage the patients, visualize their physiological parameters and adapt the scenario accordingly. The design is human-centered, thus it meets both the patients' and therapists' requirements. In our opinion the human-centered design for software means also to understand people (feelings, emotions, ideals, aspirations, needs, habits, motivations, and so on) and provide software tailored to each individual.

In this phase of research, we collect data from the users and from the therapists (biophysical signals, actions performed in the virtual environment, user behavior, general performance, the modality in which the clinical specialist reacts to the patient's performance and physiological data, adapting the exposure scenario accordingly). This data will be used for constructing a computational model with various feature extraction and machine learning techniques that will automatically recognize human emotions and adapt the virtual exposure in real time.

The paper is organized as follows: Sect. 2 presents existing systems for phobia therapy, Sect. 3 describes the emotion models, Sect. 4 presents the human-centered paradigm, Sect. 5 is dedicated to our proposed human-centered VRET system design methodology and Sect. 6 introduces a case study, the development of a VRET system for acrophobia treatment. Finally, we show the study's conclusions and provide future directions of research.

2   Virtual Reality Systems for Phobia Therapy

In order to perform a comprehensive analysis of the existing Virtual Reality (VR) systems for phobia therapy, we considered 3 main categories: platforms, applications for desktop and mobile devices and systems developed within an academic research.

2.1   Platforms

C2Phobia software [10] is composed of more than 70 configurable exposure environments (the therapist can add/remove elements from the environment) for treating a wide range of phobic conditions: Acrophobia, Agoraphobia, Claustrophobia, Ochlophobia, Arachnophobe, Aviophobia, School phobia, Fear of public speaking, Fear of pigeons, Fear of dogs, Fear of cats, Fear of the hospital. The patient is exposed gradually to different levels of anxiety according to his pathologies. PSIOUS [11] provides over 50 resources (VR and augmented reality environments, 360° videos) with real-time view of what the patient is seeing during the session. Stim Response Virtual Reality [12] offers fully modular environments for acrophobia, fear of flying and fear of public speaking therapy. The events from the virtual or augmented world and the physiological data (ECG, EEG, EOG, EMG, EGG, EDA, temperature, respiration, pulse) are synchronized. Virtual Reality Medical Center (VRMC) [13] uses VRET in combination with biofeedback and CBT to treat phobias (fear of flying, fear of driving, fear of heights, fear of public speaking, claustrophobia, agoraphobia), anxiety (including pre-surgical anxiety), stress and chronic pain. This system is used also for treating post-traumatic stress disorder caused by military deployment. Each stage can be repeated until the client feels comfortable. At every step, the therapist can see and hear what the client is experiencing. If the level of anxiety becomes too high, the user can return to a lower level or exit the virtual world. Virtually Better [14] offers Bravemind, a system for alleviating the psychological repercussions of war for the soldiers who served in Iraq or Afghanistan. Bravemind is accompanied by vibrotactile feedback (sensations associated with engine rumbling, explosions, firefights), ambient noises and scent machines. Limbix [15] offers VR environments built from panoramic images and videos. The scenes are interactive, so that the therapists can change them in real-time. PHOBOS [16] is designed for individuals, professionals and organizations. It ensures gradual exposure to stimuli and interactive 3D environments that address agoraphobia, social anxiety disorders and specific phobias.

2.2   Applications for Desktop and Mobile Devices

For acrophobia therapy, the most popular games are The Climb [17], Ritchie's Plank Experience [18], Samsung Fearless Cityscapes [19] for Gear VR, Samsung Fearless Landscapes [20]. In Arachnophobia [21], the user looks at specific spots on a piece of paper in front of him and is able to control the amount of exposure to virtual spiders. Limelight [22] for HTC Vive puts the user on stage in front of a virtual crowd that can change its mood and behavior. For treating fear of public speaking, he can give presentations in business meetings, small classrooms or large halls.

2.3   Systems Developed Within the Academic Context

Acrophobia Therapy with Virtual Reality (AcTiVity-System) [23] uses Oculus Rift to render the 3D scenes, a Microsoft Kinect for motion tracking and a heart rate sensor. A large experiment, involving 100 users, took place in order to evaluate the system and the results showed that all the participants in the VR group recorded a certain level of fear reduction, with the average reduction being 68%. Half of the participants in the VR group had a reduction in fear of heights by over three quarters. VR Phobias [24] contains a static environment depicting the view of a hotel balcony. The results of an experiment involving 15 users showed the same rates of success for the users treated in a virtual environment and for those exposed to a real-world environment. However, the virtual sessions were shorter (22 min), compared to the real-world ones (51 min). The acrophobia system developed at University of Amsterdam and Delft University of Technology [25] comprises three different virtual environments: a mall, a fire escape and a roof garden. 29 patients have been exposed to these virtual environments in the presence of the therapist. At the end of the experiment, the subjects have reduced their anxiety and avoidance levels.

3   Emotion Models

Some of the most challenging subjects in psychology are related to emotions, emotional-eliciting stimuli and the modalities of measuring affective changes. There are many theories of emotion, with each author offering his own perspective on the topic. In 1969, Izard concluded that the area of emotional experience and behaviour is one of the most confused and ill-defined in psychology [26]. The most relevant researcher in the field, Paul Ekman, stated the following about basic emotions and their facial expressions-based recognition: My views over the past 40 years have changed radically from my initial view that: (a) a pleasant-unpleasant and active-passive sale were sufficient to capture the differences among emotions: and (b) the relationship between a facial configuration and what it signified is socially learned and culturally variable. I was forced to adopt the opposite view by finding from my own and others' cross-cultural studies of facial expressions [27].

Emotions have a complex and multi-aspect nature. According to H. Hockenbury & E. Hockenbury, emotion is seen as a complex psychological state that involves three distinct components: a subjective experience, a physiological response and a behavioral or expressive response [28].

Cabanac proposed the following definition: *emotion is any mental experience with high intensity and high hedonicity (positive or negative)* [29]. The causes of emotions are various and they can be recognized through *signs of emotions, as sweating, tachycardia, facial expressions.*

While a review on emotion literature in psychology is beyond the scope of this paper, we adopt the definition proposed by H. Hockenbury & E. Hockenbury and present the most relevant emotion models and key concepts used in emotion recognition.

Regarding the emotion models, there are mainly two perspectives: discrete and dimensional. In the discrete model, it is assumed the existence of a basic set of emotions. Ekman and Friesen identified six basic emotions: anger, disgust, fear, happiness, sadness, and surprise [30]. Later, the list was updated including embarrassment, excitement, contempt, shame, pride, satisfaction, amusement, guilt, relief, wonder, ecstasy and sensory pleasure. In the dimensional model, an emotion is described by two or three dimensions, which represent fundamental properties. Russel suggested in his circumplex model of affect the usage of two dimensions: the arousal or activation dimension to express the intensity of emotion and the valence dimension to express the way in which the emotion is felt, either positive or negative [31]. Dominance was related to the extent to which a person can control his behavior. Nowadays, valence, arousal and dominance are still used as three basic dimensions to express the emotional states. Each discrete emotion can be viewed as a combination of two or three dimensions [32, 33]. For example, fear is characterized by negative valence, high arousal and low dominance.

Complex emotions can be constructed from combinations of basic emotions. Robert Plutchik introduced the famous wheel of emotions to illustrate how basic emotions (joy versus sadness; anger versus fear; trust versus disgust; and surprise versus anticipation) can be mixed to obtain different emotions [34]. The Pluthcik's model is not the only tool used to assess emotional reactions. Geneva emotional wheel (GEW) uses a circular structure with the axes defined by valence and control to arrange 40 emotion terms in 20 emotion families [35]. More information regarding the usage of GEW tool can be found at [36].

Many laboratory experiments have been carried out in order to study emotions. In [37], a comparative study regarding the capacities of pictures and films to induce emotions is provided. The Self-Assessment Manikin scale was used to rate the emotion and arousal states [38]. The results obtained were unexpected: films were less effective than pictures stimuli. Two stimuli were used in [39] to induce emotional states: self-induced emotional imagery and audio/video clips. Electroencephalography (EEG) brain signals were automatically analyzed and used to recognize human emotions. Facial expressions, posture, voice, body motion reflect emotional states [40–43]. With the development of technology, various data could be acquired and processed, thus leading to automatic emotion recognition systems development. The best performance is achieved by multi-modal emotion recognition.

4   The Human-Centered Paradigm

Nowadays, we are witnessing the explosion of the Human-Centered paradigm. There are many definitions which attempt to encompass various aspects of human-centered.

We find human-centered related to with different concepts such as computing, design, systems, machine learning, software engineering and so forth.

In the final report of the workshop Human-Centered Systems (HCS): Information, Interactivity, and Intelligence, 1997, the participants agreed and defined the human-centered systems as *an emerging discipline that combines principles from cognitive science, social science, computer science and engineering to study the design space of systems that support and expand fundamental human activities* [44]. Jaimes et al. notice that the aim of Human-Centered Computing (HCC) is the tight integration of human sciences and computer science to build computing systems with a human focus from beginning to end [43].

Human-centered Machine Learning (HML) proposes a new approach for Machine Learning (ML) algorithms. They consider human goals and contexts in designing ML algorithms, so that ML becomes more useful and usable [45]. The human and the computer have to adapt to each other: the human can change the behavior of the machine and the machine can change the human's goals. Applied ML is seen as a co-adaptive process with the computers being part of human design process [45].

Generally speaking, the Human-Centered Design (HCD) deals with those methods and principles used to design and develop any types of services or products for people, taking into account the utility, pleasure and meaning parameters [42]. van der Bijl-Brouwer and Dorst developed the NADI model based on four layers of human Needs and Aspirations for Application in a Design and Innovation process [9]:

I Solutions – shows what the people want or need

II Scenarios – describes how the people interact with a solution in a specific context of use

III Goals and **IV Themes** – are the deepest levels and describe the reasons why people want a certain solution. The authors showed the difference between goals and themes: the goals take into account the context of the problem, while themes deal with the context-free analysis of underlying needs and aspirations.

NADI is a general model for product design; it is not dedicated to software. It focuses on needs and aspirations in order to capture the long-term desires, hopes and ambitions.

In 2003, Seffah and Andreevskaia noted that the HCD techniques are still insufficiently integrated in software engineering methodologies [45]. They provided a comprehensive guide to teach engineering programming in terms of the human/user-centered design (UCD).

Considering the movement of software engineering from the traditional software development to the human-centered development, Seffah, Gulliksen, and Desmarais proposed the following process features: user-driven; solution focus; multidisciplinary teamwork including users, customers, human factor experts; focus on external attribute (look and fell, interaction); quality defined be user satisfaction and performance (quality in use); implementation of user-validated solution only; understanding the context of use (user, task, work environment) [46].

In [47] a Human-Centered Distributed Information Design (HCDID) methodology is introduced and it is demonstrated on electronic medical records systems. HCDID is based on the theory of distributed cognition, which claims that the unit of analysis is the system composed of human and artificial agents, the pattern of information distribution among human and artificial agents can radically change the behavior of the distributed system, the behavior of a distributed system should be described by the information flow dynamics [47].

HCDID comprises two related parts: the first part includes multiple levels of analysis for single user human-centered design (user, functional, representational, and task analysis); the second part is dedicated to additional analysis for designing distributed human-centered systems. We did not intend to design a distributed VRET system; therefore we only considered the first part of HCDID.

From our perspective, a human-centered design for software must care about people's feelings, emotions, ideals, aspirations, needs, habits and motivations. Medical software strongly requires considering human emotions, so our methodology takes care of it.

5 A Human-Centered VRET System Design Methodology

VRET systems comprise various technologies: VR, AR and ML. Related to VR, Jerald noted in his book that We must create VR experiences with both emotion and logic [47]. In our methodology for Human-Centered VRET (HCVRET) systems development (Fig. 1), we use a layers-based analysis adopted from the HCDID model and from the NADI model of van der Bijl-Brouwer and Dorst [9]. For the HCVRET implementation, we consider the dimensional model of emotions.

The layers-based analysis for designing a human-centered VRET system comprises 4 levels. Level 1 is dedicated to the users' analysis: patients and therapists, goals and theme analysis. Users' patterns and features of these patterns are identified at this stage. It is important to know their medical history, motivation, education, data about the phobia condition. We are interested in the gaming and computer abilities of the patients, as our intention is to develop a game-based VRET system. The therapists also use the system. They supervise the therapy and can intervene during the game. Also, we need a clear statement of the goals and themes. The goals are formulated in terms of improving the patients' condition and the theme underlying the goals is comfort. Level 1 provides information to the following levels. Level 2 deals with the system analysis requirements, emotion models and knowledge about the mental illness. All information is modeled and encoded to be computationally processed. The VRET system contains a series of tasks which are undertaken by the patients in the therapy. All tasks and subtasks are analyzed at Level 3. Each task has a hierarchical structure: high level tasks related to a goal and subtasks related to sub-goals. Also, there are defined the tasks performed by the therapists: for example, the task of setting the next game level in the therapy. The patients, the therapists and the machines need to communicate in a simple and efficient way. Task analysis involves defining the work procedures. An example of procedure is: the patient plays no more than 15 min followed by a relaxation period of 10 min. In this way, the game-based VRET system is designed to be adaptable to the model of the patient. At Level 4, we identify the patients' and therapists' preferences for colors or sounds, for a certain game, for urban or natural landscapes, for certain technologies and so on. All the information acquired at this stage is used for implementing the VRET system.

We could not find a general methodology for designing virtual reality-based medical software. The proposed methodology is dedicated to this type of application

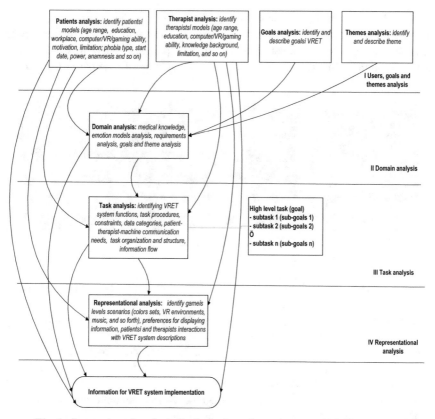

Fig. 1. Layers-based analysis for designing a human-centered VRET systems

and combines human-based product design strategies with medical software design strategies.

6 Case Study: Development of a VRET System for Acrophobia Treatment

6.1 Software Architecture

In this chapter we present the development of a VRET system for treating acrophobia. Our virtual environment is rendered via HTC Vive and depicts a natural setting (a mountain scene with hills and valleys, peaks, forests, a lake, river, transparent platform above a canyon and a transparent bridge) during daytime. The VR environment has been developed using the C# programming language and the Unity graphics engine. The software architecture is composed of the following modules:

Users Manager (Fig. 2) – manages the patients, being dedicated to the therapist. New patients can be added to the system and information about them introduced – name, age, height, sex. Also, each patient selects at this stage his favorite song/picture/quote, which will be presented during the virtual exposure whenever he considers that he needs to relax and calm down. This module also manages existing users, replays sessions and allows the therapist to see statistics concerning the patients' performance. The Users Manager module is connected to a SQL database that stores all the participants' data.

Fig. 2. Users Manager interface

Resources Manager - loads and caches all resources needed at runtime (the patient's profile, scenes, game objects, assets, etc.).

Graphics Manager – ensures graphics rendering and processing, input & output windows and UI (User Interface) display.

Input Manager – manages user input from the HTC Vive controllers. The patient interacts with the virtual environment – displacement, objects selection, menu selection, buttons pressing via the HTC Vive controllers.

Audio Manager – audio rendering management: environmental soundscapes (birds chirping, the sound of the wind), auditory icons when the user selects something from the menu, enters or exits the game, audio cues, plays the user's favorite music clip whenever he needs to relax and take a break from the virtual exposure.

Scenes Manager – manages the scenes (Fig. 3). The user can select any of the following 3 scenes: a ride by cable car a ride by ski lift and a walk by foot. Throughout any of these routes, there are 10 stop points where a mathematical quiz is applied in order to detach the patient from the virtual exposure, deactivate the right brain hemisphere responsible with emotional processing and activate the left one which manages logical and rational responses. After the user correctly answers the mathematical question (Fig. 4), he is required to select his valence, arousal and dominance levels using Self-Assessment Manikins. If he does not correctly answer the current mathematical question, another one appears on the screen and the process is repeated. At the end of the route, the user is returned to the main menu to select another ride, if he wants. At each moment of time, he can stop the cable car or ski lift from moving, as well as to get down and return to the main menu. At any time, the user can choose to take a pause to relax and listen to his favorite piece of music, see a photo depicting something he enjoys and read his favorite quote.

Physiological Monitoring Module – records physiological data (heart rate (HR) and galvanic skin response GSR)). High HR and increased GSR (skin conductivity) are associated with anxiety and fear. Both the user and the therapist can visualize and

Fig. 3. Game scenarios

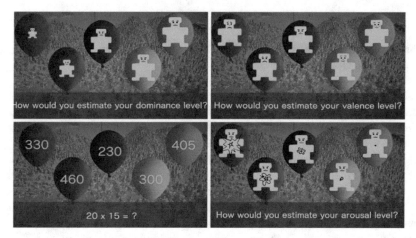

Fig. 4. Applied questions

monitor these parameters and the therapist can also modify the patient's exposure level whenever he considers that the biophysical signals exceeded a critical threshold.

Event System Module - triggers various actions during gameplay like saving statistics, recording valence/arousal/dominance rates, rendering events, animation events and any kind of communication between completely various modules or game objects.

Game Manager – integrates and operates all the modules mentioned above.

The software architecture is presented in Fig. 5.

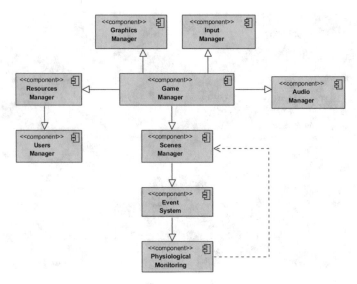

Fig. 5. Acrophobia VRET system software architecture

6.2   Development Methodology

In this section we present the detailed steps of our development methodology for the acrophobia VRET system we propose.

Level I – Users, Goals and Themes Analysis

At this stage, we identified the goal and theme: the goals refer to improving the patients' phobia-related conditions and the themes represent the comfort and safety. So, our main concern was to achieve the goals that ensure patients' comfort during the game.

Also, we identified the patients' and therapists' profiles, as well as what they expect from the system. The patients expect an immersive virtual environment, with a high level of realism, accessible tasks and a diverse range of in-game activities. For this, we developed the Scenes Manager module with increased attention to details in order to ensure a high level of immersion. All the 3 scenes – cable car, ski lift and walking route are carefully designed, having their graphics adapted to be rendered via the HTC Vive glasses. The input modality is also accessible and easy to be used. Thus, the patient interacts with the environment by pressing a few buttons from the Vive controller to teleport himself in the scene, select his responses to the mathematical questions and introduce the valence/arousal/dominance ratings, start, stop or exit the game, select the preferred scenario. The patients are however reluctant towards heavy and uncomfortable biophysical equipment. Thus, even if at the beginning of our research we pursued the idea of recording EEG data, we finally dropped it out and kept only GSR and HR. These biophysical signals have been recorded using the Shimmers Multisensory device which has integrated compatibility with the C# programming language through its API [48]. The therapists expect a reliable system, with a high level and realism and immersion, visualization of what the patient is seeing in the virtual environment, as well as of his biophysical signals, so that they can easily adapt the exposure scenario. In addition, they want to have access to recordings of the users' performance in order to calculate statistics and perform post-therapy analyses. To accomplish these requests, we developed the Physiological Monitoring module and the Users Management module.

Level II – Domain Analysis

At this stage of development, we interacted with psychologists and psychotherapists, in order to understand the emotional profile of the people suffering from acrophobia. Here we researched the domain of affective computing and defined fear as an emotion with low valence, high arousal and low dominance. The psychologists advised us to repeatedly ask the patients for their self-reported valence, arousal and dominance ratings, but before it is recommendable to detach them from the current intense emotional state, deactivate the right hemisphere and activate the left one by applying some mathematical quizzes. By listening to his favorite piece of music, look at a picture or read his preferred quotation, the patient also achieves a high state of relaxation, being at the same time an effective self-reward solution. The person rewards himself from time to time after experiencing a stressful situation or expecting to reach a certain game level, so that he can take a break, stop the exposure temporarily and enjoy a short, but pleasant activity. The data collected (biophysical signals and valence/arousal/dominance ratings) will be further used for designing an additional module, called Fear Estimation. Several machine and deep learning techniques will be used to construct a model that automatically determines the patient's current level of fear, so that the therapist will know not only the biophysical raw values, but also whether the user experiences low/medium/high fear. In this way, he can adapt the exposure scenarios more easily. Future plans include the development of an Automatic Exposure Adaptation module, where, based on the knowledge collected from the therapist, the patients' biophysical data and fear level estimation, a virtual therapist will adapt the level of exposure automatically, without or with minimum intervention from the human expert. In addition, in our future research, we intend to integrate a form of neurofeedback, so that the elements from the virtual environment would change their appearance according to the user's emotional state. So, the sky can become cloudier or darker when the patient feels anxious, clearer when he is calm and change dynamically during the session. By being provided with this form of feedback, the patient can struggle to relax and induce himself a state of relaxation in order to change the appearance of the natural elements from the virtual environment.

Level III – Task Analysis

Here we identified the tasks and corresponding subtasks. The user can select at the beginning the route he wants to take – a ride by cable car, ski lift or a walk by foot. Throughout any of these routes, there are 10 stop points where a mathematical quiz is applied. After the user correctly answers the mathematical question, he is required to select his valence, arousal and dominance levels using Self-Assessment Manikins. We established the interaction between the human and the machine, communication protocols, user interfaces. All the system's tasks – patients management, virtual exposure management, physiological monitoring, application logic, flow control – have been designed and implemented at this step.

Level IV – Representational Analysis

Here we established which will be the virtual scenarios, with both their graphical and audio components. Such, we designed a landscape with forests, cliffs, canyons, peaks, a cable car, a ski lift, a transparent platform and all the visual elements. As audio elements, we can mention the sound of bird chirping and the wind. At this stage of research, we have only one virtual setting, i.e. the mountain, but very shortly we will develop a cityscape with tall buildings, glass elevators, terraces and balconies.

The experimental procedure has the following steps:

– The user is informed about the purpose of the experiment and signs a consent form, a demographic questionnaire and an acrophobia questionnaire. Based on the acrophobia questionnaires, the subjects will be divided into 3 groups – low acrophobia, medium acrophobia and high acrophobia. He also fills in a mathematical questionnaire, based on which we will determine the math skills level – Novice, Medium or Expert
– We record GSR and HR in a resting position for 3 min (baseline).
– We record GSR and HR while the user performs some short movements that can cause artefacts in the signal – deep breath, left, right, up and down movement, hand raise and click on the controller with the right hand. Having the pattern of these artefacts, we can clear the signal and remove irregularities that interfere with the physiological data recorded during the game and which are not related to emotions.
– The user will play the game three times per day, for 5 days, in this order: walking, ski lift and cable car. At the end of each day, he fills in a game experience questionnaire.
– Finally, at the end of the training session, each user will fill in again the acrophobia questionnaire to see whether his acrophobic condition has improved
– The data recorded in the experiment will be used to train an artificial intelligence model that will automatically estimate fear level and adapt the game scenarios accordingly

7 Conclusions

This paper presented a human-centered methodology inspired from the HCDID model and from the NADI model of van der Bijl-Brouwer and Dorst [9] for designing and developing a VRET system. The four stages of development – Users, goals and themes analysis, Domain analysis, Tasks analysis and Representational analysis have been adapted for the development of a VRET application dedicated to acrophobia therapy. We have carefully followed these steps and, by taking into account the patients' and therapists' requirements in a human-centered fashion, succeeded to obtain 9 functional modules responsible with users management, physiological monitoring, event triggering and audio & graphical management. The human-centered perspective is ensured by the virtual environment's level of realism and real life inspired tasks, the first person perspective in the game that is adapted according to the player's height and by the fact that the scenario is receptive to the user's needs, so that he can relax anytime by looking at his favorite photo, listen to his favorite piece of music or read a quote he enjoys. This system of rewards is not only encouraging, but also motivating and pleasurable. We payed attention to the modality in which the user provides his emotion dimension ratings. At a psychologist suggestion, we provided a modality of deactivating the right cortical hemisphere responsible with affect and activate the left one that is responsible with thought and logic. Thus, the user is asked a mathematical quiz before introducing his emotional ratings. Also, in order to establish the mathematical skills, each user receives a test before starting the virtual reality exposure. Based on the results obtained in this test, he can receive either low difficulty/medium difficulty or high difficulty mathematical questions in the game.

Our system can collect and store data from the patients and from the therapists. This data will be used for constructing a computational model that will automatically recognize the patient's current fear level and adapt the scenario accordingly, without or with minimum intervention from the human specialist.

Future plans include performing a set of experiments with people suffering from acrophobia, collecting data and designing a computational model for emotion recognition and exposure adaptation by using various feature extraction and effective machine learning techniques.

Acknowledgement. The work has been funded by the Operational Programme Human Capital of the Ministry of European Funds through the Financial Agreement 51675/09.07.2019, SMIS code 125125, UEFISCDI proiect 1/2018 and UPB CRC Research Grant 2017.

References

1. Phobias Statistics. http://www.fearof.net/phobia-statistics-and-surprising-facts-about-our-biggest-fears/
2. Olesen, J.: Phobia Statistics and surprising facts about our biggest fears (2015). http://www.fearof.net/phobia-statistics-and-surprising-facts-about-our-biggest-fears/
3. Nation Wide Phobias Statistics. https://blog.nationwide.com/common-phobias-statistics/
4. Acarturk, C., Smit, F., de Graaf, R., van Straten, A., ten Have, M., Cuijpers, P.: Economic costs of social phobia: a population-based study. J. Affect. Disord. **115**, 421–429 (2009)
5. Trautmann, S., Rehm, J., Wittchen, H.-U.: The economic costs of mental disorders. EMBO Rep. **7**, 1245–1249 (2016)
6. Garcia-Palacios, A., Hoffman, H.G., Kwong See, S., Tsai, A., Botella, C.: Redefining therapeutic success with virtual reality exposure therapy. CyberPsychology Behav. **4**(3), 341–348 (2001). https://doi.org/10.1089/109493101300210231
7. Opris, D., Pintea, S., Garcia-Palacios, A., Botella, C., Szamoskozi, S., David, D.: Virtual reality exposure therapy in anxiety disorders: a quantitative meta-analysis. Depress. Anxiety **29**, 85–93 (2012)
8. Zhang, J., Patel, V.L., Johnson, K.A., Malin, J., Smith, J.W.: Designing human-centered distributed information systems. IEEE Intell. Syst. **17**(5), 42–47 (2002)
9. van der Bijl-Brouwer, M., Dorst, K.: Advancing the strategic impact of human-centered design. Des. Stud. **53**, 1–23 (2017). 0142-694X
10. C2Phobia. https://www.c2.care/en/c2phobia-treating-phobias-in-virtual-reality/
11. PSIOUS, https://www.psious.com/

12. Stim Response Virtual Reality. https://www.biopac.com/application/virtual-reality/
13. Virtual Reality Medical Center. https://vrphobia.com/
14. Virtually Better. www.virtuallybetter.com
15. Limbix. https://www.limbix.com/
16. Phobos. https://samsungvr.com/view/Uu9ME9YXR_B
17. The Climb. http://www.theclimbgame.com/
18. Ritchie's Plank Experience. https://www.viveport.com/apps/9347a360-c6ea-4e35-aaf1-9fa b4f41cb79/Richie's_Plank_Experience/
19. Samsung Fearless Cityscapes. https://www.oculus.com/experiences/gear-vr/821606624632 569/
20. Samsung Fearless Landscapes. https://www.oculus.com/experiences/gear-vr/129083575098 8761/
21. Arachnophobia. https://store.steampowered.com/app/485270/Arachnophobia/
22. Limelight. https://store.steampowered.com/app/544880/Limelight_VR/
23. Activity. https://www.unitylab.de/
24. Coelho, C.M., Silva, C.F., Santos, J.A., Tichon, J., Wallis, G.: Contrasting the effectiveness and efficiency of virtual reality and real environments in the treatment of acrophobia. Psychol. J. **6**(2), 203–216 (2008)
25. Emmelkamp, P.M., Krijn, M., Hulsbosch, A.M., de Vries, S., Schuemie, M.J., van der Mast, C.A.: Virtual reality treatment versus exposure in vivo: A comparative evaluation in acrophobia. Behav. Res. Ther. **40**, 509–516 (2002)
26. Izard, C.E.: The emotions and emotional constructs in personality and culture research. In: Cattel, R.B. (ed.) Handbook of Modern Personality Theory. Aldine, Chicago (1969)
27. Ekman, P., Cordaro, D.: What is meant by calling emotions basic. Emot. Rev. **3**(4), 364–370 (2011)
28. Hockenbury, D.H., Hockenbury, S.E.: Discovering Psychology. Worth Publishers, New York (2007)
29. Cabanac, M.: What is emotion? Behav. Process. **60**, 69–84 (2002)
30. Ekman, P., Friesen, W.V.: Constants across cultures in the face and emotion. J. Personal. Soc. Psychol. **17**, 124–129 (1971)
31. Russell, J.A.: A circumplex model of affect. J. Pers. Soc. Psychol. **39**, 1161–1178 (1980)
32. Posner, J., Russell, J.A., Peterson, B.S.: The circumplex model of affect: An integrative approach to affective neuroscience, cognitive development, and psychopathology. Dev. Psychopathol. **17**(3), 715–734 (2005)
33. Mauss, I.B., Robinson, M.D.: Measures of emotion: a review. Cogn. Emot. **23**(2), 209–237 (2009)
34. Plutchik, R.: Emotion: theory, research, and experience. In: Theories of Emotion, vol. 1. Academic, New York (1980)
35. Sacharin, V., Schlegel, K., Scherer, K.R.: Geneva Emotion Wheel Rating Study (Report). University of Geneva, Swiss Center for Affective Sciences, Geneva (2002)
36. The Geneva Emotion Wheel. https://www.unige.ch/cisa/gew/
37. Uhrig, M.K., Trautmann, N., Baumgärtner, U., Treede, R.D., Henrich, F., Hiller, W., Marschall, S.: Emotion elicitation: a comparison of pictures and films. Front. Psychol. **7**, 180 (2016)
38. Lang, P.J., Bradley, M.M., Cuthbert, B.N.: International Affective Picture System (IAPS): affective ratings of pictures and instruction manual. Technical Report A-6. Gainesville, FL: University of Florida (2005)
39. Masood, N., Farooq, H.: Investigating EEG patterns for dual-stimuli induced human fear emotional state, Sensors (2019)
40. Ekman, P.: A methodological discussion of nonverbal behaviour. J. Psychol. **43**, 141–149 (1957)

41. Reitano, N.: Digital emotions: the potential and issues of affective computing systems. M.Sc. Interactive Digital Media (2018)
42. Huang, T., Jones, P., Kasif, S.: Human centered Systems: information, interactivity, and intelligence. Report, NSF (1997)
43. Jaimes, A., Sebe, N., Gatica-Perez, D.: Human-centered computing: a multimedia perspective. In: Proceedings of the 14th ACM International Conference on Multimedia (MM 2006), pp. 855–864. ACM, New York (2006)
44. Gillies, M., Fiebrink, R., Tanaka, A., Garcia, J., Bevilacqua, F., Heloir, A., Nunnari, F., Mackay, W., Amershi, S., Lee, B., d'Alessandro, N., Tilmanne, J., Kulesza, T., Caramiaux, B.: Human-centered machine learning. In: Proceedings of the 2016 CHI Conference Extended Abstracts on Human Factors in Computing Systems (CHI EA 2016), pp. 3558–3565. ACM, New York (2016)
45. Seffah, A., Andreevskaia, A.: Empowering software engineers in human-centered design. In: Proceedings of the 25th International Conference on Software Engineering (ICSE 2003), pp. 653–658. IEEE Computer Society, Washington, DC (2003)
46. Seffah A., Gulliksen J., Desmarais M.C.: An introduction to human-centered software engineering. In: Seffah, A., Gulliksen, J., Desmarais, M.C. (eds) Human-Centered Software Engineering — Integrating Usability in the Software Development Lifecycle. Human-Computer Interaction Series, vol 8. Springer, Dordrecht (2005)
47. Jerald, J.: The VR Book: Human-Centered Design for Virtual Reality. ACM (2016)
48. Shimmer Sensing. http://www.shimmersensing.com/

Watching People Making Decisions: A Gogglebox on Online Consumer Interaction

Chris Barry[(⊠)] and Mairéad Hogan

National University of Ireland, Galway, Ireland
{chris.barry,mairead.hogan}@nuigalway.ie

Abstract. This paper presents a research study using eye tracking technology to observe user interaction with online decisions. Using a subjective measurement scale (NASA-TLX), cognitive load is measured for participants as they encounter micro-decisions in the online transactional process. It elaborates and improves on a pilot study that was used to test the experiment design. Prior research that led to a taxonomy of decision constructs encountered by participants in the online domain is also discussed. The main findings in this paper relate to participants' subjective cognitive load and task error rates. The overall rationale for the study is to probe ethics in information systems design.

Keywords: Eye tracking · Decision constructs · Cognitive load · NASA-TLX · Micro-decision

1 Introduction

This research is part of an ongoing effort to shine a light on more subtle aspects of ethics in information systems design. The research began as anecdotal, personal observations about some questionable customer service practices in the low cost carrier (LCC) sector in Ireland. Several studies, mostly qualitative, were conducted to understand and to solicit user views on design features which create distance between the consumer and the firm [1–3]. The work broadened outwards to examine how firms were presenting choices to users. The specific context of this research is the Business-to-Consumer (B2C) transactional process from consumer commitment to an online purchase to payment conclusion. This process has become crowded with an increasing number of micro-decisions, such as the purchase of additional insurance or faster delivery. These decision points are increasingly ambiguous, problematic and time-consuming [2].

This study describes an experiment that measures the cognitive load users experience when making online micro-decisions. Eye tracking equipment was used to collect physiological data on user interactions; a self-assessment survey was used to collate perceptions about cognitive load; and immediately afterwards, participants were prompted

---

A prior version of this paper has been published in the ISD2019 Proceedings (http://aisel.aisnet.org/isd2014/proceedings2019).

A. Siarheyeva et al. (Eds.): ISD 2019, LNISO 39, pp. 198–212, 2020.
https://doi.org/10.1007/978-3-030-49644-9_12

to express feelings and opinions using the Cued Retrospective Think Aloud (RTA) technique. The main focus of this paper is the analysis of the subjective cognitive load and the error rate in the interactions. The remaining data will be the subject of later reporting. The findings present some fascinating insights into how subtle differences in the design and framing of decisions can lead to significantly divergent perceptions and outcomes.

2 Analyzing Online Decision Constructs

2.1 The Influence on User Choice

The classical view of decision-making in economics is that individuals will behave rationally by objectively weighing and ranking alternative options, according to their preferences, and choosing appropriately. The model assumes the phrasing of alternatives, and the order they are presented in, makes no difference to how individuals choose. This theory has been significantly contradicted or inherently questioned by many authors [1, 4–11]. So, quite to the contrary, individuals or consumers have been shown to be:

- influenced by whether information has been positively or negatively framed
- persuaded by the context and the presentation of choice
- impacted by influential labels
- affected in their choice by default values
- influenced in their choice by opt-in or opt-out decision formats

Using a combination of the above factors, firms can frame questions and use defaults in a way that influences participants to makes choices that are to the firm's advantage.

2.2 A Taxonomy of Online Transactional Decision Constructs

Research has shown that a variety of elements can be designed to make micro-decisions unnecessarily complicated and potentially subject to error [12]. The complexity is contributed to by: question framing; default values; levels of persuasion; whether decisions are optional or necessary; how users expect decisions to be presented; and the unconventionality of some decision constructs. With this in mind the authors set about identifying an exhaustive list of decision constructs [13] and produced a taxonomy identifying seven types of decision constructs used in the B2C transactional process (see Table 1). At the macro level decisions are either essential or optional. Essential decisions are those that must be made, such as choosing a shoe size or a delivery method. Optional decisions were described as being either opt-in, opt-out or must-opt. For clarity, an opt-in exists where a user has to explicitly choose to join or permit something; a decision having the default option of exclusion or avoidance. An opt-out exists where a user has to choose explicitly to avoid or forbid something; a decision having the default option of inclusion or permission.

A must-opt decision was identified by the authors as a new type of construct – it is neither an opt-in nor an opt-out, it occurs when a user cannot continue through the transactional process without explicitly choosing to accept or decline an option. All decisions were also classified as being either pre-selected or un-selected. This refers to whether the checkbox is ticked or not. A study was conducted [14] to confirm that each construct identified in the taxonomy is used in practice. It concluded that although most constructs are not problematic, the opt-out decision construct was often presented in a way resulting in users inadvertently making unwanted choices, reinforcing the capacity for firms to make unethical design decisions. Variants of the opt-out decision construct are the subject of this study.

Table 1. Taxonomy of transactional decision constructs.

Decision construct	Default value	Normal presentation	Framing
Un-selected opt-in	Don't receive the option	Un-selected	Acceptance
Pre-selected opt-in	Don't receive the option	Selected	Rejection
Un-selected opt-out	Receive the option	Un-selected	Rejection
Pre-selected opt-out	Receive the option	Selected	Normally acceptance
Must-opt	Cannot proceed	Multiple option variants, un-selected	Normally acceptance
Un-selected essential decision	Cannot proceed	Multiple option variants, un-selected	Normally acceptance
Pre-selected essential decision	Variant selected	Multiple decision variants, one selected	Normally acceptance

2.3 Cognitive Load

According to Grimes and Valacich [15, p. 1] cognitive load, or mental workload, can be defined as: "the mental effort and working memory required to complete a task." Considerable research in the area of cognitive load in computer-based learning applications has shown it impacts negatively on learning [9, 16–18]. While less research on cognitive load in e-commerce transactions has been conducted, higher cognitive loads have been shown to negatively affect both time to complete tasks and user satisfaction in e-commerce applications [19]. Additionally, higher mental workload corresponds to lower perceived usability for webpages [20].

Cognitive load can be measured in multiple ways. The main approaches include: subjective measures; direct objective (or physiological) measures; and indirect objective measures (for example, electroencephalography (EEG) or cardiovascular metrics) [21]. The subjective measures generally use Likert scales for self-reporting of stress or other indicators of mental load. Some of the more commonly used measures include the Subjective Workload Assessment Technique (SWAT), the NASA-Task Load Index (NASA-TLX) and the Workload Profile (WP). Each of these measures lead to a global workload index that is sensitive to the level of difficulty in the task [22]. Think-aloud can also be used to qualitatively measure cognitive load [23].

2.4 Subjective Measurement Scales

Measurement scales commonly used to determine cognitive load include uni-dimensional scales, such as the Modified Cooper-Harper Scale (MCH), and the Overall Workload Scale (OW), as well as multi-dimensional scales, such as NASA-TLX and SWAT [16]. Rating scales require the user to indicate the mental effort required to complete a task. Research indicates people can put a numerical value on their perceived mental effort [24, 25], resulting in their use in much research. NASA-TLX and SWAT are the most commonly used measurement scales of subjective cognitive load [26]. However, SWAT is not sensitive for low cognitive load tasks, unlike the NASA-TLX [27]. Hence, NASA-TLX is considered to be superior to SWAT in terms of sensitivity [28] and is frequently used as a benchmark when assessing other measures [29–31].

While NASA-TLX was originally developed for use in the aviation domain, its use has spread to other areas, including the medical profession, data entry and decision-making. Additionally, it has been translated into multiple different languages. Hart [32] examined 550 studies in which NASA-TLX was used and found most of these studies were concerned with some form of question relating to interface design or evaluation. Modification of the scale occurred in many of the studies, with subscales being added, deleted or modified. Modifications include either eliminating the weighting or analyzing the subscales individually, either in conjunction with, or instead of, the overall workload measure. Hart [32, p. 907] concluded "NASA-TLX has achieved a certain venerability; it is being used as a benchmark against which the efficacy of other measures, theories, or models are judged."

2.5 Subjective Cognitive Load

Based on the research detailed above in Sect. 2.4, NASA-TLX was deemed the most appropriate measurement scale to use in this study. NASA-TLX was the culmination of a multi-year research programme that resulted in a multi-dimensional rating scale, and derives an estimate of workload that is both reliable and sensitive [33]. The research programme determined the contributing factors to an individual's subjective perception of physical and mental workload. These were narrowed down to six factors: mental demand; physical demand; temporal demand; performance; effort; and frustration level. The definitions for these can be seen in Table 2.

According to the NASA-TLX user manual [34], the participant assigns a score on a 21-point scale ranging from 0–100 on each factor. Additionally, each of these factors are weighted by the participants according to their perception of the contribution of each factor to the workload of a given task. This weighting can be done while carrying out the task, or afterwards while replaying the task, and requires the participant to weight each of the factors by indicating which one was most relevant to the task in a series of paired comparisons. However, more recent studies [15, 18, 35, 36] have used a slightly modified version of the NASA-TLX, known as NASA-Raw Task Load Index (NASA-RTLX). Rather than weighting the factors, each is assigned equal weight and the overall workload is obtained by summing the values and dividing by the number of factors used. Studies have shown [16, 32, 35, 37] this modified version to be as effective as the original, with the added benefit of being a much simpler approach.

Table 2. Rating scale definitions for NASA-TLX.

Rating scale definitions	
Scale	Definition
Mental demand	The level of mental and perceptual activity required for the task
Physical demand	The level of physical activity required for the task
Temporal demand	The level of time pressure felt
Performance	The level of success in reaching the goals of the task
Effort	The level of work, both mental and physical, required
Frustration level	The level of frustration felt during the task

In addition, Hart and Staveland [33] determined the individual factors can be used independently to garner information about the various aspects of workload. Hart [32, p. 907], in her review of the usage of NASA-TLX states the analysis of subscale ratings instead of, or in addition to, an overall rating demonstrates "one of the continuing strengths of the scale: the diagnostic value of the component subscales." Studies have also adapted the measure: using a 5-point scale [38, 39] rather than the original 21-point scale with values between 0 and 100; changing the wording to increase the relevance to the tasks [40, 41]; and using only some of the subscales [42, 43].

3   Eye Tracking Research

Another important aspect to the study was to use eye tracking technology to track users' gaze when making micro-decisions. While it is possible, and indeed desirable, to listen to users describe what they see and experience, eye tracking data contribute objective measurements of the visual pattern of the interaction.

Eye tracking technology involves the projection of a light and a video camera on a person's eye to identify where they are looking on a screen [44]. The usual pattern of eye movement on webpages is much more erratic than one might anticipate. When someone does want to concentrate on an area of interest, they fix their gaze on it and it then comes into sharp focus. The period when a user's gaze remains fixed on something for more than 3 ms is known as a fixation, while the movements in-between fixations are known as saccades.

In HCI and web usability research, eye tracking has been extensively used [45–48]. By studying what users do and do not look at, it is possible to determine where they are concentrating their attention [49]. Through the examination of eye movement patterns, conclusions may then be drawn regarding the decision-making strategies users adopt [48, 50, 51]. The potential of gathering hard, physiological data about participant behavior in interactive decision-making was a key motivation for developing an Eye Tracking Laboratory at the authors' university.

The equipment used in the study was an EyeLink 1000 Plus System distributed by SR Research. The main device is a Host PC that performs the detection and analysis of eye movement events. These events include eye fixations, blinks and saccades. The Host PC communicates with the EyeLink Camera using a Gigabit network connection. The software integrates all of the eye tracking functionality including participant set-up, calibration, transmitting real-time data and data recording. While the system is robust and reliable, setting up the parameters of the experiment with both the hardware and software is a time-consuming and complex process.

A second, Display PC is used to present the stimuli (e.g., webpages) during the experiment, via an Ethernet link, to the participant. It can control eye tracking functionality such as calibration and data collection. Using this equipment, real-time eye and gaze positioning can be observed.

4 Preparation for the Study

It was anticipated that the design and construction of a study of user decision-making in online transactional processes would be a substantial undertaking and, using research technology new to the authors, a risky process. Thus, it was decided to run a pilot study to validate the research design for a more extensive eye tracking study. The purpose was two-fold: to learn from the process of constructing an eye tracking experiment; and to fine-tune the research instruments [52].

This pilot study, using eye tracking and the qualitative Cued RTA technique, examined potentially problematic decision constructs [52]. It explored the impact of decision constructs on users' decision-making and their cognitive processes during interactions.

The main lessons ascertained were to ensure participants: are fully briefed before commencing the test; perform the interaction as instructed working with neither haste nor labouring the tasks; and are de-briefed after the test to ascertain insights into their behavior. The key contributions of the study were the identification of improvements to be made to the research design, robust experiment administration and the refinement of research instruments.

5 The Research Study

During the research study, data was collected from 114 participants, 456 experiment trials, 2736 Interest Area data sets and 23 Cued RTA sessions. The study consisted of an eye tracking experiment, self-assessment evaluations (subjective cognitive load) and Cued RTA sessions.

5.1 Eye Tracking Experiment

Significant effort was spent planning the eye tracking study. The pilot study had highlighted the risks associated with the use of the eye tracking technology. While initially it was intended to study each of the decision constructs in the taxonomy, it soon became clear that the scope of the study would be unachievable and would require thousands of test trials. Instead, opt-out decision constructs, the most problematic in the taxonomy, were selected. Indeed their problematic and ethically questionable nature has been recognized by the European Union, who prohibit their use in distance selling [53]. Each of the variants of opt-out decisions were examined: Un-selected Rejection Framing; Pre-selected Acceptance Framing; Pre-selected Rejection Framing; and Pre-selected Neutral Framing (see Table 3).

Table 3. Opt-out decision constructs.

Construct name	Construct type	Default value	Framing
Un-selected rejection	USR	Un-selected	Rejection
Pre-selected acceptance	PSA	Pre-selected	Acceptance
Pre-selected rejection	PSR	Pre-selected	Rejection
Pre-selected neutral	PSN	Pre-selected	Neutral

Four screens of consumer decisions, (each of the opt-outs in Table 3 and illustrated in Table 4) were randomized and presented to participants. The core webpage screen was a breakdown insurance product to which participants were asked if they require an enhanced monthly-costed, add-on feature. Each screen had a single decision point with a checkbox beside it. Participants were instructed to make a decision to buy or not to buy the add-on.

Table 4. Decision constructs presented to participants.

Construct type	Decision construct	
PSA	☑	Rescue Plus includes free car hire and travel expenses. I want to purchase Rescue Plus
PSN	☑	Rescue Plus
PSR	☑	Rescue Plus includes free car hire and travel expenses. If you would rather not purchase Rescue Plus, please untick this box
USR	☐	Rescue Plus includes free car hire and travel expenses. If you would rather not purchase Rescue Plus, please tick this box

5.2 Self-assessment Evaluation

After each decision, participants were presented with three onscreen scales. They were asked to rank each decision in terms of their performance, the mental demand and the level of frustration experienced. Collectively these constitute the subjective cognitive load relevant to this study. The scales are explained as follows:

- Mental Demand: How much mental and perceptual activity did you spend for this task? 1 = Low, 5 = High
- Frustration: How insecure, discouraged, irritated, stressed, and annoyed were you during the task? 1 = Low, 5 = High
- Performance: How successful do you think you were in accomplishing the task goals? 1 = Good, 5 = Poor

The pilot study had highlighted the importance of avoiding any perception that participants were under time pressure. Thus, they were instructed to work at their normal pace; not to feel under pressure to complete quickly or to over analyze it; and to look at, and read, whatever information they normally would to make the decision.

5.3 Cued RTA Sessions

Approximately one in four participants took part in a Cued RTA discussion immediately after their session. They were shown an animated playback of their interaction showing eye movements for each of the four decision screens. The lead researcher prompted the participant to articulate the thought processes and feelings they had during the interaction. Each of the sessions, taking from five to seven minutes, were documented by a scribe and an audio recording. The analysis of these sessions is the focus of a further publication.

6 Exploratory Analysis

Once the data was gathered, exploratory analysis was conducted. The main focus of this analysis was subjective cognitive load while conducting the tasks, and participant error rate, where the number of errors made by participants was examined.

The opt-out decisions presented to participants were typical of the type of micro-decisions encountered by users as they navigate the transactional process on websites. They were based on the variety of opt-out constructs identified during a desk analysis of 57 different websites [11] and are based on actual decision constructs encountered. They were all opt-out decisions, meaning the participant needed to take action to decline the purchase, with the default option being to opt-in and purchase the item. Opt-out decisions are generally recognized as being problematic, with users often inadvertently making a purchase, or opting in to a mailing list [8].

6.1 Error Rate

The first step in exploring our data was to examine the error rate for the different construct types.

As can be seen in Table 5, the number of incorrect selections varied between the construct types, with PSA having the highest number of correct selections and USR having the highest number of incorrect selections. Overall, the number of incorrect selections made by participants was quite high, ranging from 18% (PSA) to 37% (USR). Chi-square test was conducted to determine whether the relationship between construct type and error rate was significant. The test indicated significance (χ^2 (3, N = 456) =

Table 5. Error rate.

Construct type	Correct	Incorrect	Total
PSA	94 (82%)	20 (18%)	114
PSN	87 (76%)	27 (24%)	114
PSR	86 (75%)	28 (25%)	114
USR	72 (63%)	42 (37%)	114
Total	339 (74%)	117 (26%)	456

11.715, $p < 0.01$). However, the value for ϕ was 0.158, indicating the association was weak, only accounting for 2.5% of the variation.

The results from this study, whereby 26% of the decisions participants made during the experiment were incorrect, support previous research [8] that found opt-out constructs to be problematic. Additionally, the significant difference in error rates suggests that, while opt-outs in general are error prone, some are more problematic that others.

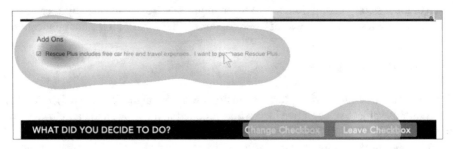

Fig. 1. Heat map of a pre-selected opt-out with acceptance framing (PSA)

The heat maps in Figs. 1 and 2 illustrate gaze concentration where green indicates less time, and red indicates more time, focusing on the text. Figure 1 is the heat map of a pre-selected opt-out with acceptance framing (PSA), the construct that had fewest errors, while Fig. 2 is the heat map of an un-selected opt-out with rejection framing (USR), the construct with the most errors. As can be seen, participants spent considerably longer examining the rejection-framed text (i.e., If you would rather not purchase…) than the acceptance-framed text (i.e., I want to purchase…). Despite spending more time reading the USR construct text, participants still made twice as many errors.

The error rate is broadly in line with the frequency of construct types found in general use by Barry et al. [14], who found most opt-outs are PSA, with considerably fewer PSN, USR and PSR. The comparatively smaller, though still high, error rate for PSA may be explained by the fact that consumers are more used to seeing opt-outs in this format and, when seeing a pre-selected checkbox, may be more likely to assume it is an opt-out, and so requires action if the user does not wish to purchase the product. In contrast, the higher rate for PSR and PSN may be explained by the rejection or neutral framing being more rarely encountered but still having the pre-selected checkbox. The pre-selected

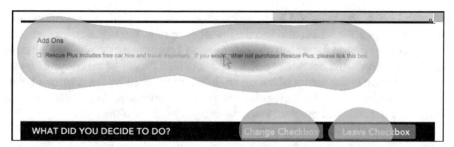

Fig. 2. Heat map of an un-selected opt-out with rejection framing (USR)

checkbox may be suggestive of an opt-out to the participant, while the unusual opt-out framing (especially for PSR) may confuse them, thus resulting in a higher error rate. The USR has an unselected checkbox, which may be more suggestive of an opt-in to the participant, and when combined with the more rarely encountered rejection framing may explain the considerably higher error rate.

6.2 Cognitive Load

The cognitive load was measured using NASA-RTLX, where participants rated their interaction with each construct type on a scale of 1–5 for three factors: Mental Demand, Frustration and Perceived Performance. It was decided to use NASA-RTLX as it is simpler to administer and has been determined to be as effective as the original [16, 32, 35, 37]. Cognitive load was determined by summing the scores for each factor and dividing by 3.

In order to assess if the participant's perceived cognitive load varied by construct type, a one-way, within-subjects ANOVA was conducted. As can be seen in Table 6, participants reported the lowest cognitive load for PSN and the highest for PSR.

Table 6. Mean cognitive load.

Construct type	Mean	Std. deviation	N
PSN	2.11	0.885	114
PSA	2.13	0.938	114
USR	2.49	0.996	114
PSR	2.54	0.956	114

Mauchly's test of sphericity was used to test the null hypothesis that the variances are equal. The test indicates the assumption of sphericity has not been violated (χ^2 (5) = 2.931, p = 0.711) and so, no corrections were required. The test showed there was a significant effect (p < 0.01) of the construct type on the participants' subjective assessment of cognitive load. The cognitive load ranged from 2.11 to 2.54 on a scale of

1–5, with 1 being very low and 5 being very high (see Table 6). The lowest cognitive load was reported for PSN, which also had the lowest error rate. The highest cognitive load was for PSR, which had the second highest error rate. Interestingly, despite the high error rate, the participants did not rate cognitive load very high for any of the construct types. This may be due to the nature of the micro-decisions required by the construct types. The micro-decisions are minor, everyday decisions, that users would encounter multiple times in the transactional process. Thus, the everyday nature of the decisions, coupled with the brevity of the text, may have made the participant feel that, even though some decisions were more difficult and complex than others, none warranted being described as imposing a major cognitive load.

6.3   Cognitive Load and Error Rate

A logistic regression was performed for each of the construct types to determine whether cognitive load, and the individual factors contributing to cognitive load, could be used to predict error rates. Firstly, the score for cognitive load was tested. For one of the constructs (PSN), the model significantly predicted the error rate. For the other three (PSA, PSR and USR), it did not.

For PSN, (omnibus Chi-square $= 4.89$, df $= 1$, p $= 0.027$), the model accounted for between 3% and 4.5% of the variance in error rate, with 100% of correct interactions successfully predicted. However, none of the predictions for unsuccessful interactions were accurate. Overall, 77.6% of predictions were accurate. The predictions for PSA, PSR and USR were not significant (omnibus Chi-square $= 2.537$, df $= 1$, p $= 0.111$), (omnibus Chi-square $= 1.711$, df $= 1$, p $= 0.191$) and (omnibus Chi-square $= 0.147$, df $= 1$, p $= 0.7$) respectively.

The measure of cognitive load was then broken down into the individual factors and the model was re-run with mental demand, frustration and perceived performance as predictor variables of error rate (see Table 7). For two of the construct types (PSA and PSN), the full model significantly predicted error rate. For the other two construct types, it did not.

Table 7. Cognitive load factors and error rate.

Construct type	Correct predicted	Incorrect predicted	Total predicted	p value
PSA	96.6%	8.7%	72.1%	0.031
PSN	97.7%	10.8%	78.2%	0.001
PSR	100%	0%	78.2%	0.325
USR	100%	0%	65.5%	0.612

For PSA, (omnibus Chi-square $= 8.873$, df $= 3$, p $= 0.031$), the model accounted for between 5.2% and 7.5% of the variance in error rate, with 96.6% of correct inter-actions successfully predicted. However, only 8.7% of the predictions for unsuccessful interactions were accurate. Overall, 72.1% of predictions were accurate. When the individual factors were assessed, only perceived performance significantly contributed to the prediction of error rate.

For PSN, (omnibus Chi-square = 15.808, df = 3, p = 0.001), the model accounted for between 9.1% and 13.9% of the variance in error rate, with 97.7% of correct interactions successfully predicted. However, only 10.8% of the predictions for unsuccessful interactions were accurate. Overall, 78.2% of predictions were accurate. When the individual factors were assessed, it was again only perceived performance which significantly contributed to the prediction of error rate.

The only construct for which cognitive load was a significant predictor of error rate was PSN, although it predicted only correct interactions. When cognitive load was broken down into its constituent factors, they significantly predicted error rates for PSA and PSN, although for each, the only factor that contributed to the prediction was perceived performance. The model did not significantly predict error rate in PSR or USR.

Where perceived performance significantly predicted error rate, it predicted correct interactions at a considerably higher level than incorrect interactions (see Table 7). This suggests that participants were less likely to believe they had performed poorly on the tasks and perceived their accuracy in making the micro-decisions to be higher than it actually was. This is consistent with Bellman et al.'s [8] findings that opt-outs are error prone. Early analysis of the Cued RTA sessions would also indicate over-confidence on the part of many participants who actually had high error rates. If users perceive these micro-decisions to be relatively easy to make, as suggested by their self-reported cognitive load; and erroneously over-estimate their performance when making these micro-decisions; they are more likely to inadvertently make a purchase or sign-up to a mailing list. This phenomenon may encourage firms to deliberately use design features to trick users into making inadvertent choices.

7   Conclusions and Future Direction

The study set out to examine whether participants were able to correctly make decisions in respect of multiple, micro-decisions involved in online, commercial transactions. All the decisions were opt-outs, and while each is generally recognized as being problematic, a certain construct (the USR) hugely distorted expectations of error rates. The take-away finding here is that should a firm wish to nudge consumers toward a preferred outcome then the deliberate choice of framing and default values constitute a potent combination.

The self-reported cognitive load on participants, while not at the high end of the NASA-RTLX scales, was evident at modest levels amongst participants. Given that the micro-decisions were completed in just seconds, the manifestation of cognitive load was clearly evident. The analysis also clearly found that the construct type had a significant effect on the participants' subjective assessment of cognitive load. Not surprisingly the error rate was lowest for the decision that bore the least cognitive load, while the constructs with the higher cognitive load tallied with the higher error rates.

Where cognitive load was tested to see if it was a good predictor of error rate, the data was less convincing. Only for pre-selected neutrally-framed decisions was cognitive load a significant predictor of error rate. What was interesting was that perceived performance predicted correct interactions to a much greater extent than incorrect interactions. The implication is that participants had a much greater confidence that they were making correct decisions than was born out by their actual accuracy. The clear inference that can be drawn here is that such over-confidence leads to error rates where participants are more likely to inadvertently, and unknowingly, make decisions not in their interest, reinforcing the temptation for firms to use ambiguous design strategies.

The study also yielded an enormous quantity of physiological participant data such as fixation count, fixation duration, dwell time, blink count and saccade information – not reported here. The data will be parsed on the basis of construct type, interest area, trial analysis and gender. The granularity of the data is microscopic and initial probing indicates some promising results. The near future direction of analysis and publication will be fixed firstly on the physiological data, then the qualitative Cued RTAs and ultimately to effectively combine the three data dimensions. More Gogglebox episodes to follow!

References

1. Barry, C., Torres, A.M.: Tricks and clicks - how low-cost carriers ply their trade through self-service websites. In: Oliver, D., Romm Livermore, C., Sudweeks, F. (eds.) Self-Service in the Internet Age - Expectations and Experiences, pp. 111–137. Springer, New York (2009)
2. Barry, C., Hogan, M., Torres, A.: Low-cost carriers and high-tech barriers - user views on questionable web design practices in Ireland. Irish J. Manag. **31**(1), 43–58 (2011)
3. Barry, C., Hogan, M., Torres, A.M.: Perceptions of low cost carriers' compliance with EU legislation on optional extras. In: 20th International Conference on Information Systems Development, Edinburgh, Scotland (2011)
4. Tversky, A., Kahneman, D.: The framing of decisions and the psychology of choice. Science **211**(4481), 453–458 (1981)
5. Kahneman, D., Miller, D.T.: Norm theory: comparing reality to its alternatives. Psychol. Rev. **93**(2), 136 (1986)
6. Samuelson, W., Zeckhauser, R.: Status quo bias in decision making. J. Risk Uncertain. **1**(1), 7–59 (1988)
7. Levin, I.P., Schneider, S.L., Gaeth, G.J.: All frames are not created equal: a typology and critical analysis of framing effects. Organ. Behav. Hum. Decis. Process. **76**(2), 149–188 (1998)
8. Bellman, S., Johnson, E.J., Lohse, G.L.: On site: to opt-in or opt-out?: it depends on the question. Commun. ACM **44**(2), 25–27 (2001)
9. Johnson, E.J., Goldstein, D.G.: Do defaults save lives? Science **302**, 1338–1339 (2003)
10. Lai, Y.-L., Hui, K.-L.: Internet opt-in and opt-out: investigating the roles of frames, defaults and privacy concerns. In: Proceedings of the 2006 ACM SIGMIS CPR Conference on Computer Personnel Research: Forty Four Years of Computer Personnel Research: Achievements, Challenges & the Future, pp. 253–263. ACM, Claremount (2006)
11. Barry, C., Hogan, M., Torres, A.M.: Framing or gaming? Constructing a study to explore the impact of option presentation on consumers. In: Information System Development: Transforming Healthcare Through Information Systems, pp. 111–124. Springer (2016)
12. Anaraky, R.G., Nabizadeh, T., Knijnenburg, B.P., Risius, M.: Reducing default and framing effects in privacy decision-making. In: SIGCHI 2018, San Francisco, CA, pp. 1–6 (2018)
13. Hogan, M., Barry, C., Torres, A.M.: Theorising and testing a taxonomy of decision constructs. J. Cust. Behav. **13**(3), 171–185 (2014)

14. Barry, C., Hogan, M., Torres, A.M.: Confirming a taxonomy of decision constructs in business-to-consumer commercial transactions. In: 23rd International Conference on Information Systems Development, Varaždin, Croatia (2014)
15. Grimes, G.M., Valacich, J.S.: Mind over mouse: the effect of cognitive load on mouse movement. In: Thirty Sixth International Conference on Information Systems, Forth Worth, USA (2015)
16. Miller, S.: Literature review - workload measures. National Advanced Driving Simulator (2001)
17. Brunken, R., Plass, J.L., Leutner, D.: Direct measurement of cognitive load in multimedia learning. Educational Psychologist. **38**(1), 53–61 (2003)
18. Hoonakker, P., Carayon, P., Gurses, A., Brown, R., McGuire, K., Khunlertkit, A., Walker, J.M.: Measuring workload of ICU nurses with a questionnaire survey: the Nasa task load index (TLX). IIE Trans. Healthc. Syst. Eng. **1**(2), 131–143 (2011)
19. Schmutz, P., Heinz, S., Métrailler, Y., Opwis, K.: Cognitive load in eCommerce applications - measurement and effects on user satisfaction. Adv. Hum.-Comput. Interact. **2009**, 1–9 (2009)
20. Longo, L., Rusconi, F., Noce, L., Barrett, S.: The importance of human mental workload in web design. In: WEBIST 2012 8th International Conference on Web Information Systems and Technologies, pp. 403–409 (2012)
21. Martin, S.: Measuring cognitive load and cognition: metrics for technology-enhanced learning. Educ. Res. Eval. **20**(7–8), 592–621 (2014)
22. Rubio, S., Díaz, J.E., Martín, J., Puente, J.M.: Evaluation of subjective mental workload: a comparison of SWAT, NASA-TLX, and workload profile methods. Appl. Psychol.: Int. Rev. **53**(1), 61–86 (2004)
23. Eveland, W.P., Dunwoody, S.: Examining information processing on the world wide web using think aloud protocols. Media Psychol. **2**(3), 219–244 (2000)
24. Gopher, D., Braune, R.: On the psychophysics of workload: why bother with subjective measures? Hum. Factors **26**(5), 519–532 (1984)
25. Paas, F.: Training strategies for attaining transfer of problem-solving skill in statistics: a cognitive-load approach. J. Educ. Psychol. **84**(4), 429–434 (1992)
26. Galy, E., Cariou, M., Melan, C.: What is the relationship between mental workload factors and cognitive load types? Int. J. Psychophysiol. **83**(3), 269–275 (2012)
27. Luximon, A., Goonetilleke, R.S.: Simplified subjective workload assessment technique. Ergonomics **44**(3), 229–243 (2001)
28. Hill, S.G., Ianecchia, H.P., Byers, J.C., Bittner, A.C., Zakland, A.L., Christ, R.E.: Comparison of four subjective workload rating scales. Hum. Factors **34**(4), 429–439 (1992)
29. Albers, M.: Tapping as a measure of cognitive load and website usability. In: 29th ACM International Conference on Design of Communication, pp. 25–32. ACM, Pisa (2011)
30. Zheng, B., Jiang, X., Tien, G., Meneghetti, A., Panton, O.N., Atkins, M.S.: Workload assessment of surgeons: correlation between NASA TLX and blinks. Surg. Endosc. **26**(10), 2746–2750 (2012)
31. Finomore, V.S., Shaw, T.H., Warm, J.S., Matthews, G., Boles, D.B.: Viewing the workload of vigilance through the lenses of the NASA-TLX and the MRQ. Hum. Factors: J. Hum. Factors Ergon. Soc. **55**(6), 1044–1063 (2013)
32. Hart, S.G.: Nasa-task load index (NASA-TLX); 20 years later. In: Proceedings of the Human Factors and Ergonomics Society Annual Meeting, pp. 904–908 (2006)
33. Hart, S.G., Staveland, L.E.: Development of NASA-TLX (task load index): results of empirical and theoretical research. Adv. Psychol. **52**, 139–183 (1988)
34. NASA: NASA TLX paper and pen manual. http://humansystems.arc.nasa.gov/groups/tlx/paperpencil.html

35. Wiebe, E.N., Roberts, E., Behrend, T.S.: An examination of two mental workload measurement approaches to understanding multimedia learning. Comput. Hum. Behav. **26**(3), 474–481 (2010)
36. Colligan, L., Potts, H.W., Finn, C.T., Sinkin, R.A.: Cognitive workload changes for nurses transitioning from a legacy system with paper documentation to a commercial electronic health record. Int. J. Med. Inform. **84**(7), 469–476 (2015)
37. Nygren, T.E.: Psychometric properties of subjective workload measurement techniques: implications for their use in the assessment of perceived mental workload. Hum. Factors **33**(1), 17–33 (1991)
38. Goodman, J., Brewster, S.A., Gray, P.: How can we best use landmarks to support older people in navigation? Behav. Inf. Technol. **24**(1), 3–20 (2005)
39. Smuts, M., Scholtz, B., Calitz, A.P.: Usability guidelines for designing information visualisation tools for novice users. In: Beyond Development. Time for a New ICT4D Paradigm? Proceedings of the 9th IDIA Conference, IDIA2015, Nungwi, Zanzibar, pp. 148–162 (2015)
40. Hayashi, T., Kishi, R.: Utilization of NASA-TLX for workload evaluation of gaze-writing systems. In: IEEE International Symposium on Multimedia, pp. 271–272 (2014)
41. Mohamed, R., Raman, M., Anderson, J., McLaughlin, K., Rostom, A., Coderre, S.: Validation of the national aeronautics and space administration-task load index as a tool to evaluate the learning curve for endoscopy training. Can. J. Gastroenterol. Hepatol. **28**(3), 155–160 (2014)
42. González Gutiérrez, J.L., Jiménez, B.M., Hernández, E.G., López López, A.: Spanish version of the swedish occupational fatigue inventory (SOFI): factorial replication, reliability and validity. Int. J. Ind. Ergon. **35**(8), 737–746 (2005)
43. Wesiaka, G., Steinera, C.M., Moore, A., Dagger, D., Power, D., Bertholda, M., Alberta, D., Conlan, O.: Iterative augmentation of a medical training simulator: effects of affective metacognitive scaffolding. Comput. Educ. **76**, 13–19 (2014)
44. Nielsen, J., Pernice, K.: Eyetracking Web Usability. New Riders, Berkeley (2010)
45. Djamasbi, S., Siegel, M., Tullis, T., Dai, R.: Efficiency, trust, and visual appeal: usability testing through eye tracking. In: 43rd Hawaii International Conference on System Sciences (HICSS), pp. 1–10. IEEE (2010)
46. Di Stasi, L.L., Antolí, A., Cañas, J.J.: Main sequence: an index for detecting mental workload variation in complex tasks. Appl. Ergon. **42**(6), 807–813 (2011)
47. Djamasbi, S., Siegel, M., Skorinko, J., Tullis, T.: Online viewing and aesthetic preferences of generation Y and the baby boom generation: testing user web site experience through eye tracking. Int. J. Electron. Commer. **15**(4), 121–158 (2011)
48. Huang, Y.-F., Kuo, F.-Y.: An eye-tracking investigation of internet consumers' decision deliberateness. Internet Res. **21**(5), 541–561 (2011)
49. Pernice, K., Nielsen, J.: Eyetracking methodology: how to conduct and evaluate usability studies using eyetracking. Technical report in Nielsen Norman Group (2009)
50. Day, R.F., Shyi, G.C.W., Wang, J.C.: The effect of flash banners on multiattribute decision making: distractor or source of arousal? Psychol. Mark. **23**(5), 369–382 (2006)
51. Glöckner, A., Herbold, A.K.: An eye-tracking study on information processing in risky decisions: evidence for compensatory strategies based on automatic processes. J. Behav. Decis. Mak. **24**(1), 71–98 (2011)
52. Hogan, M., Barry, C., Torres, A.M.: An eye tracking pilot study on optionality - some lessons learned. In: 17th Irish Academy of Management Annual Conference, Galway (2015)
53. European-Union: Directive on Consumer Rights. In: European-Union (ed.) 2011/83/EU (2011)

Author Index

A. Siarheyeva et al. (Eds.): ISD 2019, LNISO 39, p. 213, 2020.
https://doi.org/10.1007/978-3-030-49644-9

Printed in the United States
By Bookmasters